D1592881

SALES
COMPENSATION
ALMANAC
2022

DAVID J. CICHELLI

About The Alexander Group, Inc.

The Alexander Group (www.alexandergroup.com) provides revenue growth consulting services to the world's leading sales, marketing and service organizations. Founded in 1985, the firm combines deep experience, proven methodologies and data-driven insights to help revenue leaders anticipate change, align their go-to-customer resources with company goals and make better informed decisions with one goal in mind—to grow revenue. The Alexander Group has offices in Atlanta, Chicago, London, New York, San Francisco, São Paulo, Scottsdale, and Vero Beach.

Our Sales Compensation Consulting Services

As the leading firm in sales compensation design, we help our clients create incentive plans that align selling resources with corporate objectives. The Alexander Group is the recognized thought leader in sales compensation solutions, as widely acknowledged by clients and professional associations. We have helped thousands of clients, including worldwide sales organizations, realize the full benefits of effective sales compensation programs to reward and recognize high-performing sales resources.

From strategic alignment to design, market pricing and program implementation, we can help with all elements of your sales compensation program.

AGI Press

2022 Sales Compensation Almanac

ISBN: 978-1-7358646-4-8

This publication is designed to provide accurate and authoritative information in regards to the subject matter covered. It is sold with the understanding that neither the author nor the publisher are engaged in rendering legal, accounting or other professional service. If legal advice or other expert assistance is required, the services of a competent professional person should be sought.

—*From a Declaration of Principles Jointly Adopted by a Committee of the American Bar Association and a Committee of Publishers and Associations.*

For information about this title or to order other books, contact us at www.alexandergroup.com.

TABLE OF CONTENTS

ACKNOWLEDGMENTS

The Alexander Group's *Sales Compensation Almanac* is now in its eighth year. The *2022 Sales Compensation Almanac* provides contemporary reference information, research findings and case studies reflecting the Alexander Group's sales compensation consulting practice leadership.

I would like to extend my gratitude to those who have contributed to this resource book.

Some of the high-value features of the *Almanac* are the market survey trends and practices reports. Thank you to the hundreds of sales compensation professionals, who carefully and thoroughly complete the survey questionnaires each year. Your submissions provide the basis for leading-edge reports on contemporary sales compensation practices.

Thank you to the companies that participated in our *Sales Compensation Administration Vendors Guide.* I would like to recognize the Alexander Group's benchmarking team for assembling this guide.

Thank you to the many companies who develop and provide market pay surveys. These companies have completed and submitted their product profiles featured here. I would like to recognize Emily Schur of the Alexander Group for compiling the *Reference Guide to Sales Compensation Surveys.*

This year, the Almanac features the work of several Alexander Group consultants, who have prepared case studies and insightful whitepapers for this edition. They are Andrea Farinelli, Daniel Kravitz, Parker Hoffman, Mark O'Donnell and Kelly Rue.

Thanks to Lori Feuer, editor-in-chief, who has edited and managed the production and distribution of this edition.

Finally, to my wife, Kathleen, thanks for your loving support.

INTRODUCTION

INTRODUCTION

Welcome to the eighth annual *Sales Compensation Almanac! The 2022 Sales Compensation Almanac* provides the latest trends, resources and insights into sales compensation solutions.

What is the *Sales Compensation Almanac?*

For many sales entities, sales compensation is an important management tool, yet needs constant attention. Excellent designs one year may give way to necessary updates and revisions the following year. Sales compensation stakeholders, including executive management, sales leaders, finance, and HR professionals, are often looking for specific resources, survey findings and publications to address sales compensation design and administration challenges. The *Sales Compensation Almanac* provides the latest research and resources in this space.

2022 Edition Sections

This year's edition contains the following sections:

2021 Sales Compensation Trends Survey. Conducted each November to December and published in January of the following year, the *Sales Compensation Trends Survey* provides a look back at the previous year and a look forward to the next fiscal year on key sales compensation metrics, such as budgets, costs, turnover, program changes, and program effectiveness. The survey also presents the results of select topics regarding specific and topical sales compensation challenges. The full survey results are available to survey participants exclusively for six months.

2020 Sales Compensation Hot Topics Survey. Each year, the sales compensation "hot topics" survey provides in-depth insight into select sales compensation practices. The *2020 Sales Compensation Hot Topics Survey* examined recent and popular topics in sales compensation practices, including COVID-19 pay protection practices, sales restart after COVID-19, recurring revenue and renewals, program late start practices, and pre-booking incentives.

Multiyear Research Findings–Trends and Practices Surveys. Our many years of sales compensation research offer compelling multiyear observations.

Sales Compensation Market Pay Surveys. Need to locate a sales compensation market pay survey? The *Reference Guide to Sales Compensation Surveys* catalogs many of the available surveys on sales compensation pay levels. Use these vendor products to price and manage your sales compensation costs.

Sales Compensation Administration Vendors. Sales compensation administration software and service providers use powerful administration tools to track, report and model sales compensation transactions. Use this list of vendors to locate and assess the right administration software to help manage your pay program.

Educational and Publication Resources. Use these resources to help gain leading-edge knowledge about sales compensation concepts and principles.

Sales Compensation Case Studies. Learn how other companies examine and update their sales compensation practices with case studies from the Alexander Group's client engagements. Our mid-career consultants prepare these case studies; they add to our catalog of hundreds to thousands of client engagements. This year's case studies include:

- Distribution (2)
- Healthcare
- Internet Security
- Record and Information Management
- Technology (3)

Whitepapers. Explore select topics authored by the Alexander Group's consultants. This year's whitepapers feature the following topics:

- How to Compensate Customer Success Roles in High-Growth Software Companies
- How to Use Spiffs to Reward Sellers
- Sales Compensation: How to Reduce Base Pay and Increase Pay at Risk
- Sales Compensation: Rewarding Team Selling
- Sales Compensation Cost Modeling: Determining Methodology and Components

Recent Articles of Interest. Finally, view our listing of the latest published sales compensation articles.

SALES COMPENSATION SERVICES

SALES COMPENSATION ALMANAC • 2022

Sales Compensation Services

The Alexander Group is the Sales Compensation Market Leader. We are the premier provider of sales compensation design services to Global 2000 companies. Let us help you improve sales results by ensuring your sales force has best-in-class sales compensation solutions.

Harness the Best Design Solutions

The Alexander Group optimizes sales compensation solutions for revenue organizations. From strategic alignment and program management to design, market pricing and automation, we help improve all elements of your sales compensation effectiveness.

Revenue Growth Model™

Revenue Leadership

STRATEGY			STRUCTURE			MANAGEMENT		
1	2	3	4	5	6	7	8	9
Revenue Segments	Value Propositions	Engagement & Motions	Channel Coverage	Organization & Job Design	Sizing & Deployment	Talent & Enablement	Metrics & Quotas	Performance & Rewards

Revenue Operations

With a history that spans thousands of clients, including global sales organizations, we will help you realize the full benefits of an effective sales compensation program to reward and recognize your dedicated sales force. Recognized by clients and professional associations alike, we are the thought leader in sales compensation solutions.

Don't allow your sales compensation plans to become obsolete. A well-designed sales compensation plan ensures alignment between sales force efforts and business objectives. Best-in-class sales organizations use the right sales compensation plans to motivate performance and drive business results.

Whether your pay plans require a tune-up, an update or a major overhaul, the Alexander Group can devise an incentive compensation plan that optimizes your high-performance sales team.

We have helped Global 2000 companies align business priorities to salespeople for more than 30 years with end-to-end sales compensation design services.

Learning—Briefings and Seminars. Leading companies must challenge existing practices. The Alexander Group facilitates knowledge transfer through full- and half-day briefings on key concepts in sales compensation. These instructive sessions instill a deep understanding of sales compensation design principles—the practices that really work. The full-day workshop includes specific design discussions about your plans. Let us educate your stakeholders in sales compensation best practices.

www.alexandergroup.com

WORLD-CLASS SALES COMPENSATION SOLUTIONS

Assessment. The Alexander Group's program assessment incorporates a review of your current practices and objectives. The assessment report encompasses a checklist of action items and suggestions for further consideration. Our assessment report answers your most pressing question: "How well is the current plan working?" Our team can determine if your current practices are effective, need minor modification or a major redesign.

Design. During our design engagements, the Alexander Group reviews the results of the fact-finding efforts, provides alternative designs for evaluation and helps with the selection of preferred plans. Once your management team selects the plan, the focus shifts to the development phase to estimate costs and document the new plans. Finally, implementation includes the creation of all supporting materials to train managers and communicate the new plan to staff.

Depending on your firm's needs and circumstances, the Alexander Group can help reconfigure your support programs, including quota allocation, sales crediting, account management, and plan automation.

Implementation. We provide hands-on implementation support, including creating program collateral, training managers and ensuring program adoption. Additional services ensure that your administration team has all of the plan elements fully defined in order to automate the new pay program.

Program Management. Need sales compensation program management protocols? We can create design principles, plan parameters, platform jobs, and governance and program accountabilities. Use these program management solutions to keep widely dispersed stakeholders aligned with best practices and sanctioned corporate policies.

The Alexander Group's consultants have helped nearly half of the Fortune 1000 increase sales and profits through the effective design and implementation of sales strategies and solutions. Our incentive compensation solutions leverage the best ideas and adapt them to your organization's needs and circumstances.

OFFICES

Atlanta 404.249.1338

Chicago 312.357.0500

London +4420 3455 9603

New York 646.891.4445

San Francisco 415.391.3900

Scottsdale 480.998.9644

Vero Beach 772.226.6715

2021 SALES COMPENSATION TRENDS SURVEY

SALES COMPENSATION ALMANAC • 2022

2021 SALES COMPENSATION TRENDS SURVEY

Conducted each December and published in January of the following year, the *Sales Compensation Trends Survey* provides a look back at the previous year and a look forward to the next fiscal year on key sales compensation metrics, such as budgets, costs, turnover, program changes, and program effectiveness. The survey also presents the results of select topics regarding specific and topical sales compensation challenges.

IN THIS SECTION

- Executive Summary
- Multiyear Trends
- Sales Department Trends 2020 and 2021
- Sales Compensation–What Happened in 2020?
- Sales Compensation–What Will Happen in 2021?
- Sales Compensation Changes Planned for the Primary Sales Job in 2021
- Quotas
- COVID-19: Sales Compensation–What Did You Do?
- Trending Topics
- Demographics

EXECUTIVE SUMMARY

Overview

2020 was a COVID-19 upheaval year with some sectors suffering significantly, others meeting goals and some even prospering. Sales departments increased sales volume only 2% in 2020. This was less than the growth estimate of 6% projected at the end of December 2019 for 2020 performance. Meanwhile, sales leaders expect sales revenue to grow a remarkable 8% in 2021.

For those planning base pay increases in 2021, 3% is the projected increase in budget. -1.5% was the median decrease in incentive costs in 2020. 2% is the projected increase in incentive payments for 2021.

Introduction

109 sales departments participated in this year's 19th annual *2021 Sales Compensation Trends Survey*©. Participants provided data in November and December 2020 on what occurred in 2020 and what they plan for 2021. Results published in January 2021.

KEY METRICS

Actual Revenue Growth in 2020

10th Perc	25th Perc	50th Perc	75th Perc	90th Perc	Average
−12	−5	2	8	19.8	3

Expected Revenue Growth in 2021

10th Perc	25th Perc	50th Perc	75th Perc	90th Perc	Average
0	4	8	15	24.8	10.9

2020 Change in Sales Incentive Costs

10th Perc	25th Perc	50th Perc	75th Perc	90th Perc	Average
−20	−10	−1.5	1.5	10	−3.5

2021 Planned Base Pay Increases

10th Perc	25th Perc	50th Perc	75th Perc	90th Perc	Average
0	2	3	3.5	8.1	3.1

2021 Planned Incentive Plan Budget Increase

10th Perc	25th Perc	50th Perc	75th Perc	90th Perc	Average
0	0	2	5	10	3.8

MULTIYEAR TRENDS

2016 to 2021 Sales Revenue Trends

8% revenue increase for 2021 suggests optimistic revenue growth.

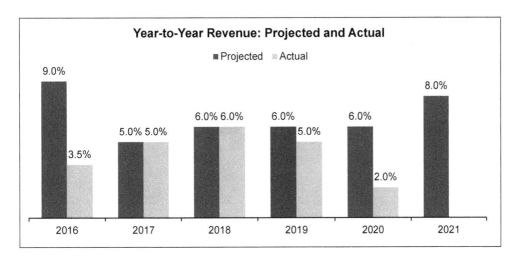

2017 to 2021 Staffing Changes

17.5% will reduce headcount in 2021; a jump from previous years.

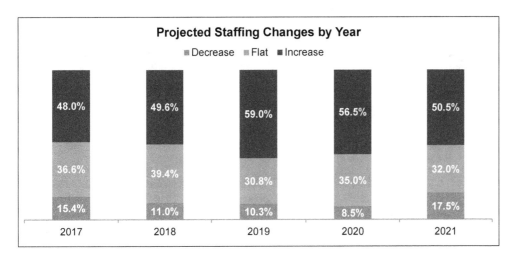

2016 to 2021 Sales Compensation Incentive Payouts

–1.5% was the incentive decline in 2020; the most recent decline was in 2009.

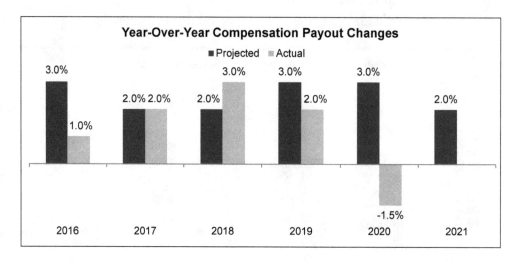

2016 to 2020 Sales Compensation Plan Effectiveness

46.3% rated pay plans effective; a major drop from previous years.

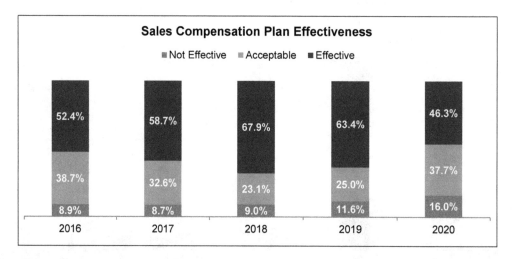

2017 to 2021 Next Year's Sales Compensation Challenges

62.6% cite correct goal/quota setting as the major challenge for 2021.

New challenges added in 2021 Survey: 34.6% Uncontrollable External Factors. 27.1% COVID-19 Pay Mitigation Practices.

2017 to 2021 Most Common Plan Changes

40.2% will make changes to performance measures.

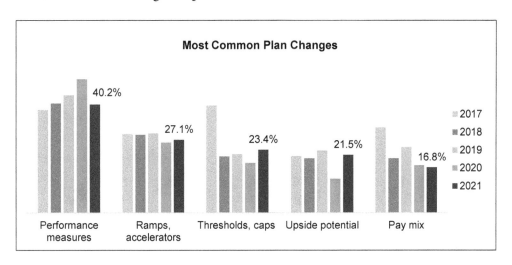

18.7% will make sales crediting practice changes, too.

2017 to 2021 Planned Program Changes

100% plan to make changes to the 2021 sales compensation plan.

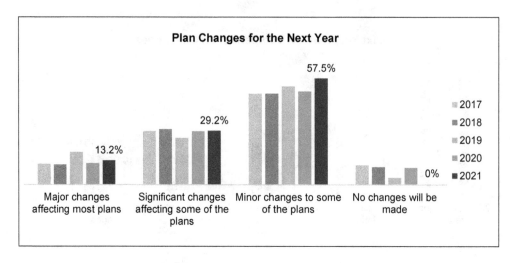

First time in 19 years of the survey, all participants plan to make changes to next year's sales compensation plan.

2017 to 2021 Most Common Performance Measures

85.7% selected sales revenue as the primary pay plan measure for 2021.

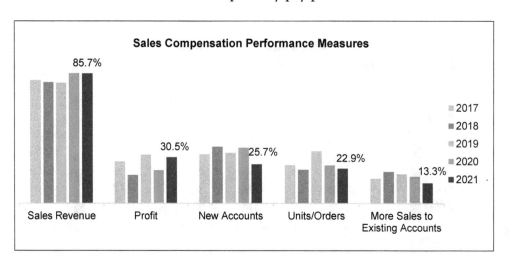

Other important measures include: 22.9% Renewals. 18.1% New Contracts.

SALES DEPARTMENT TRENDS 2020 AND 2021*

- 2% growth was the revenue performance for 2020.
- 90% to budget was the revenue performance for 2020.
- 8% is the projected revenue growth for 2021.
- 49.5% expect minor improvement in 2021 for their industry sector.
- 63.5% will maintain or increase spending in 2021.
- 67% will focus on growing existing business in 2021.
- 76% have average or above average sales confidence for 2021.
- 36.6% lost headcount in 2020; 28.7% gained headcount.
- 50.5% will increase headcount in 2021; 17.5% will reduce headcount.
- 55.4% had 1% to 5% of sales positions open during 2020.
- 5% was the 2020 turnover rate.
- 5% is the expected 2021 turnover rate.
- 68% say growing revenue/bookings/units is the top focus in 2021.
- 39% want to improve sales productivity in 2021; objectives vary.

Highest Response or Median for the Question

2020 Actual Percent Revenue Performance: For your division sales unit, what percentage change in revenue performance occurred from 2019 to 2020?

10th Perc	25th Perc	50th Perc	75th Perc	90th Perc	Average
−12	−5	2	8	19.8	3

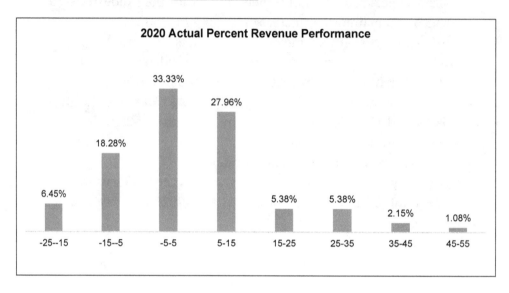

Survey Findings. 2% growth was the revenue performance for 2020.

2020 Sales Compared to Budget: How did your actual sales performance compare to budget?

10th Perc	25th Perc	50th Perc	75th Perc	90th Perc	Average
0.2	76	90	99	103.6	75.1

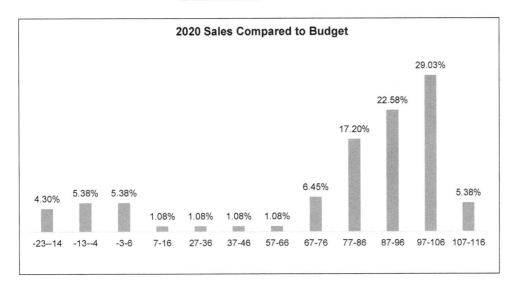

Survey Findings. 90% to budget was the revenue performance for 2020.

2021 Revenue Expectations: For your division sales force, 2021 fiscal year revenue performance is forecasted to increase or decrease by what percent as compared to actual 2020?

10th Perc	25th Perc	50th Perc	75th Perc	90th Perc	Average
0	4	8	15	24.8	10.9

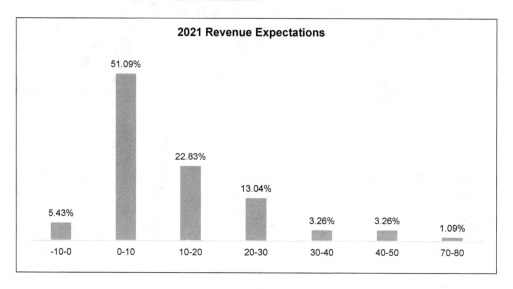

Survey Findings. 8% is the projected revenue growth for 2021.

Your Industry Sector Economic Sentiment for 2021: As you can best estimate, for your industry sector, what is the economic sentiment of your executive leaders for 2021 as compared to 2020?

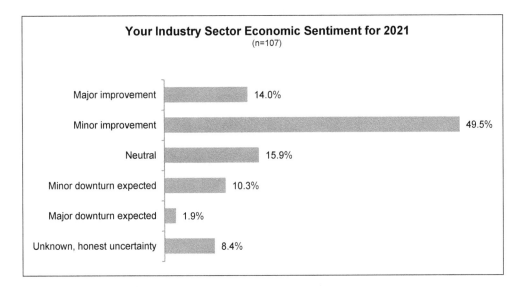

Survey Findings. 49.5% expect minor improvement in 2021 for their industry sector.

Spending Expectations for 2021: As now planned, what is the spending expectation for the company in 2021?

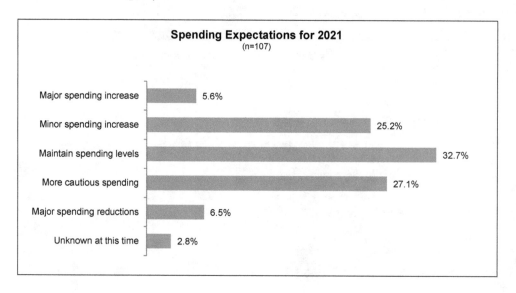

Survey Findings. 63.5% will maintain or increase spending in 2021.

Primary Strategic Objectives: In your opinion, what is the primary (top three) strategic objectives of senior management?

Survey Findings. 67% will focus on growing existing business in 2021.

2021 Sales Confidence: How would you rate your company's sales confidence—the ability to meet and exceed 2021 revenue goals?

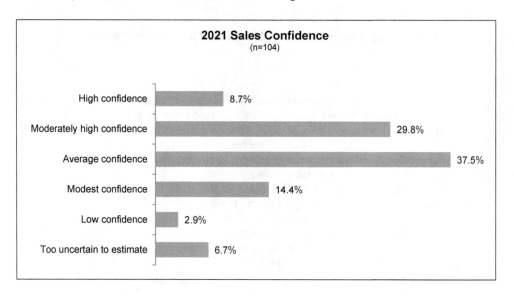

Survey Findings. 76% have average or above average sales confidence for 2021.

2020 Headcount Changes: Did your sales force headcount change in 2020 for the division sales unit?

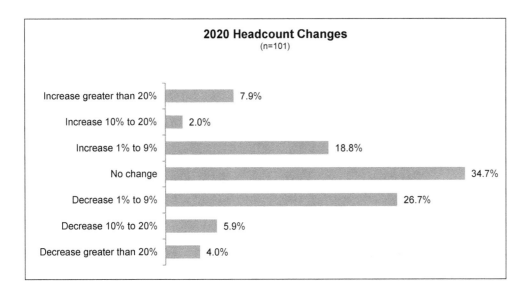

Survey Findings. 36.6% lost headcount in 2020; 28.7% gained headcount.

2021 Expected Headcount Changes: How do you expect 2021 sales force staffing levels to change as compared to 2020 for the division sales unit?

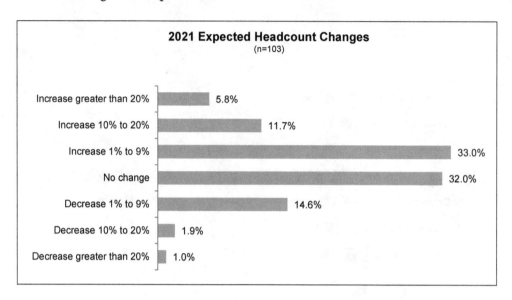

Survey Findings. 50.5% will increase headcount in 2021; 17.5% will reduce headcount.

2020 Open Positions: At any given time during 2020, what was the average percent of open sales positions compared to the total approved headcount?

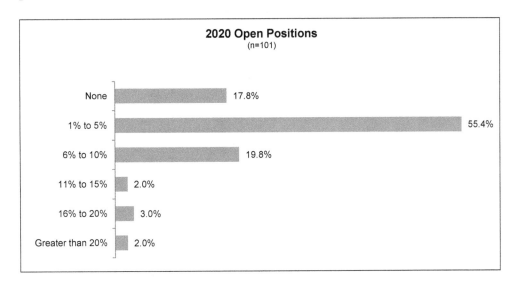

Survey Findings. 55.4% had 1% to 5% of sales positions open during 2020.

2020 Turnover: What was your turnover percent rate (voluntary and involuntary) for sales personnel in 2020 for the division sales unit?

10th Perc	25th Perc	50th Perc	75th Perc	90th Perc	Average
1	3	5	13	22.5	8.5

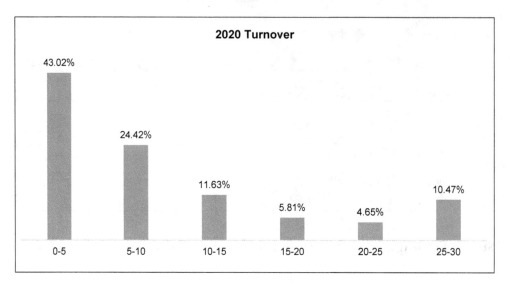

Survey Findings. 5% was the 2020 turnover rate. 5% is half the traditional turnover rate of 10%.

2021 Projected Turnover: What is your anticipated/projected 2021 percent turnover rate (voluntary and involuntary) for sales personnel in the division sales unit?

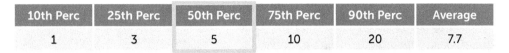

10th Perc	25th Perc	50th Perc	75th Perc	90th Perc	Average
1	3	5	10	20	7.7

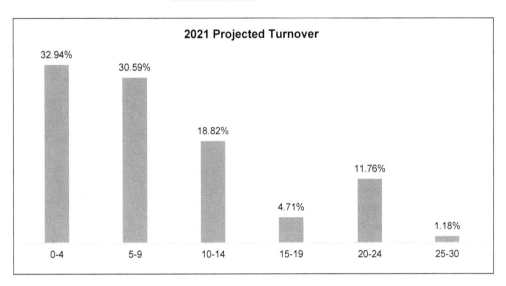

Survey Findings. 5% is the expected 2021 turnover rate. 5% is less than the traditional expected turnover of 8% to 11%.

2021 Performance Objectives: What are the top achieve and exceed sales performance objectives for 2021?

Survey Findings. 68% say growing revenue/bookings/units is the top focus in 2021.

2021 Sales Effectiveness Initiatives: What are the expected top three key sales effectiveness initiatives for the sales department in 2021?

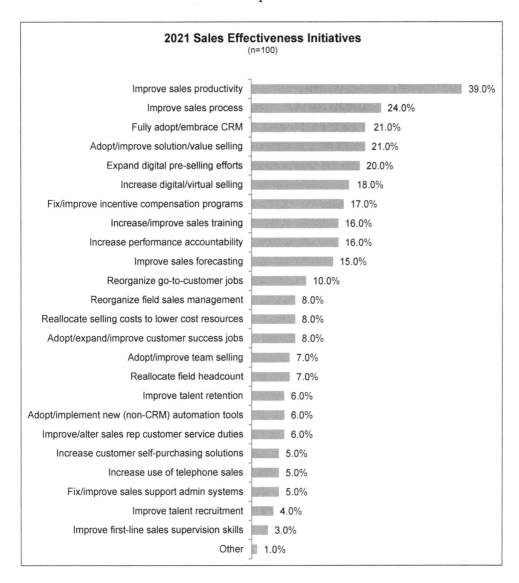

2021 Sales Effectiveness Initiatives
(n=100)

Initiative	Percentage
Improve sales productivity	39.0%
Improve sales process	24.0%
Fully adopt/embrace CRM	21.0%
Adopt/improve solution/value selling	21.0%
Expand digital pre-selling efforts	20.0%
Increase digital/virtual selling	18.0%
Fix/improve incentive compensation programs	17.0%
Increase/improve sales training	16.0%
Increase performance accountability	16.0%
Improve sales forecasting	15.0%
Reorganize go-to-customer jobs	10.0%
Reorganize field sales management	8.0%
Reallocate selling costs to lower cost resources	8.0%
Adopt/expand/improve customer success jobs	8.0%
Adopt/improve team selling	7.0%
Reallocate field headcount	7.0%
Improve talent retention	6.0%
Adopt/implement new (non-CRM) automation tools	6.0%
Improve/alter sales rep customer service duties	6.0%
Increase customer self-purchasing solutions	5.0%
Increase use of telephone sales	5.0%
Fix/improve sales support admin systems	5.0%
Improve talent recruitment	4.0%
Improve first-line sales supervision skills	3.0%
Other	1.0%

Survey Findings. 39% want to improve sales productivity in 2021; objectives vary.

SALES COMPENSATION—WHAT HAPPENED IN 2020*?

- 84% report the 2020 sales compensation program acceptable or better.
- 64.1% made mid-year sales compensation plan changes in 2020.
- 74.3% found the 2020 plan mostly or completely aligned with strategy.
- 82.1% said most or all of their sellers understood their 2020 pay plan.
- 67.6% said the 2020 plan payouts mostly or fully matched sales results.
- −1.5% was the median drop in 2020 incentive payment costs.
- 90.5% was the incentive payout as compared to budget.
- 50% of sellers will reach target payout in 2020.
- 100% of target incentive would be paid for 100% quota performance.

* Highest Response or Median for the Question

2020 Sales Compensation Program Effectiveness: In 2020, how effective was the overall sales compensation program?

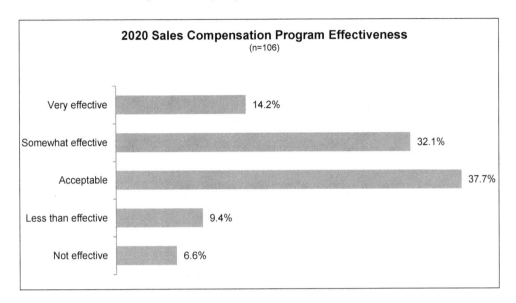

Survey Findings. 84% report the 2020 sales compensation program acceptable or better.

2020 Mid-Year Changes: During 2020, did you have to make any mid-year changes to the sales compensation program?

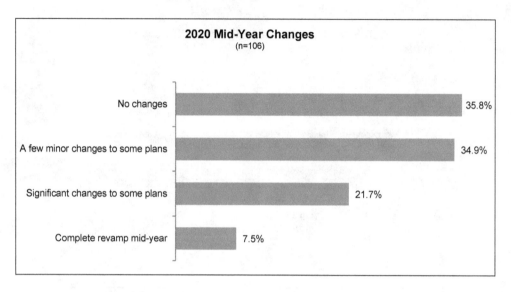

Survey Findings. 64.1% made mid-year sales compensation plan changes in 2020.

2020 Plan Alignment: How well did the 2020 sales compensation program align sales efforts with company business objectives?

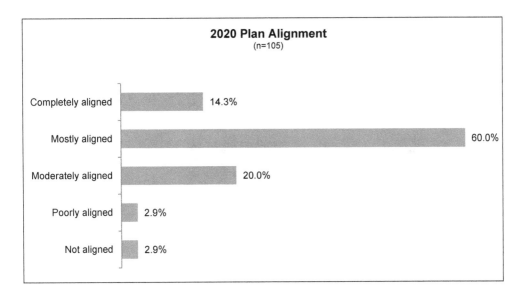

Survey Findings. 74.3% found the 2020 plan mostly or completely aligned with strategy.

2020 Plan Understanding: How well did sales personnel understand their 2020 sales compensation plan?

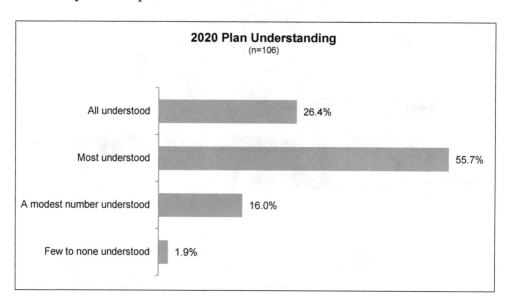

Survey Findings. 82.1% said most or all of their sellers understood their 2020 pay plan.

2020 Plan Rewards: How well did payouts match performance?

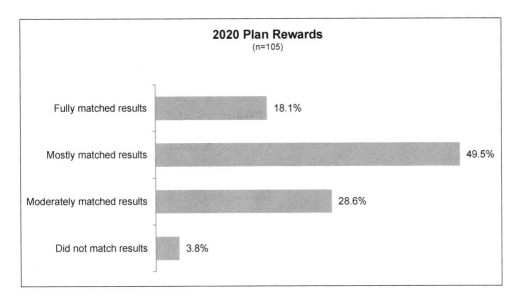

Survey Findings. 67.6% said the 2020 plan payouts mostly or fully matched sales results.

2020 Incentive Payments Costs: By what percentage did actual incentive pay-outs for sales personnel change from 2019 to 2020?

10th Perc	25th Perc	50th Perc	75th Perc	90th Perc	Average
−20	−10	−1.5	1.5	10	−3.5

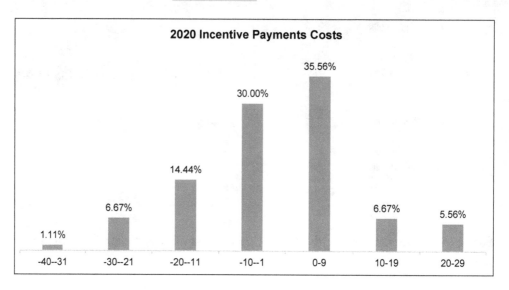

Survey Findings. −1.5% was the median drop in 2020 incentive payment costs.

2020 Expected Total Incentive Payments: What are the estimated total incentive payments for 2020 (include extra bonuses and spiffs) as compared to 100% incentive budget (excluding extra bonuses and spiffs)?

10th Perc	25th Perc	50th Perc	75th Perc	90th Perc	Average
50	80	90.5	100	109.7	84.8

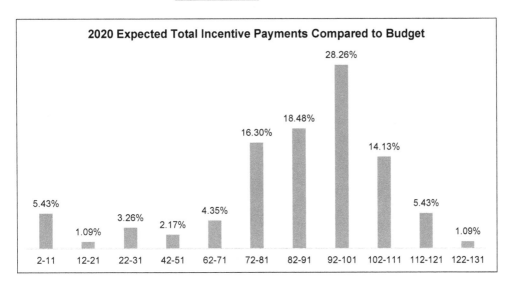

Survey Findings. 90.5% was the incentive payout as compared to budget.

2020 Target Incentive Participation Rate: For the primary sales job, what percent of sales personnel will reach and exceed their target or on-par expected incentive amount? Include extra bonuses and spiffs.

10th Perc	25th Perc	50th Perc	75th Perc	90th Perc	Average
10	36	50	65	89.2	50.7

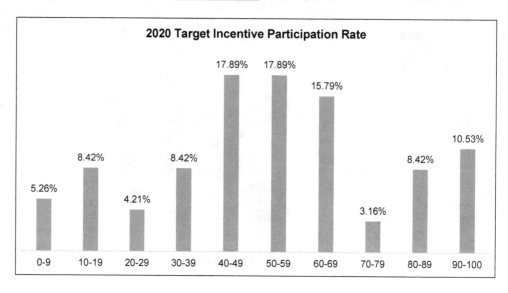

Survey Findings. 50% of sellers will reach target payout in 2020.

2020 Payout Estimate Variance: If your company achieved 100% of its sales objective, how much would the incentive plan pay compared to the incentive plan target budget? Include add-on bonuses, contests and spiffs.

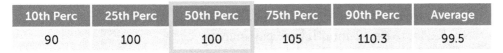

10th Perc	25th Perc	50th Perc	75th Perc	90th Perc	Average
90	100	100	105	110.3	99.5

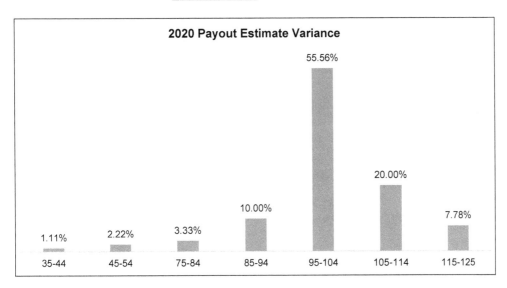

Survey Findings. 100% of target incentive would be paid for 100% quota performance.

SALES COMPENSATION PROGRAM—WHAT WILL HAPPEN IN 2021*?

- 66% will grant a base pay increase in 2021.
- 3% increase in base pay planned for 2021.
- 72.4% use a 12-month base pay increase cycle.
- 100% will make changes to the 2021 sales compensation program.
- 62.6% say correct goal/quota setting is the top challenge for 2021.
- 41% will make changes to the 2021 plan to improve strategy alignment.

* Highest Response or Median for the Question

2021 Base Pay Changes: Will you make base pay changes for eligible sales employees in 2021?

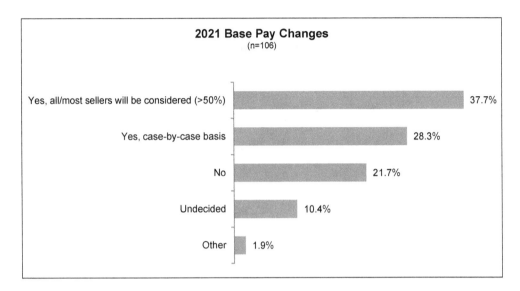

Survey Findings. 66% will grant a base pay increase in 2021.

2021 Average Percent Change in Base Pay: If you answered yes to making a base pay change in 2021, what do you expect the average percent change in base pay to be for those receiving an increase?

10th Perc	25th Perc	50th Perc	75th Perc	90th Perc	Average
0	2	3	3.5	8.1	3.1

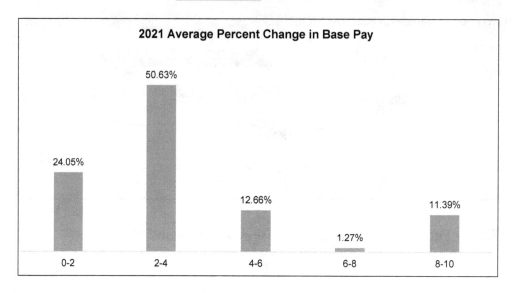

Survey Findings. 3% increase in base pay planned for 2021.

2021 Base Pay Increase Cycle: For incumbents in the primary sales job, how long is the normal duration between base pay changes? (absent temporary COVID-19 practices)

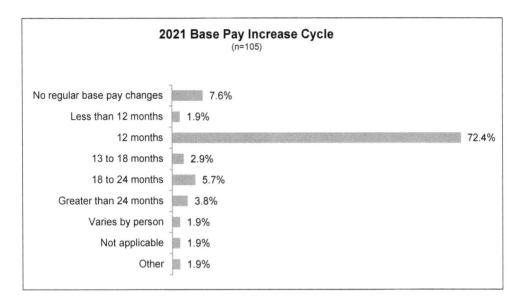

Survey Findings. 72.4% use a 12-month base pay increase cycle.

2021 Sales Compensation Program Changes: For 2021, what are the extent of changes you plan to make to your sales compensation program?

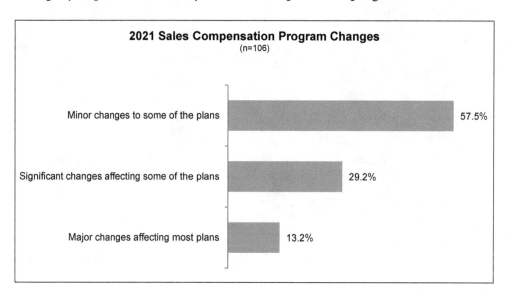

Survey Findings. 100% will make changes to the 2021 sales compensation program.

2021 Sales Compensation Challenges: What sales compensation challenges do you expect in 2021?

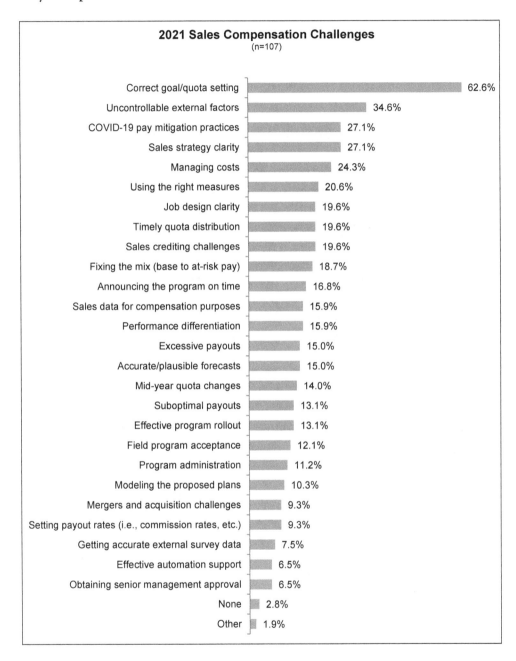

Survey Findings. 62.6% say correct goal/quota setting is the top challenge for 2021.

2021 Plan Revision Reason: Why will you change your sales compensation plan for next fiscal year?

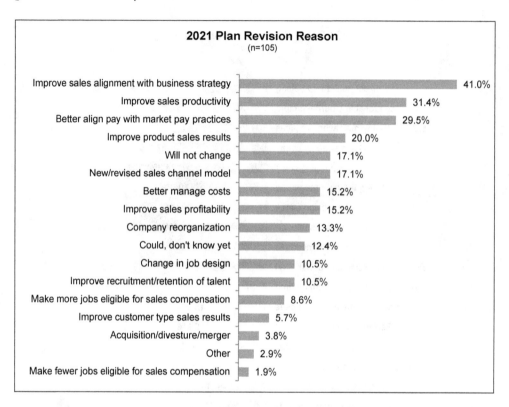

Survey Findings. 41% will make changes to the 2021 plan to improve strategy alignment.

SALES COMPENSATION CHANGES PLANNED FOR THE PRIMARY SALES JOB IN 2021*

- 2% is the target total earnings planned increase in 2021.
- 41.1% will change the performance measures for the primary sales job.
- 85.7% report sales revenue as the key measure in the pay plan.
- 29.7% use annual objectives with monthly payouts but practices vary.
- 80.3% use three or fewer measures in the 2021 pay plan.
- 82.3% will tie payout to individual performance.
- 79.8% do not use an MBO component in the sales compensation plan.
- 20% is the weighting of the MBO component for the 12.1% using MBOs.
- 42% use a bonus formula paid against quota achievement.
- 33% use a 50/50 pay mix (base/target); practices vary.
- 67.3% have no pay caps for sellers in the primary sales job.
- 27.6% provide 2x the target incentive as upside earnings potential; practices vary.
- 58.1% use a performance threshold for the primary sales job.
- 67.3% use clawbacks if orders do not fully transact.
- 35.6% place new hires on a fixed guarantee.

Highest Response or Median for the Question

Type of Sales Job: Select your primary sales job type used in this section.

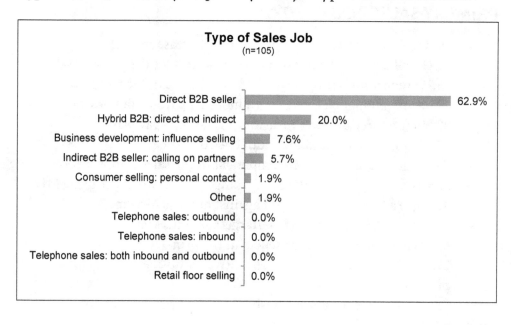

2021 Percent Change in Target Total Earnings: In 2021, what percent will the official (or unofficial) target earnings (base salary plus amount of incentive an average performer will earn) for the primary sales job change from 2020?

10th Perc	25th Perc	50th Perc	75th Perc	90th Perc	Average
0	0	2	5	10	3.8

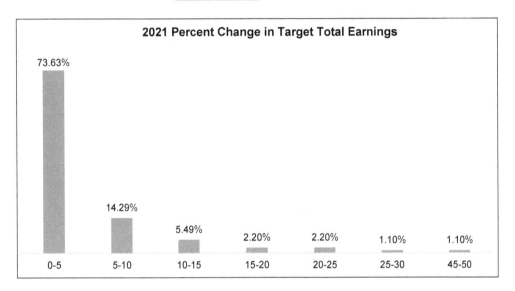

Survey Findings. 2% is the target total earnings planned increase in 2021.

2021 Plan Changes: For the primary sales job, the following elements of the incentive plan will be changed in 2021 (exclude quota changes):

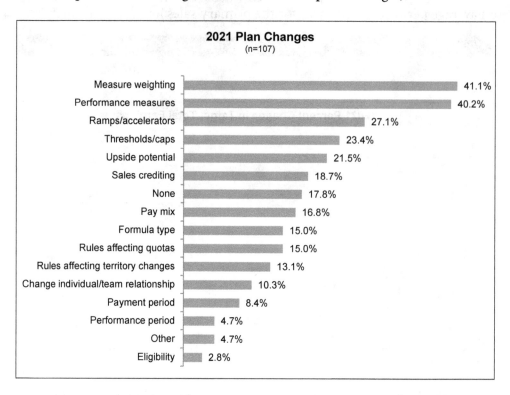

2021 Plan Changes
(n=107)

Element	Percentage
Measure weighting	41.1%
Performance measures	40.2%
Ramps/accelerators	27.1%
Thresholds/caps	23.4%
Upside potential	21.5%
Sales crediting	18.7%
None	17.8%
Pay mix	16.8%
Formula type	15.0%
Rules affecting quotas	15.0%
Rules affecting territory changes	13.1%
Change individual/team relationship	10.3%
Payment period	8.4%
Performance period	4.7%
Other	4.7%
Eligibility	2.8%

Survey Findings. 40.2% will change the performance measures for the primary sales job.

2021 Performance Measures: In 2021, the sales compensation plan for the primary sales job will use which of the following distinct performance measures:

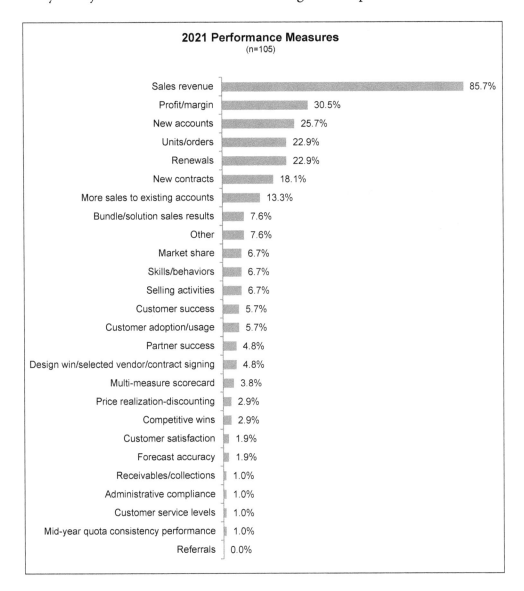

2021 Performance Measures
(n=105)

Measure	Percentage
Sales revenue	85.7%
Profit/margin	30.5%
New accounts	25.7%
Units/orders	22.9%
Renewals	22.9%
New contracts	18.1%
More sales to existing accounts	13.3%
Bundle/solution sales results	7.6%
Other	7.6%
Market share	6.7%
Skills/behaviors	6.7%
Selling activities	6.7%
Customer success	5.7%
Customer adoption/usage	5.7%
Partner success	4.8%
Design win/selected vendor/contract signing	4.8%
Multi-measure scorecard	3.8%
Price realization-discounting	2.9%
Competitive wins	2.9%
Customer satisfaction	1.9%
Forecast accuracy	1.9%
Receivables/collections	1.0%
Administrative compliance	1.0%
Customer service levels	1.0%
Mid-year quota consistency performance	1.0%
Referrals	0.0%

Survey Findings. 85.7% report sales revenue as the key measure in the pay plan.

2021 Measurement and Payment Period: In 2021, the primary performance measure will be measured and paid primarily in the following fashion.

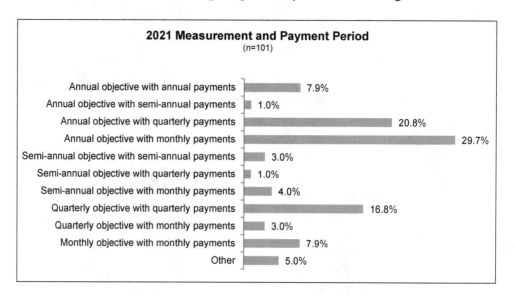

Survey Findings. 29.7% use annual objectives with monthly payouts but practices vary.

2021 Number of Performance Measures: The incentive plan for the primary sales job has how many distinct performance measures?

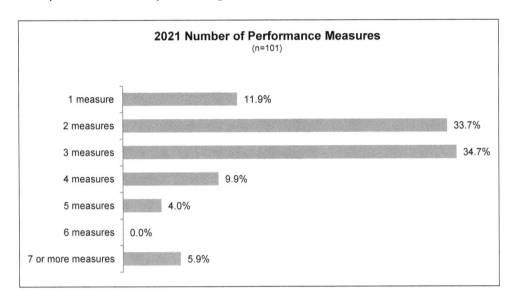

Survey Findings. 80.3% use three or fewer measures in the 2021 pay plan.

2021 Average Target Payout: The average target payout will be a mix of what percent? Enter the percentage; all five must sum to 100%.

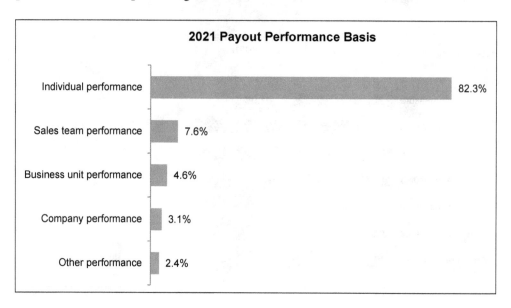

Survey Findings. 82.3% will tie payout to individual performance.

2021 MBO Component: Does the incentive plan for the primary sales job have an MBO (management by objectives) component?

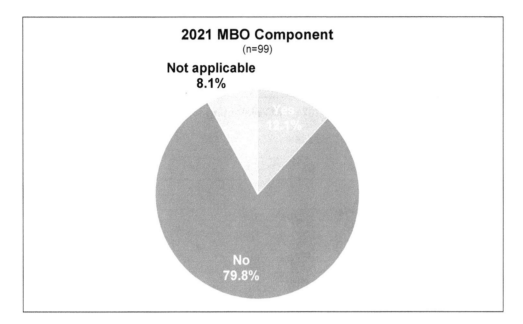

Survey Findings. 79.8% do not use an MBO component in the sales compensation plan.

2021 MBO Weighting: If you have an MBO component, what percent of target incentive does it represent? Leave blank if you do not have an MBO component; enter whole number percent.

10th Perc	25th Perc	50th Perc	75th Perc	90th Perc	Average
10	20	20	32.5	70	31.4

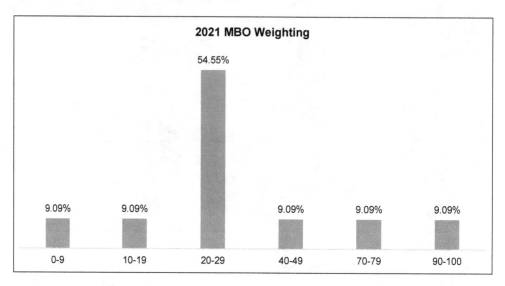

Survey Findings. 20% is the weighting of the MBO component for the 12.1% using MBOs.

2021 Calculation Method: What is the calculation method for the key performance measure of the primary sales job?

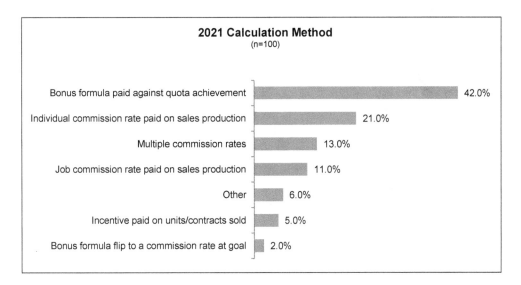

Survey Findings. 42% use a bonus formula paid against quota achievement.

2021 Pay Mix: What is the target pay mix—split of target total pay between base and incentive (e.g., 60/40) for the primary sales job?

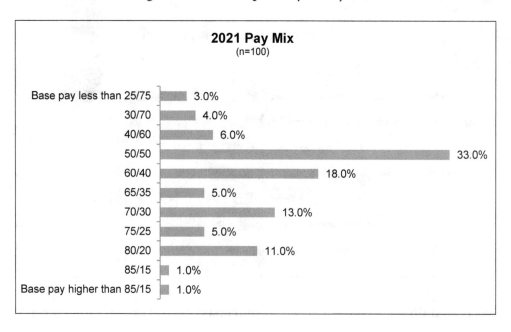

Survey Findings. 33% use a 50/50 pay mix (base/target); practices vary.

2021 Pay Caps: Does the pay plan have an absolute cap on compensation earnings for the primary sales job?

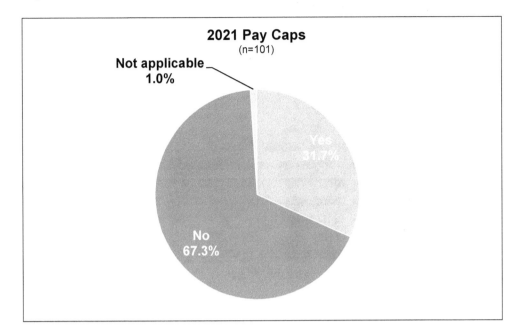

Survey Findings. 67.3% have no pay caps for sellers in the primary sales job.

2021 Leverage/Upside: The best performers (~90th percentile of performance) in the primary sales job can earn how many total incentive dollars as a multiple of the at-risk target incentive dollars?

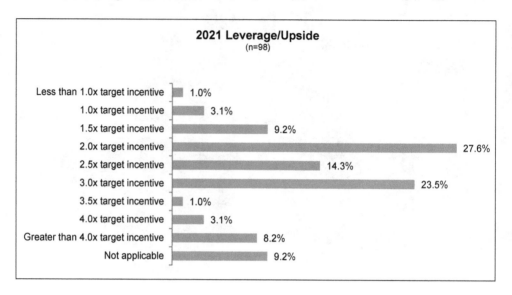

2021 Leverage/Upside
(n=98)

Category	Percentage
Less than 1.0x target incentive	1.0%
1.0x target incentive	3.1%
1.5x target incentive	9.2%
2.0x target incentive	27.6%
2.5x target incentive	14.3%
3.0x target incentive	23.5%
3.5x target incentive	1.0%
4.0x target incentive	3.1%
Greater than 4.0x target incentive	8.2%
Not applicable	9.2%

Survey Findings. 27.6% provide 2x the target incentive as upside earnings potential; practices vary.

Threshold: Does the 2021 sales compensation plan for the primary sales job have a threshold—a minimum level of performance for the key revenue measure before sellers earn incentive?

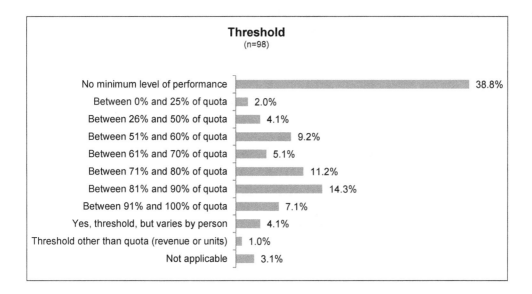

Threshold
(n=98)

Category	Percent
No minimum level of performance	38.8%
Between 0% and 25% of quota	2.0%
Between 26% and 50% of quota	4.1%
Between 51% and 60% of quota	9.2%
Between 61% and 70% of quota	5.1%
Between 71% and 80% of quota	11.2%
Between 81% and 90% of quota	14.3%
Between 91% and 100% of quota	7.1%
Yes, threshold, but varies by person	4.1%
Threshold other than quota (revenue or units)	1.0%
Not applicable	3.1%

Survey Findings. 58.1% use a performance threshold for the primary sales job.

2021 Clawbacks: Can all or any part of the incentive payment be clawed back (repaid to the company) for any reason?

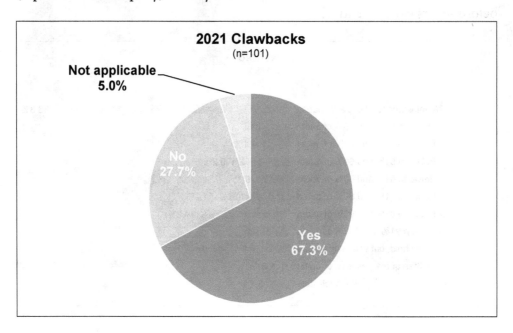

Survey Findings. 67.3% use clawbacks if orders do not fully transact.

2021 New Hires: What is your incentive practice for new hires into the primary sales job?

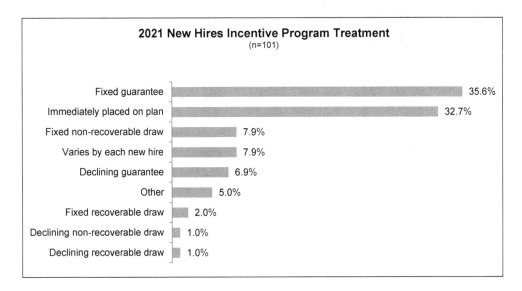

Survey Findings. 35.6% place new hires on a fixed guarantee.

QUOTAS*

- 45.5% of sellers will reach quota in 2020.
- 49% made mid-year 2020 quotas changes.
- 100% of full sales credit matched actual revenue in 2020.
- 85% was the median quota performance in 2020.
- 43.7% of companies over assigned 2021 quotas.
- 41.9% use a combination of top-down and bottom-up to set 2021 quotas.

* Highest Response or Median for the Question

2020 Achieving/Exceeding Quota Percent: What percent of sales personnel in the primary sales job met or exceeded quota in 2020? (e.g., 45%, 65%, 75%)

10th Perc	25th Perc	50th Perc	75th Perc	90th Perc	Average
13.2	28.8	45.5	60.2	75	44.8

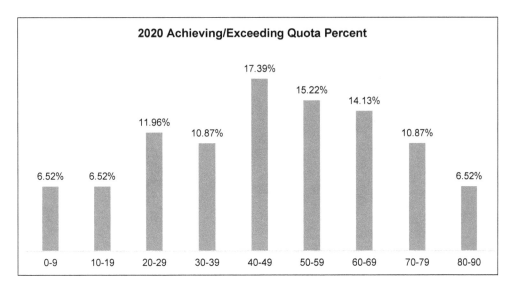

Survey Findings. 45.5% of sellers will reach quota in 2020.

2020 Quotas Changes: In 2020, what percent of incumbents in the primary sales job had their quotas changed mid-performance period?

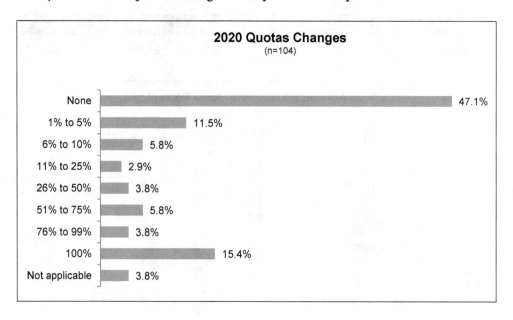

Survey Findings. 49% made mid-year 2020 quotas changes.

2020 Sales Crediting: Is your sales crediting for compensation purposes different than your actual revenue? Estimate the compensable revenue as a percent of actual revenue in 2020 (e.g., 92%, 102%, 126%). Exclude sales crediting for supervisors and managers.

10th Perc	25th Perc	50th Perc	75th Perc	90th Perc	Average
12.7	90.5	100	100	100	82.2

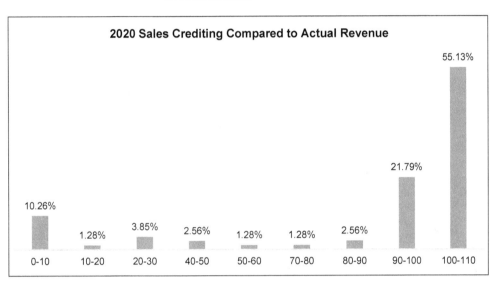

2020 Sales Crediting Compared to Actual Revenue

Survey Findings. 100% of full sales credit matched actual revenue in 2020.

2020 Average Quota Performance: What is the anticipated average (not median) percent sales quota achievement in 2020 for incumbents in the primary sales job? [express as a percent of goal/quota, e.g., 85%, 97%, 101%, 110%] Leave blank if you did not have quotas or goals.

10th Perc	25th Perc	50th Perc	75th Perc	90th Perc	Average
60	74	85	95	100	83.2

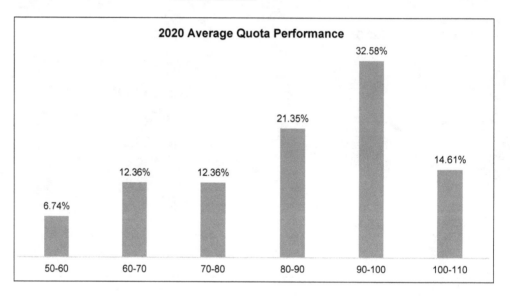

Survey Findings. 85% was the median quota performance in 2020.

2021 Quotas Compared to Forecast: For 2021, how does the summation of assigned quotas to sales personnel compare to the sales department's objective (e.g., over assignment, match or under assignment)?

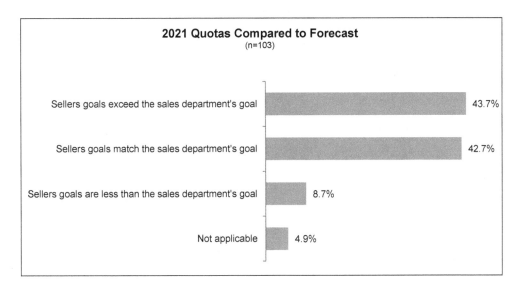

Survey Findings. 43.7% of companies over assigned 2021 quotas.

2021 Quota Allocation Method: Which of the following methods does the company use to allocate sales goals to sales personnel in the primary sales job?

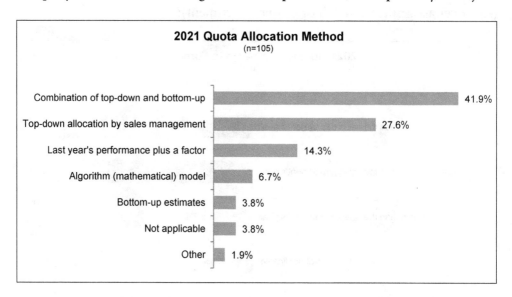

Survey Findings. 41.9% use a combination of top-down and bottom-up to set 2021 quotas.

COVID-19: SALES COMPENSATION—WHAT DID YOU DO?*

- 63% made a change to their incentive plans due to COVID-19.
- 64.5% have no plans for sales restart incentives.
- 2.8% made base pay adjustments for relocated sellers; most did not have relocated sellers.

Highest Response or Median for the Question

Program Changes: Did you make mid-year pay adjustments affecting incentive payments for the primary sales job?

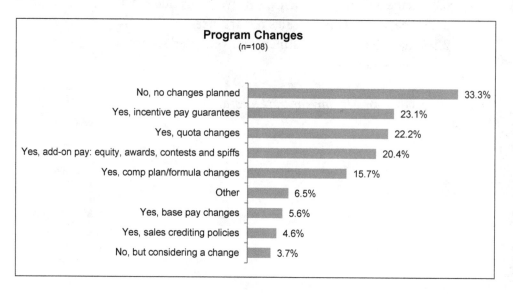

Survey Findings. 63% made a change to their incentive plans due to COVID-19.

Sales Restart Incentives: What additional restart incentives do you plan to provide (or have already provided) for the primary sales jobs?

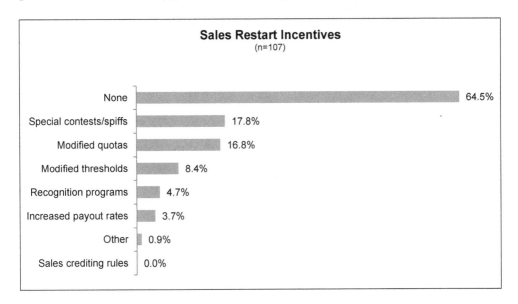

Survey Findings. 64.5% have no plans for sales restart incentives.

Work From Home Base Pay Adjustments: Some companies allowed select employees to relocate from a high-cost area to a low-cost area. Did you change the base pay of these individuals?

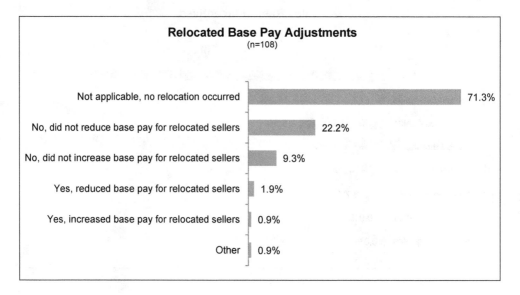

Relocated Base Pay Adjustments
(n=108)

Not applicable, no relocation occurred	71.3%
No, did not reduce base pay for relocated sellers	22.2%
No, did not increase base pay for relocated sellers	9.3%
Yes, reduced base pay for relocated sellers	1.9%
Yes, increased base pay for relocated sellers	0.9%
Other	0.9%

Survey Findings. 2.8% made base pay adjustments for relocated sellers; most did not have relocated sellers.

TRENDING TOPICS*

- 31.1% identified sales managers/sales operations responsible for plan design.
- Twelve weeks is typical maternity leave.
- 62.5% make pay and/or quota adjustments for maternity leave.
- Six weeks is the median paternity leave.
- 57.3% make pay and/or quota adjustments for paternity leave.
- 89.4% do not plan to examine sales job FLSA exemption status due to virtual selling.
- 43.3% provide incentives to lead generation representatives.
- 46.2% reward revenue from new customers/accounts differently; practices vary.
- Three FTEs assigned to administer plan; 91 payees.
- 33% use desktop solutions to administer pay plan; 25.5% use SaaS provider.
- 48.6% will make changes/investments to the automation system.
- 47.1% provide mobile access to incentive reporting.
- 62.4% have or plan to examine pay equity (gender) among sellers.
- Internal automation solutions are the top two applications.

Highest Response or Median for the Question

Responsible for Plan Design: Who is responsible for designing the sales compensation plans (leads the process, suggests and selects design changes)?

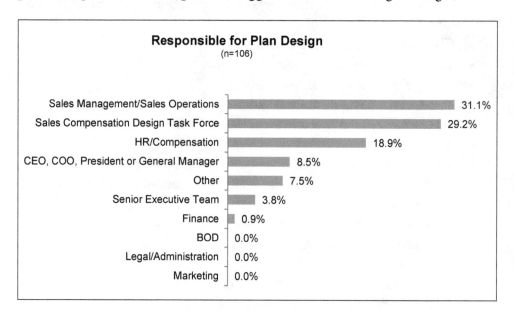

Survey Findings. 31.1% identified sales managers/sales operations responsible for plan design.

Maternity Leave of Absence: How many weeks of maternity/adoption leave of absence do you provide to sellers (not to exceed)?

10th Perc	25th Perc	50th Perc	75th Perc	90th Perc	Average
6	8.5	12	12	16	11.8

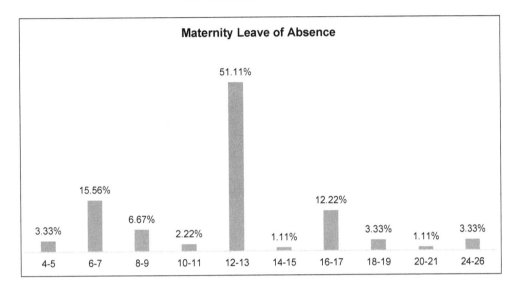

Survey Findings. Twelve weeks is typical maternity leave.

Maternity Leave of Absence Incentive Earnings: How do you treat maternity/ adoption leave of absence incentive earnings?

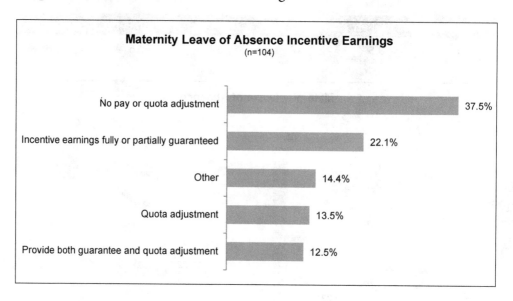

Survey Findings. 62.5% make pay and/or quota adjustments for maternity leave.

Paternity Leave of Absence: How many weeks of paternity/adoption leave of absence do you provide to sellers (not to exceed)?

10th Perc	25th Perc	50th Perc	75th Perc	90th Perc	Average
1.5	4	6	12	12	7.8

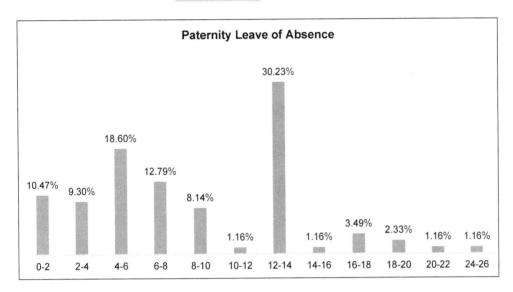

Survey Findings. Six weeks is the median paternity leave.

Paternity Leave of Absence Incentive Earnings: How do you treat paternity/adoption leave of absence incentive earnings?

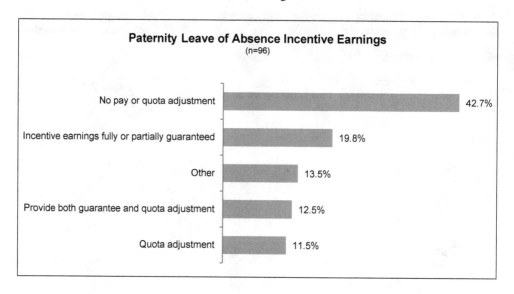

Survey Findings. 57.3% make pay and/or quota adjustments for paternity leave.

Sales Job FLSA Exemption Status: Are you considering changing the exempt status of sales jobs to non-exempt status due to changes in selling practices for the primary sales job, i.e., virtual selling?

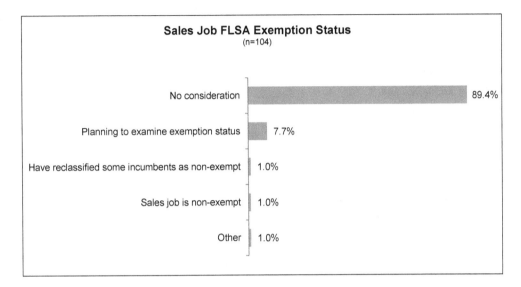

Survey Findings. 89.4% do not plan to examine sales job FLSA exemption status due to virtual selling.

Incentives for Lead Generation Jobs: Do you provide incentives for your dedicated lead generation jobs?

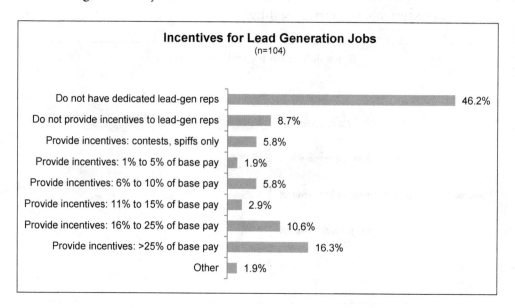

Survey Findings. 43.3% provide incentives to lead generation representatives.

New Customers/Accounts: Do you have any special incentives for new-account selling?

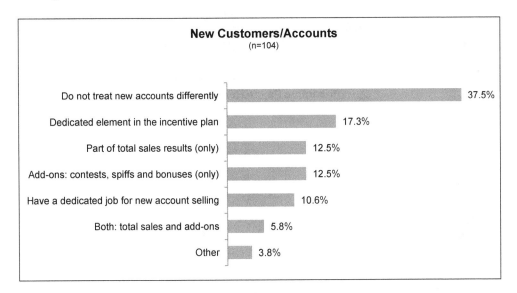

Survey Findings. 46.2% reward revenue from new customers/accounts differently; practices vary.

Incentive Payee Headcount: How many customer contact personnel are eligible for performance incentives?

10th Perc	25th Perc	50th Perc	75th Perc	90th Perc	Average
1.5	15	90.5	318.8	1450	404

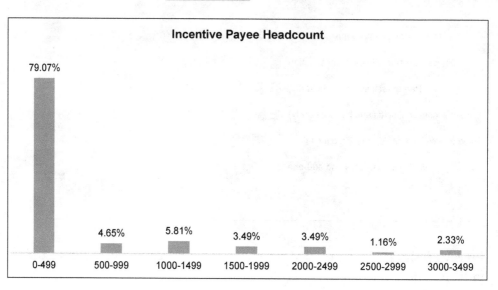

Incentive Program FTE Plan Administration: How many full-time equivalent (FTE) personnel provide ongoing plan administration support (exclude design or program management)?

10th Perc	25th Perc	50th Perc	75th Perc	90th Perc	Average
1	1	3	6	14	6.8

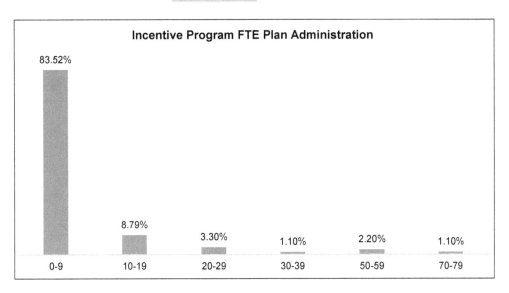

Survey Findings. Three FTEs assigned to administer plan; 91 payees.

Automated Administration Solution: For your largest sales population, how do you currently administer your sales compensation plan?

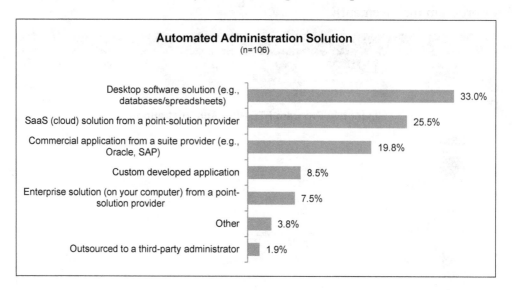

Survey Findings. 33% use desktop solutions to administer pay plan; 25.5% use a SaaS provider.

Automation Investment: In 2021, do you plan to make investments in your automation solution?

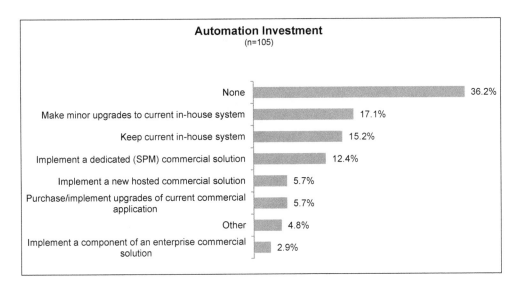

Survey Findings. 48.6% will make changes/investments to the automation system.

Mobile Access: Do sales personnel have access to sales compensation reports via their mobile devices (smart phone and tablets)?

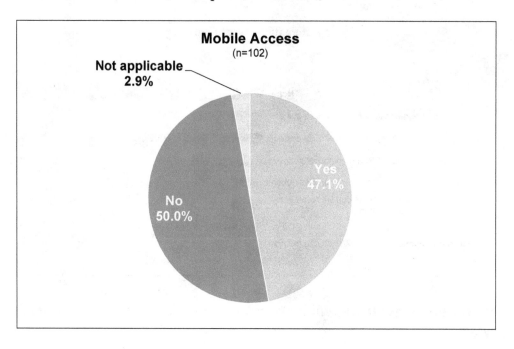

Survey Findings. 47.1% provide mobile access to incentive reporting.

Pay Equity: Has the company conducted a formal assessment of sales compensation pay equity examining gender pay variance among job incumbents within the last two years?

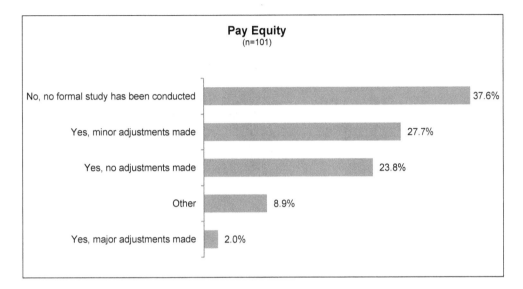

Pay Equity
(n=101)

No, no formal study has been conducted	37.6%
Yes, minor adjustments made	27.7%
Yes, no adjustments made	23.8%
Other	8.9%
Yes, major adjustments made	2.0%

Survey Findings. 62.4% have or plan to examine pay equity (gender) among sellers.

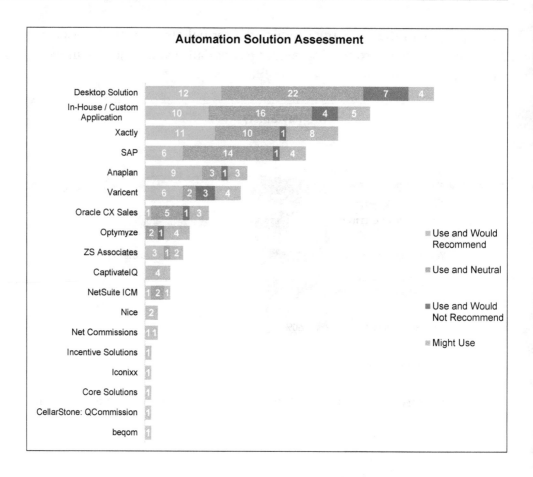

Other Automation Vendors Cited
- Leaptree Incentivize
- Sage
- MS Dynamics
- KMK
- Canidium
- Forma.ai

Quota System Vendors Used
- Alteryx
- Anaplan (3)
- Adaptive Insights
- TerrAlign

Survey Findings. Internal automation solutions are the top two applications. Vendors continue to make improvements to their automation applications. Investigate current functionality to best evaluate offerings.

DEMOGRAPHICS

Fiscal Year: In what month does your fiscal 2021 year begin?

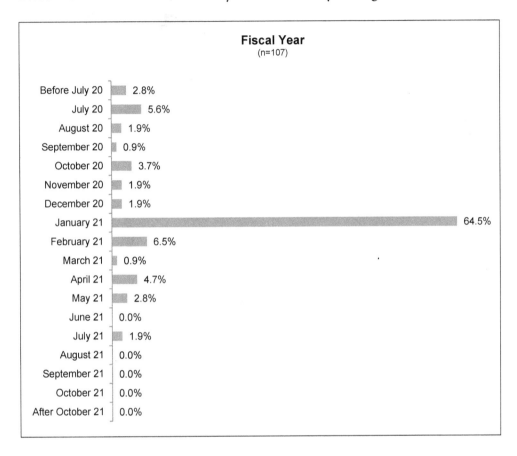

Number of Eligible Participants: For your division sales unit, how many employees are eligible to participate in the sales compensation program? Enter a whole number; an estimate is acceptable.

10th Perc	25th Perc	50th Perc	75th Perc	90th Perc	Average
30.8	70.5	150	635	2000	595.9

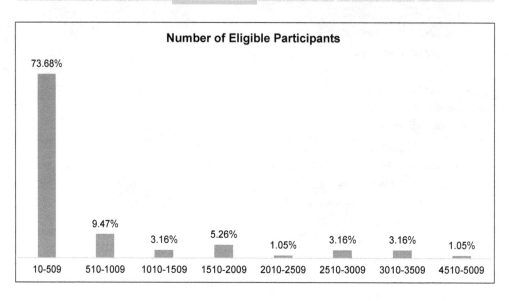

Type of Product/Service: What type of product does your division sell?

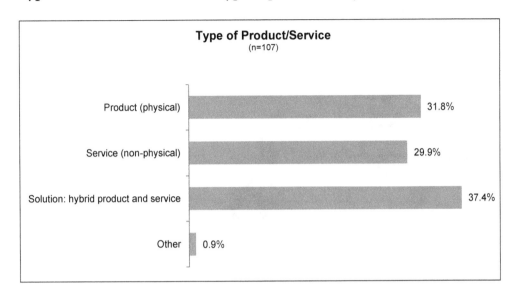

Sales Model: What is the primary sales model for the division sales unit?

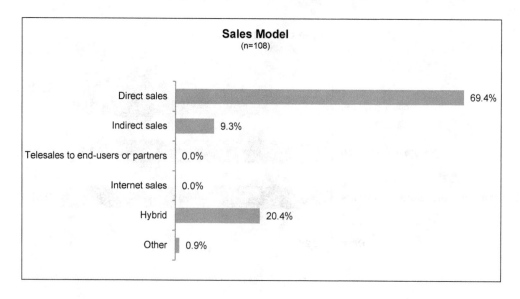

Revenue Type: What is the primary revenue objective?

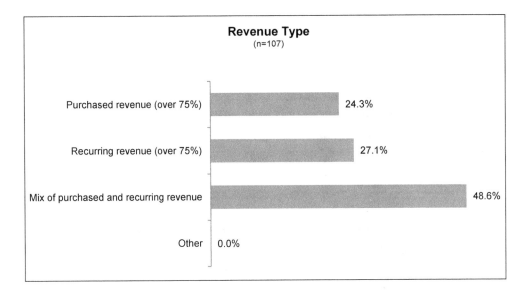

Revenue Type
(n=107)

Purchased revenue (over 75%)   24.3%

Recurring revenue (over 75%)   27.1%

Mix of purchased and recurring revenue   48.6%

Other   0.0%

Industry Category: What is the industry for the division sales unit?

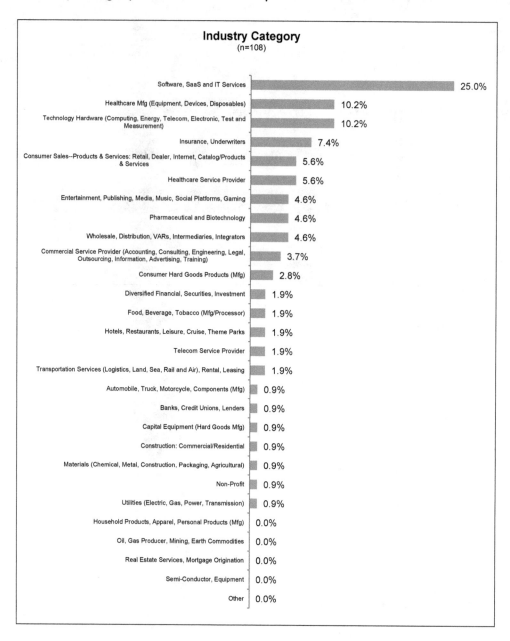

Industry Category
(n=108)

Industry	Percent
Software, SaaS and IT Services	25.0%
Healthcare Mfg (Equipment, Devices, Disposables)	10.2%
Technology Hardware (Computing, Energy, Telecom, Electronic, Test and Measurement)	10.2%
Insurance, Underwriters	7.4%
Consumer Sales--Products & Services: Retail, Dealer, Internet, Catalog/Products & Services	5.6%
Healthcare Service Provider	5.6%
Entertainment, Publishing, Media, Music, Social Platforms, Gaming	4.6%
Pharmaceutical and Biotechnology	4.6%
Wholesale, Distribution, VARs, Intermediaries, Integrators	4.6%
Commercial Service Provider (Accounting, Consulting, Engineering, Legal, Outsourcing, Information, Advertising, Training)	3.7%
Consumer Hard Goods Products (Mfg)	2.8%
Diversified Financial, Securities, Investment	1.9%
Food, Beverage, Tobacco (Mfg/Processor)	1.9%
Hotels, Restaurants, Leisure, Cruise, Theme Parks	1.9%
Telecom Service Provider	1.9%
Transportation Services (Logistics, Land, Sea, Rail and Air), Rental, Leasing	1.9%
Automobile, Truck, Motorcycle, Components (Mfg)	0.9%
Banks, Credit Unions, Lenders	0.9%
Capital Equipment (Hard Goods Mfg)	0.9%
Construction: Commercial/Residential	0.9%
Materials (Chemical, Metal, Construction, Packaging, Agricultural)	0.9%
Non-Profit	0.9%
Utilities (Electric, Gas, Power, Transmission)	0.9%
Household Products, Apparel, Personal Products (Mfg)	0.0%
Oil, Gas Producer, Mining, Earth Commodities	0.0%
Real Estate Services, Mortgage Origination	0.0%
Semi-Conductor, Equipment	0.0%
Other	0.0%

Sales Volume: The division's sales for 2020 will be (approximately):

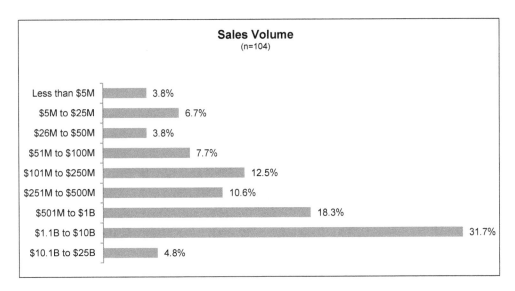

Sales Volume
(n=104)

Less than $5M	3.8%
$5M to $25M	6.7%
$26M to $50M	3.8%
$51M to $100M	7.7%
$101M to $250M	12.5%
$251M to $500M	10.6%
$501M to $1B	18.3%
$1.1B to $10B	31.7%
$10.1B to $25B	4.8%

SALES
COMPENSATION:
MULTIYEAR TRENDS

SALES COMPENSATION ALMANAC • 2022

MULTIYEAR TRENDS DATA

Conducted each year since 2003, the *Sales Compensation Trends Survey* captures a moving history of sales compensation program trends. Economic cycles affect certain outcomes such as revenue, quota performance and pay increase amounts. The data and charts reveal the impact of these cycles. Other practices remain relatively constant.

LISTING OF CHARTS

- Change in Annual Revenue—Projected Versus Actual
- Sales Force Actual Headcount Changes
- Turnover Rate
- Sales Compensation Program Effectiveness
- Payouts and Performance
- Extent of Program Changes
- Average Quota Achievement
- Percent Achieving Quota
- Projected Change in Total Earnings
- Actual Change in Incentive Payments

Change in Annual Revenue—Projected Versus Actual

Each year, The Alexander Group asks survey participants two questions: How much did revenue grow in the previous year? How much revenue growth do you expect next year? Revenue projections affect quota setting, which affects sales compensation plan payouts. The more accurate the revenue forecast (as compared to the actual), the more likely sales personnel will have stretch but achievable sales quotas. When the two numbers vary (either the actual is above or below the projected revenue growth), variance in plan payouts will most likely occur. 2020 saw the projected and actual growth vary substantially due to the pandemic. Revenue management expected growth of 6% but only achieved 2%. Other survey research confirmed that companies with significant declines in revenue provided partial pay protection to sellers during 2020. Revenue leaders expect a strong 8% revenue growth in 2021.

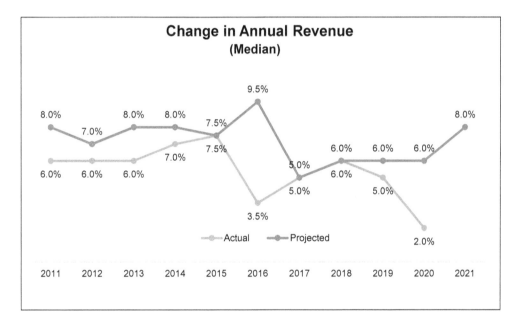

Sales Force Actual Headcount Changes

After a peak hiring year in 2018, actual headcount changes declined. In 2018, 59% increased headcount. In 2020, only 28.7% increased headcount. In 2018, only 10.3% decreased headcount. By 2020, 36.6% decreased headcount. The 2020 headcount changes reflect the pandemic-induced economic contraction.

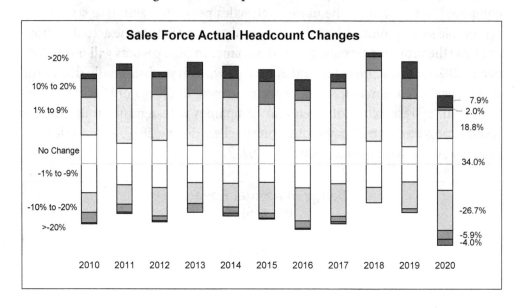

Turnover Rate

2020 saw a significant drop in turnover. Many companies were not hiring during the pandemic. Employment choices for salespeople were curtailed. As compared to the norm of 10% turnover rate, 2020 recorded a turnover rate of 5%. These turnover statistics represent both voluntary and involuntary turnover. A typical turnover rate for sales teams is close to 10%. We expect this trend to return.

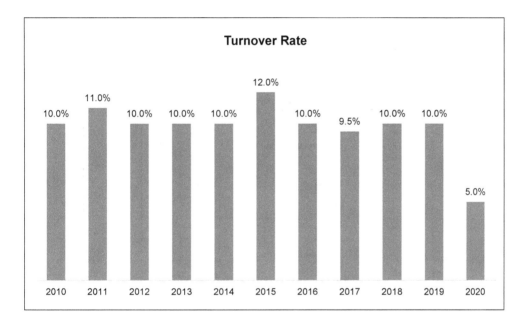

Sales Compensation Program Effectiveness

During the past 10 years, most companies have viewed their sales compensation plans as acceptable and better. However, 2020 saw a large jump in sales leaders giving their sales compensation plan a less than acceptable rating. In 2020, 16% of sales leaders rated their sales compensation as less than acceptable. This is a significant jump from the 11.6% rating of less than acceptable recorded in 2019.

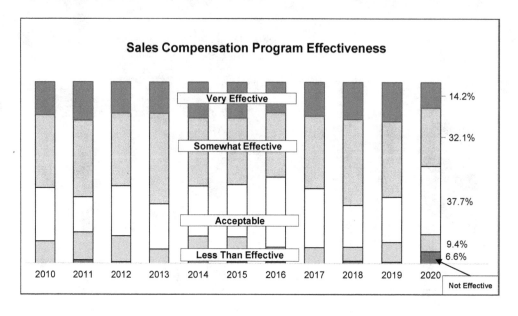

Payouts and Performance

Examining how well payouts matched performance helps assess program effectiveness. The closer payouts match performance, the more effective the program. In 2020, the year of the pandemic, 32.4% said their pay plan either moderately matched or did not match performance. This is the largest mismatch between payouts and performance recorded in the previous 10 years.

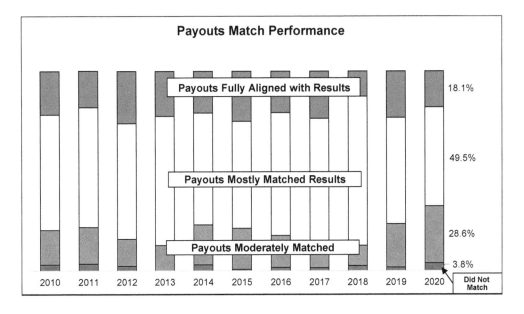

Extent of Program Changes

Sales management makes sales compensation program changes to keep the pay program aligned with sales objectives. Often, management makes changes to the performance measures to ensure strategic alignment. 7.3% is the average "no changes" made to the pay plan for the last 10 years. The exception is 2021 where all companies made changes to their pay plans for 2021.

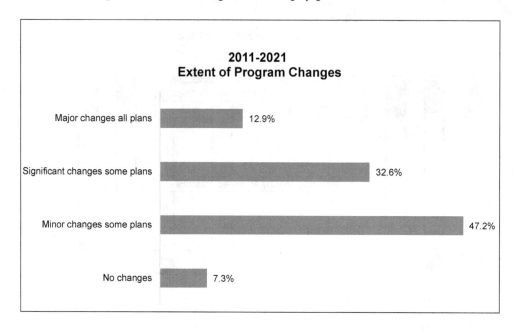

2011-2021
Extent of Program Changes

Major changes all plans	12.9%
Significant changes some plans	32.6%
Minor changes some plans	47.2%
No changes	7.3%

Average Quota Achievement

Average quota achievement gives an overall summary of the sales team's sales success. The average quota achievement includes all participants, both low performers and high performers. The average quota performance for 2020 was 85%, the lowest recorded in 10 years.

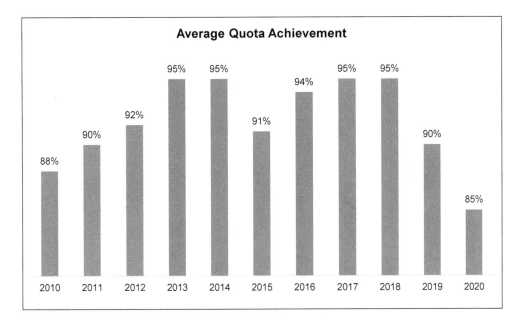

Percent Achieving Quota

Most companies target 60% to 70% of all sellers to achieve quota. Both 2019 and 2020 saw less than 50% of the sellers reaching quota; 45% in 2019 and 46% in 2020. The more typical outcome is for approximately 50% of all sellers to reach and exceed quota.

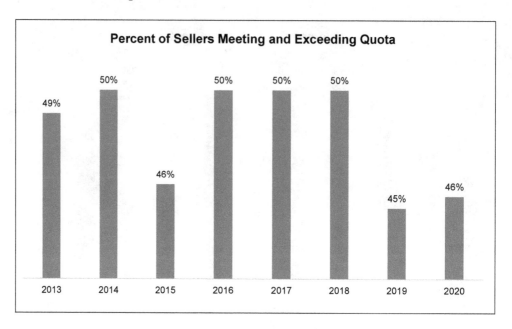

Projected Change in Total Earnings

Each year's wage inflation moves total earnings for all sellers. Estimated wage inflation (the increase in total earnings including base pay and incentive earnings) continues to track between 2% and 3%. These modest planned increases reflect low wage inflation.

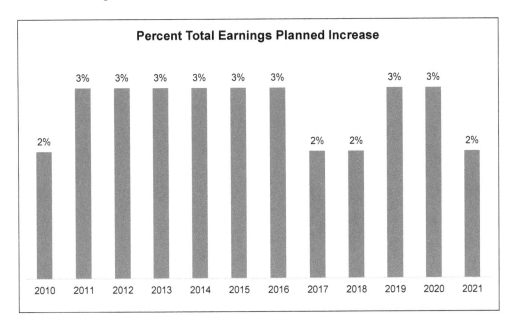

Actual Change in Incentive Payments

Year-to-year change in incentive payments (median) fluctuates. The change in actual incentive payments is an outcome of sales performance affected by market trends, competitor actions and quota difficulty. Due to the pandemic, 2020 overall incentive payments declined –1.5%. The last recorded decline was in 2008.

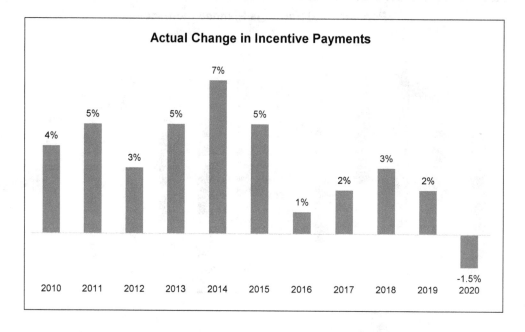

2020 SALES COMPENSATION HOT TOPICS SURVEY

SALES COMPENSATION ALMANAC • 2022

2020 SALES COMPENSATION HOT TOPICS SURVEY

Each year, the sales compensation "hot topics" survey provides in-depth insight into select sales compensation practices. The *2020 Sales Compensation Hot Topics Survey* examined recent and popular topics in sales compensation practices.

IN THIS SECTION

- Executive Summary
- COVID-19 Pay Protection Practices
- Sales Restart After COVID-19
- Recurring Revenue and Renewals
- Program Late Start Practices
- Pre-Booking Incentives
- Demographics

EXECUTIVE SUMMARY

Each year, the Alexander Group conducts the *Sales Compensation Hot Topics Survey* to capture current trends, answer popular questions and examine topics of interest. We ask both our clients and our consultants to suggest topics for consideration. Thank you to the 135 participating companies that contributed their professional perspectives.

We gathered data in June 2020 and published in July 2020.

Noteworthy Highlights

- **COVID-19 Pay Protection Practices.** 64.2% of the companies will make changes to sellers' compensation due to COVID-19. For companies where the negative impact on revenue was greater than 15%, 70.8% of the responding companies will provide some form of partial incentive compensation pay protection. The common method is a pay guarantee, but other techniques are prevalent, too.

- **Sales Restart After COVID 19.** Half of the companies plan to provide additional seller and buyer incentives to help restart sales.

- **Recurring Revenue.** Account managers and territory representatives are frequently responsible for renewal revenue. Half of the companies treat new and renewal revenues the same for compensation purposes. For the most part, revenue crediting occurs at time of sale regardless of contract expiration date.

- **Program Late Start Practices.** Most companies implement their pay programs on time. One-third of the companies provide a draw to offset any program late start.

- **Pre-Booking Incentives.** Almost half of the companies use pre-booking incentives for one or more of their customer contact jobs.

COVID-19 PAY PROTECTION PRACTICES

COVID-19 caused a disruption in revenues. In some cases, the change in revenue was modest. In other cases, it was significant. Among sales personnel, the impact was not uniform. Some saw only a minor impact on their territory revenue, while select peers saw a major impact. 64.2% of the companies will make changes to sellers' compensation due to COVID-19. For companies where the negative impact on revenue was greater than 15%, 70.8% of the companies will provide some form of incentive pay protection.

The most popular method is to provide a guarantee (29.9%), some amount greater than 50% of target incentive. Other pay protection techniques include compensation sales plan/formula changes (21.6%) and quota adjustments (16.4%). 57% of the companies used multiple methods, including one-off adjustments for specific territories.

Program Changes: Did you make mid-year pay adjustments affecting incentive payments for the primary sales job?

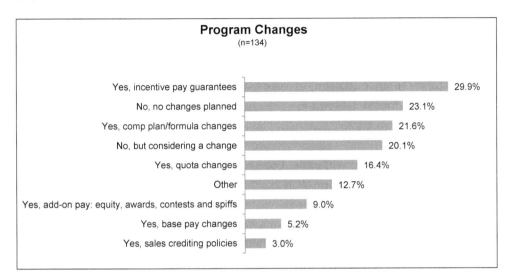

Program Changes
(n=134)

Category	Percentage
Yes, incentive pay guarantees	29.9%
No, no changes planned	23.1%
Yes, comp plan/formula changes	21.6%
No, but considering a change	20.1%
Yes, quota changes	16.4%
Other	12.7%
Yes, add-on pay: equity, awards, contests and spiffs	9.0%
Yes, base pay changes	5.2%
Yes, sales crediting policies	3.0%

Survey Findings. Sales leaders in 64.2% of the reporting companies will make changes to sellers' pay as a result of COVID-19 impact on compensation earnings. The most popular change is pay guarantees (29.9%) followed by formula changes (21.6%) and quota changes (16.4%). Some companies use multiple techniques: 24.4% will use one pay adjustment method; 22.2% will use two methods and 10.4% will use three methods.

Other Program Changes

Cap for incentive

With regards to "no, but considering a change," we are still looking into mid-year quota changes

No, but considering a change among select impacted population only

Reduced quotas and added team component

We did guarantee and comp plan change, but only for a narrow slice of the org.

Considering additional

Negative forgiveness—no paybacks for YTD components

Considering plan/quota be on July-Dec. Jan-June had no quota change, but was guaranteed

Considering LATAM region: yes, comp plan/formula changes plus pay guarantees

Plan to add an "attainment boost" for quota carrying sellers

Bonus target indexation based on revenue performance

We made some quarterly exceptions

Considering account changes, spiffs and bonuses—quota changes as last resort

Guaranteed minimum incentive for Q2 with obligation to pay back through future production

Temporary pay reductions to both base and VC

Backstop repayable loan program

Made adjustments to our quota-setting process

Accelerator for revenue attained between March and July

Adjusted targets for fall

Goals have been revised

Revenue/Bookings: Do you expect the COVID-19 crisis to have an impact on your annual revenue/bookings?

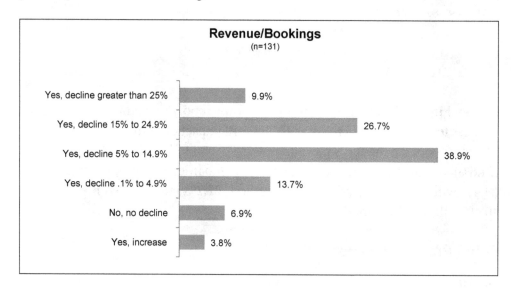

Sales Compensation Impact: Without management intervention, what impact could COVID-19 have on your sellers' annual incentive earnings?

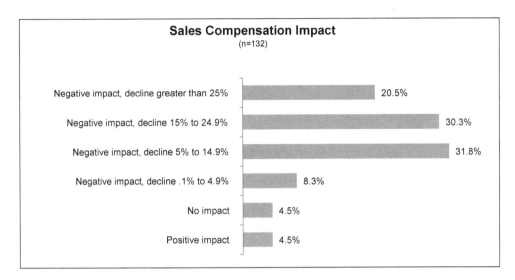

Survey Findings. 50.8% would see a decline in sellers' earnings of greater than 15% without pay protection intervention.

Incentive Replacement: What level of target or expected incentive replacement do you plan to provide to sellers?

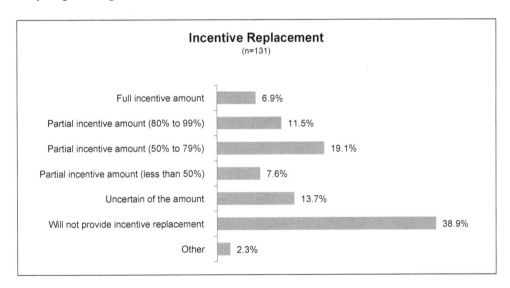

Duration of Changes: What is the expected duration for pay adjustment changes to the primary sales job? For those whose response might be "don't know," make your best guesstimate.

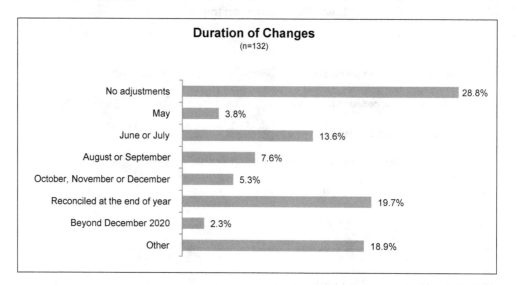

Duration of Changes
(n=132)

- No adjustments — 28.8%
- May — 3.8%
- June or July — 13.6%
- August or September — 7.6%
- October, November or December — 5.3%
- Reconciled at the end of year — 19.7%
- Beyond December 2020 — 2.3%
- Other — 18.9%

Survey Findings. Of the companies providing incentive replacement, 19.1% will provide 50% to 79% of target incentive. The planned duration of pay adjustments varies significantly by company, with no clear pattern. 19.7% doing final reconciliation at year-end. Regardless, most all companies expect any special pay practices to terminate between now and the end of the calendar year.

SALES RESTART AFTER COVID-19

Companies are eager to "restart" their sales efforts. With the arrival of COVID-19, most sales teams quickly pivoted to "COVID-19 selling:" virtual selling, social distancing and stay-at-home practices.

28.7% will reduce headcount.

For those needing to "restart sales," 54.1% plan to provide additional seller incentives. 53.4% plan to offer buyer incentives.

Headcount: What mid-year 2020-headcount changes will sales leadership make/have made?

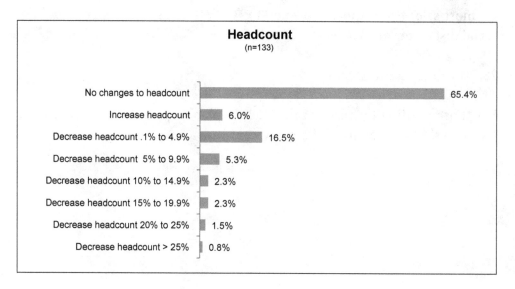

Survey Findings. 65.4% made no mid-year seller headcount changes. 28.7% will reduce seller headcount; 6% will increase headcount.

Sales Force Additional Restart Incentives: What additional mid-year 2020-restart incentives do you plan to provide (or have already provided) for the primary sales jobs?

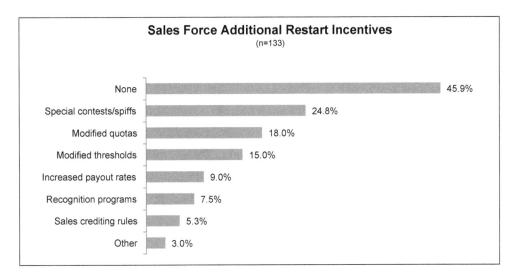

Buyer Incentives: What type of new buyer incentives is your company offering to encourage customer purchasing?

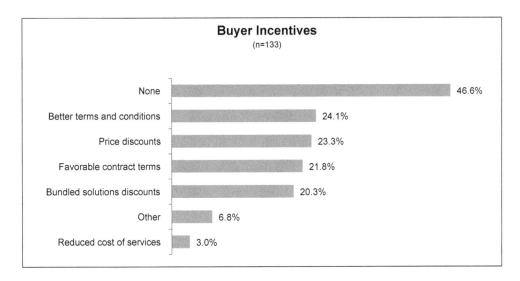

Survey Findings. 54.1% will use additional restart seller incentives. 53.4% plan to provide buyer incentives. Slightly more than the majority of companies will use additional seller and buyer incentives.

RECURRING REVENUE AND RENEWALS

Recurring Revenue

Across many industries, companies provide products and services supported by recurring revenue. The customer does not purchase the product, but "rents" the functionality on a monthly basis; thus, the seller/provider earns "recurring revenue." 68.7% of the survey participants earn recurring revenue for some set of products and services.

Renewals

Companies plan for renewals of recurring revenue contracts. These renewals will be incorporated into the seller's quota. Here is the sales compensation challenge: What happens to incentive pay if the seller has the customer renew the contract prior to the performance period containing the anticipated quota? Only 14.1% make quota, credit or timing adjustments. Likewise, what if the seller closes the contract after the expiration date, causing it to fall into the next performance period? Regardless of quota implications, most companies credit at time of sale. However, 20.3% will make some type of adjustment to the credit timing or amount for late signing.

Types of Revenue: What purchase types do you provide to customers?

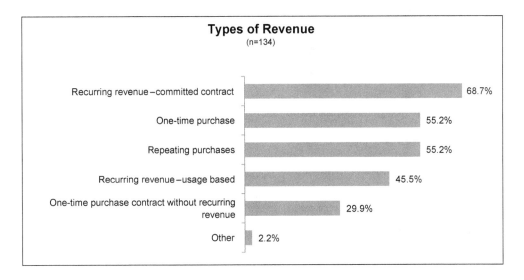

Recurring Revenue Measurement: How do you measure recurring revenue?

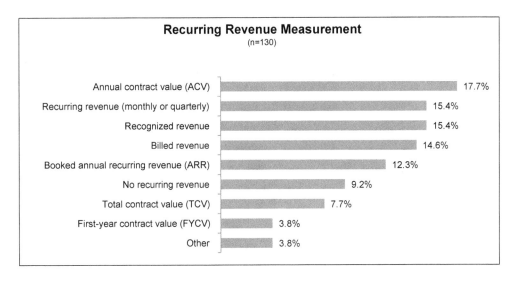

Survey Findings. Most companies have multiple different revenue types. 68.7% have recurring revenue with a committed contract. The most common measurement of recurring revenue for incentive purposes is annual contract value (ACV) (17.7%).

Renewal Responsibility: Which jobs in your company are responsible for closing renewal business?

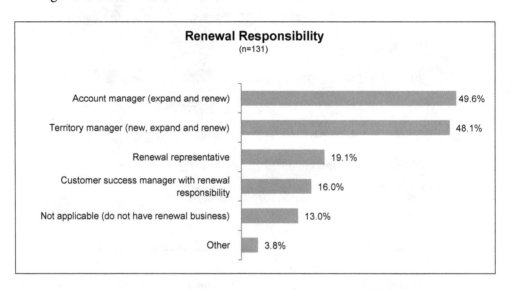

Compensating the Primary Sales Job on Renewals: How does your company compensate your core sales role on renewals?

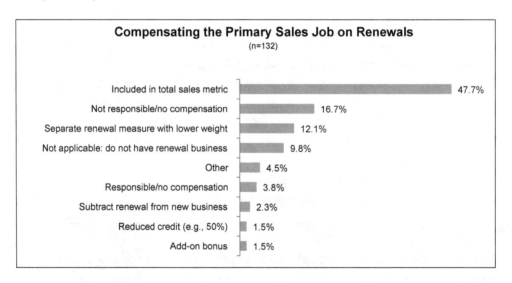

Survey Findings. Account managers (49.6%) and territory managers (48.1%) are responsible for renewals. Renewals are an important element of the revenue goal. Often, the account manager/territory representative is responsible for these revenue dollars, which are part of the total sales goal and compensated accordingly. Renewal revenue is often included in the total sales metric (47.7%).

Early Renewal Contract Signing: How does your company compensate a seller who closes a renewal in a fiscal period prior to expected renewal date (e.g., closed a FY21 renewal in FY20)?

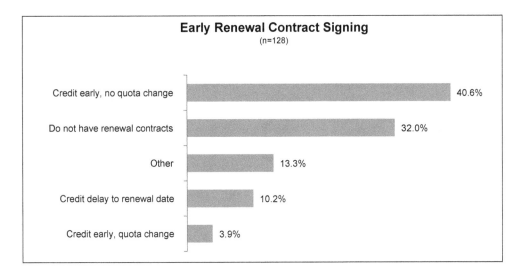

Late Renewal Contract Signing: How does your company compensate a seller who closes a renewal in a fiscal period after an expected renewal date (e.g., closed a FY20 renewal in FY21)?

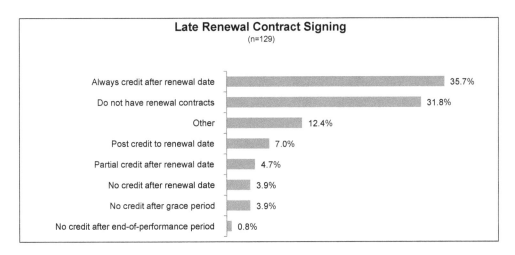

Survey Findings. Early/late renewals: Do they affect sales compensation? The most prevalent practices are to not adjust payments for early renewals (40.6%); and to not adjust for late renewals (35.7%). Off schedule renewals can cause unexpected payments if quotas anticipate the target date for the renewals. 14.1% make adjustments for early renewals. 20.3% will make some type of adjustment to the credit timing or amount for late renewals.

PROGRAM LATE START PRACTICES

While not the intention, there are many reasons why sales compensation plans are late. The goal is to implement the new sales compensation plan at the start of the fiscal year. Numerous reasons, such as late quotas (13.4%) or late formula design (11.9%), cause the delay.

33.9% provide a draw to incumbents as they await their "late" sales compensation plans to arrive.

Start of Year Recoverable Draw Practice: Does your company provide "start of year" recoverable draws and, if so, for what reason?

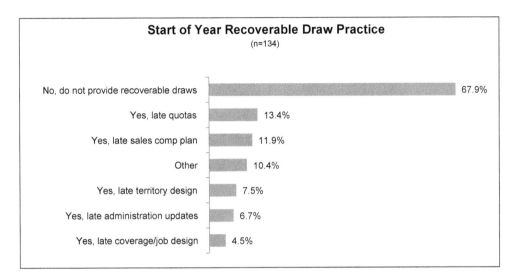

Survey Findings. 33.9% provide a draw for "late" sales compensation plans. The top two reasons causing a late launch to the new fiscal year plan are late quotas (13.4%) and late plan designs (11.9%).

Start of Year Recoverable Draw Duration: How long does your company provide "start of year" recoverable draws?

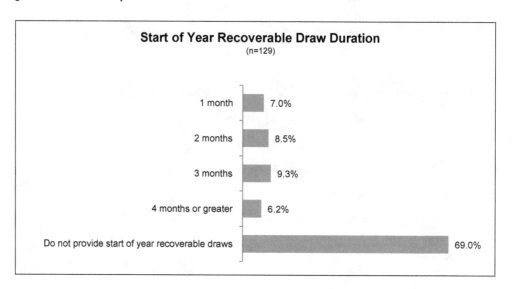

Start of Year Recoverable Draw Amount: What percent of the target incentive does your company provide in its "start of year" recoverable draw?

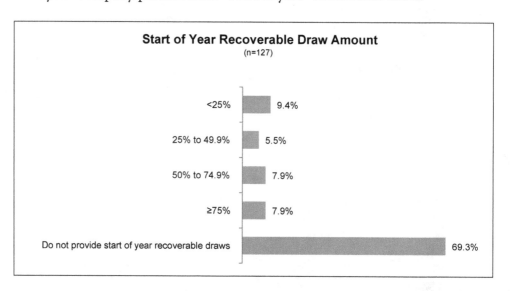

Survey Findings. Of the companies providing a draw, 80% of the draws last less than 4 months. 9.4% provide a draw of less than 25% of the target incentive. Generally, start of year draws for late program implementation are not prevalent.

PRE-BOOKING INCENTIVES

One of the tenets of sales compensation design is to "pay for results." That is, the incentive program pays for confirmed sales bookings or revenue received. Any measure prior to the official acceptance of an order (and invoice issued) is considered a "pre-booking" event or activity. 48.1% of the reporting companies have one or more jobs paying incentives on pre-booking milestones or activities.

Reasons for providing pre-booking activities could include one or more of the following.

- **Teaching:** For some jobs, sales leadership uses the incentive plan to teach the "right" sales behaviors.

- **Execution Excellence:** Sales management might have a tightly engineered "successful selling process" that sellers must follow. Sales leadership rewards sellers for compliance to this preferred selling model.

- **Only Accountabilities Are Pre-Booking Actions:** Finally, some jobs only focus on pre-billing activities such as "securing qualified leads." In such cases, the only measurements available for incentive purposes are pre-booking milestones or activities.

Jobs Eligible for Pre-Booking Rewards: Which jobs are eligible for financial or non-financial incentives for milestones or activities prior to sales bookings?

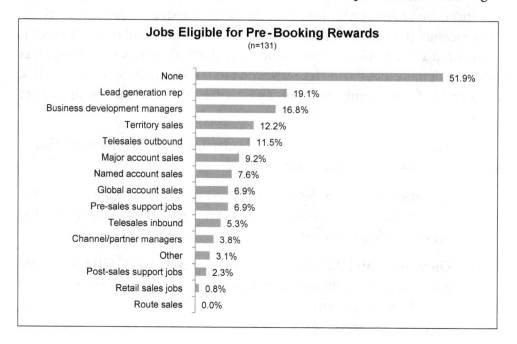

Functionality: Regardless of practice, does your organization have the tracking structure to measure pre-booking sales milestones or activities for some or all jobs?

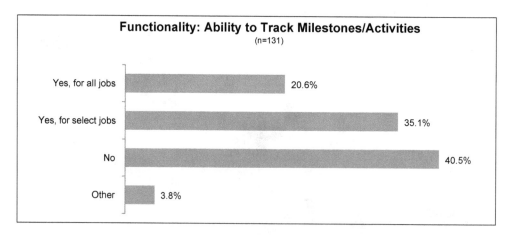

Survey Findings. 48.1% use pre-booking incentives for one or more jobs. Lead generation reps (19.1%), business development managers (16.8%) and territory sales (12.2%) are the most common jobs earning pre-booking incentives. 20.6% have suitable milestone/activity tracking systems; 40.5% do not.

Pre-Booking Sales Milestones: For customer contact jobs, do you provide any rewards for the following pre-booking sales milestones?

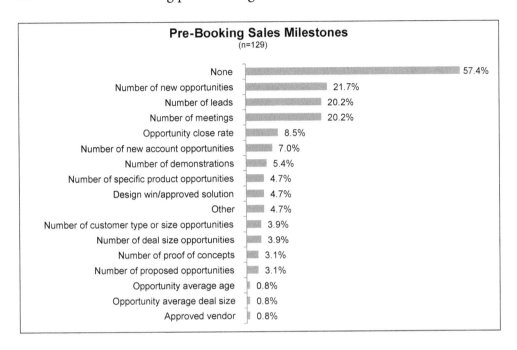

Pre-Booking Sales Milestone Award Types: What awards, if any, do you provide for pre-sales milestones?

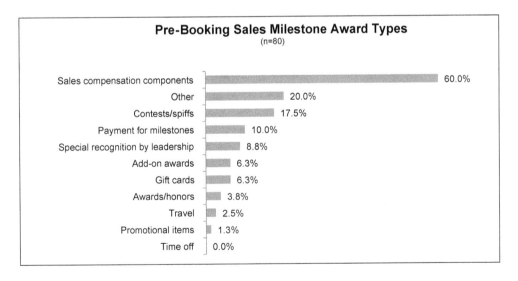

Survey Findings. 42.6% report using pre-booking milestones. If used, the milestone component is part of the sales compensation plan (60%). Milestones are sales progression efforts leading to a sale.

Pre-Booking Sales Activities: For customer contact jobs, do you provide any rewards for the following pre-booking sales activities?

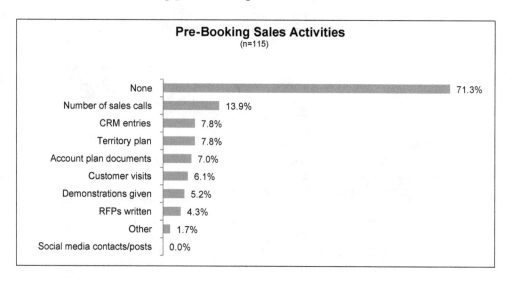

Pre-Booking Sales Activities Award Types: What awards, if any, do you provide for pre-sales activities?

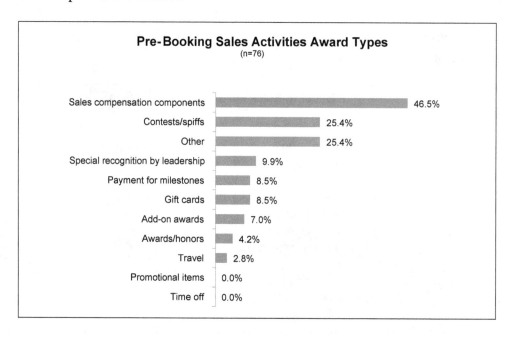

Survey Findings. 71.3% do not reward sales activities. If rewarded, it's found in the sales compensation plan (46.5%). Activities may or may not contribute to sales progression.

DEMOGRAPHICS

Type of Product/Service: Your division sales unit is primarily selling a:

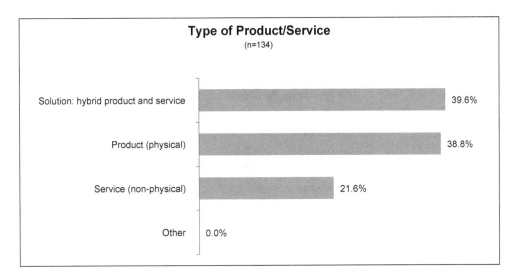

Sales Model: Your primary sales model for the division sales unit is:

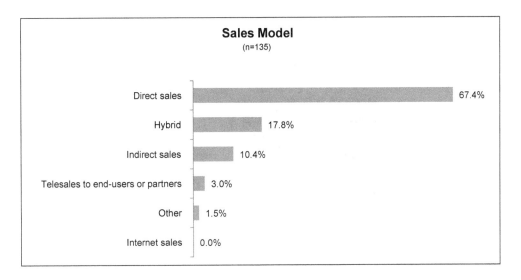

Industry Category: For the division sales unit, your industry is:

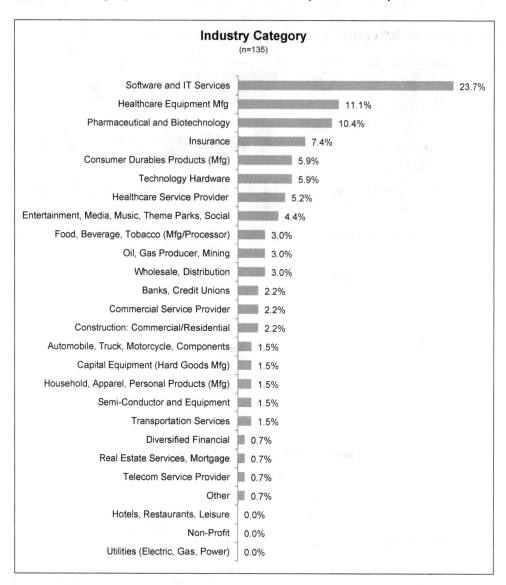

Industry Category
(n=135)

Category	Percentage
Software and IT Services	23.7%
Healthcare Equipment Mfg	11.1%
Pharmaceutical and Biotechnology	10.4%
Insurance	7.4%
Consumer Durables Products (Mfg)	5.9%
Technology Hardware	5.9%
Healthcare Service Provider	5.2%
Entertainment, Media, Music, Theme Parks, Social	4.4%
Food, Beverage, Tobacco (Mfg/Processor)	3.0%
Oil, Gas Producer, Mining	3.0%
Wholesale, Distribution	3.0%
Banks, Credit Unions	2.2%
Commercial Service Provider	2.2%
Construction: Commercial/Residential	2.2%
Automobile, Truck, Motorcycle, Components	1.5%
Capital Equipment (Hard Goods Mfg)	1.5%
Household, Apparel, Personal Products (Mfg)	1.5%
Semi-Conductor and Equipment	1.5%
Transportation Services	1.5%
Diversified Financial	0.7%
Real Estate Services, Mortgage	0.7%
Telecom Service Provider	0.7%
Other	0.7%
Hotels, Restaurants, Leisure	0.0%
Non-Profit	0.0%
Utilities (Electric, Gas, Power)	0.0%

Sales Volume: The division's sales for 2019 will be (approximately):

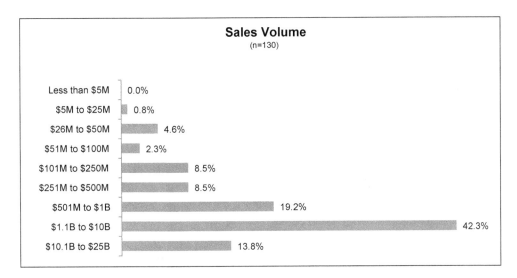

Estimate Number of Eligible Participants: For your division sales unit, how many employees are eligible to participate in the sales compensation program: include all–not just the primary sales job?

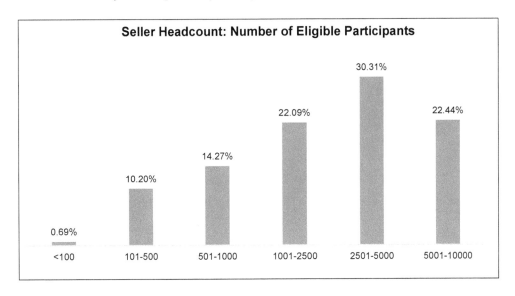

REFERENCE GUIDE TO SALES COMPENSATION SURVEYS©

SALES COMPENSATION ALMANAC • 2022

ABOUT THIS SURVEY REFERENCE GUIDE

Welcome to the *Reference Guide to Sales Compensation Surveys©*. This Guide is a resource for locating sales compensation surveys.

Published continually by the Alexander Group since 2000, the Guide profiles sales compensation surveys that provide benchmark pay data. The Guide also includes an index of compensation surveys by industry, allowing users to easily locate surveys that best meet their needs.

Inclusion—Survey Sources

Survey publishers provided the information in this Guide. In order to be included in the Guide, a survey must be administered by a third-party survey company, consulting firm or an association. The survey provider must publish the survey on a regular basis. Surveys must include pay information on customer contact jobs such as sales personnel, customer service, field technical support and related supervisory and management positions.

If you are aware of additional surveys that should be included in future editions, please contact me at david.cichelli@alexandergroup.com.

The Alexander Group would like to thank each individual at the survey organizations who contributed information to this Reference Guide.

Enjoy!
David Cichelli
Editor

TABLE OF CONTENTS

Compensation Surveys by Sector

Company Name/Survey Name	Media	IT/High-Tech	Manufacturing	General	Healthcare/ Life Sciences/ Medical	Financial/ Insurance	Consumer/ Retail
American Society of Employers Office, Clerical and Technical Compensation Survey	✓		✓		✓	✓	✓
American Society of Employers Supervisory, Managerial and Professional Compensation Survey	✓		✓		✓	✓	✓
BDO USA, LLP BDO CRO Industry Global Compensation and Turnover Survey					✓		
BDO USA, LLP BDO Health Insurance Industry Sales Compensation Survey						✓	
Culpepper and Associates Culpepper Sales Compensation Survey	✓	✓		✓	✓		
DGL Consultants Defined Contribution (401k, 403b and 457 Plans) Retirement Plan Sales Compensation Survey: Large Plan Markets						✓	
DGL Consultants Defined Contribution (401k, 403b and 457 Plans) Retirement Plan Sales Compensation Survey: Small to Midsize Plan Markets						✓	
Economic Research Institute Sales and Marketing Salary Survey				✓			
Employer Associations of America National Sales Compensation Survey	✓		✓		✓	✓	✓
Fitzgerald's Compensation Consulting Services 2020 Agency/Brokerage Insurance Positions Survey						✓	
Fitzgerald's Compensation Consulting Services 2020 Call Center Insurance Positions Survey						✓	
Fitzgerald's Compensation Consulting Services 2020 Executive Insurance Positions Survey					✓	✓	
Fitzgerald's Compensation Consulting Services 2020 Health Insurance Positions Survey					✓	✓	
MedReps.com MedReps 2020 Medical Sales Salary Report					✓		
Mercer Canadian Mercer Life Sciences Compensation Survey					✓		
Mercer US Mercer SIRS® Medical Device Sales Compensation Survey					✓		

Company Name/Survey Name	Media	IT/High-Tech	Manufacturing	General	Healthcare/ Life Sciences/ Medical	Financial/ Insurance	Consumer/ Retail
Mercer | Comptryx Mercer | Comptryx		✓					
MRA—The Management Association Benchmark Compensation Survey	✓		✓		✓	✓	✓
Pearl Meyer CHiPS One World		✓	✓				
Pearl Meyer Forest Products Industry Compensation Survey			✓				
Pearl Meyer HR Alliance Compensation Survey		✓					
Pearl Meyer National Engineering and Construction Salary Survey			✓				
Pearl Meyer The Executive Compensation and Benchmarking Survey				✓			
Radford Radford Global Compensation Database—Sales Roles Job Module	✓	✓	✓	✓	✓		✓
Salary.com IPAS® Global Benchmark Survey				✓			
Salary.com IPAS® Global Consumer Industry Survey							✓
Salary.com IPAS® Global High Technology Compensation Salary Survey		✓					
The Croner Company C2HR Content Developers Compensation Survey	✓						
The Croner Company C2HR Content Providers Compensation Survey	✓						
The Croner Company Croner Digital Content and Technology Survey		✓					
The Croner Company Croner Entertainment Survey	✓						
The Croner Company Croner Local Media Survey	✓						
The Croner Company Croner Software Games Survey	✓						
Western Compensation & Benefits Consultants Marketing & Sales Compensation Survey			✓	✓	✓	✓	✓
Western Management Group Retail Sales Compensation Survey							✓

Company Name/Survey Name	Media	IT/High-Tech	Manufacturing	General	Healthcare/ Life Sciences/ Medical	Financial/ Insurance	Consumer/ Retail
Western Management Group Sales and Service Compensation Survey	✓	✓					✓
Willis Towers Watson 2020 Sales Compensation and Design Survey – U.S.				✓	✓	✓	✓

American Society of Employers

Office, Clerical and Technical Compensation Survey
5505 Corporate Drive, Suite 200 Troy, MI 48098
(248) 353-4500
www.aseonline.org

Survey Overview

The survey report is part of a three-volume set and is one of the most comprehensive compensation surveys in the state of Michigan. Covering data for over 100 positions across 17 job families, including Accounting/Financial, Administrative, Banking, Creative/Advertising, Design/Drafting, Engineering Support, Field Service/Sales, Human Resources, Information Systems, Legal, Medical, Quality Control/Assurance/Safety, Research/Scientific, Sales/Marketing, Scheduling, Supply Chain/Logistics and Technicians.

Survey Editor

Jason Rowe, jrowe@aseonline.org
(248) 223-8053

General Information

Industries Covered

Goods Producing, Non-Manufacturing (Natural Resources/Mining, Utilities, Construction), Non-Durable Goods Manufacturing, Durable Goods Manufacturing, Trade & Services (Retail Trade, Wholesale Trade, Transportation/Warehousing, Information (Communication/Broadcasting), Professional/Business Services, Leisure/Hospitality Services, Services not elsewhere classified), Government & Financial Services (Financial Activities & Public Administration), Educational & Health Services (Education Services, Health Services, Social Services)

Survey Specifications

Range of Revenue of Reporting Companies . . . . $0–$500M
Frequency of Survey Updates . . . . Annual/Specific Date
Annual Publication Date . . . . Late May
First Year of Publication. 1952
Restrictions . . . . None
Data Delivery Methods . . . . Electronic/Soft Copy, Online
Non-Participant Report Available . . . . Yes
Custom Reporting. . . . . Online Access/User Defined
Data from World Regions . . . . North America
Number of Companies. 406

Number of Sales Jobs 9
Data Submitted . . . . Incumbent Level
Sales Volume by Job Title. . . . . No

Practices

Plan Performance Metrics. . . . . No
Formula Mechanics . . . . No
Benefits . . . . No
Allowances (e.g., Car, Mobile Devices, Internet) . . . No
Contests/Spiffs. . . . . No
Long-Term Incentives (e.g., Stock, RSU) . . . . No

Compensation Data

	Base Salary	Incentive Earnings	Total Compensation
Target	No	Yes	No
Actual	Yes	Yes	No

Major Sales/Customer Contact Job Families Featured in the Survey

Call Center Representative I, Call Center Representative II, Customer Service Representative I (Advanced), Customer Service Representative II (Experienced), Customer Service Representative III (Entry), Proposal Writer, Sales Order Clerk, Sales/Marketing Assistant, Social Media Coordinator

American Society of Employers

Supervisory, Managerial and Professional Compensation Survey
5505 Corporate Drive, Suite 200 Troy, MI 48098
(248) 353-4500
www.aseonline.org

Survey Overview

This survey report is part of a three-volume set and is one of the most comprehensive compensation surveys in the state of Michigan. Covering data for over 300 positions across 22 job families, including Accounting/Financial, Administrative, Behavior Health, Construction Engineering Creative/Advertising, Design/Drafting, Engineering, Engineering Management, Engineering Program/Project Management, Engineering Support, Field Service/Sales, General Executive, Human Resources, Information Systems, Legal, Medical, Plant Management, Quality Control/Assurance/Safety, Research/Scientific, Sales/Marketing, Scheduling and Supply Chain/Logistics.

Survey Editor

Jason Rowe, jrowe@aseonline.org
(248) 223-8053

General Information

Industries Covered

Goods Producing, Non-Manufacturing (Natural Resources/Mining, Utilities, Construction), Non-Durable Goods Manufacturing, Durable Goods Manufacturing, Trade & Services (Retail Trade, Wholesale Trade, Transportation/Warehousing, Information (Communication/Broadcasting), Professional/Business Services, Leisure/ Hospitality Services, Services not elsewhere classified), Government & Financial Services (Financial Activities & Public Administration), Educational & Health Services (Education Services, Health Services, Social Services)

Survey Specifications

Range of Revenue of Reporting Companies . . . . $0–$500M
Frequency of Survey Updates . . . . Annual/Specific Date
Annual Publication Date . . . . Late May
First Year of Publication. 1952
Restrictions . . . . None
Data Delivery Methods . . . . Electronic/Soft Copy, Online
Non-Participant Report Available . . . . Yes
Custom Reporting. . . . . Standard Report, Online
Access/User Defined

Data from World Regions . . . . North America
Number of Companies. 450
Number of Sales Jobs 30
Data Submitted . . . . Incumbent Level
Sales Volume by Job Title. . . . . No

Practices

Plan Performance Metrics. . . . . No
Formula Mechanics . . . . No
Benefits. . . . . No
Allowances (e.g., Car, Mobile Devices, Internet) . . . No
Contests/Spiffs. . . . . No
Long-Term Incentives (e.g., Stock, RSU) . . . . No

Compensation Data

	Base Salary	Incentive Earnings	Total Compensation
Target	No	Yes	No
Actual	Yes	Yes	No

Major Sales/Customer Contact Job Families Featured in the Survey

Advertising/Sales Promotions Manager, Business Development Manager, Call Center Manager, Customer Service Director, Customer Service Manager, Customer Service Supervisor, General Sales Manager (2nd Level of Management), Inside Sales Representative, Inside Sales Representative, Sr., International Sales Representative/Account Executive, Marketing Director, Marketing Generalist I, Marketing Generalist II, Marketing Generalist III, Marketing Manager, Marketing Research Analyst I (Advanced), Marketing Research Analyst II (Experienced), Marketing Research Analyst III (Entry), Marketing Research Manager, National Accounts Manager, Order Processing Supervisor, Outside Sales Representative/Account Executive, Outside Sales Representative/Account Executive, Sr., Outside Sales Representative, Jr., Public Relations Manager, Public Relations Representative I, Public Relations Representative II, Sales Manager, Top Sales & Marketing Executive, Top Sales Executive

BDO USA, LLP

**BDO CRO Industry Global Compensation and
  Turnover Survey**
1801 Market Street, Suite 1700, Philadelphia, PA 19103
(215) 636-5635
https://www.bdo.com/services/tax/global-employer-services/
compensation-consulting

Survey Overview

Survey covers clinical research outsourcing companies.

Survey Editor

Judy Canavan, jcanavan@bdo.com
(215) 636-5635

General Information

Industries Covered

Clinical Research Outsourcing

Survey Specifications

Range of Revenue of Reporting Companies....... (Left Blank)
Frequency of Survey Updates .... Annual/Specific Date
Annual Publication Date .... September
First Year of Publication...................... 1999
Restrictions .... Industry
Data Delivery Methods .... Electronic/Soft Copy
Non-Participant Report Available .... No
Custom Reporting............................ Standard Reporting
Data from World Regions .... North America, Europe, Asia,
                                             Middle East, Other Americas
Number of Companies........................ 20+
Number of Sales Jobs 30
Data Submitted .... Incumbent Level
Sales Volume by Job Title..................... No

Practices

Plan Performance Metrics . . . . Yes
Formula Mechanics . . . . No
Benefits . . . . Yes
Allowances (e.g., Car, Mobile Devices, Internet) . . . Yes
Contests/Spiffs . . . . No
Long-Term Incentives (e.g., Stock, RSU) . . . . Yes

Compensation Data

	Base Salary	Incentive Earnings	Total Compensation
Target	No	Yes	Yes
Actual	Yes	Yes	Yes

Major Sales/Customer Contact Job Families Featured in the Survey

Business Development: Contract Management, Project Budget Analysis, Proposal Writing, Sales, Strategic Account Management

BDO USA, LLP

BDO Health Insurance Industry Sales
  Compensation Survey
1801 Market Street, Suite 1700, Philadelphia, PA 19103
(215) 636-5635
https://www.bdo.com/services/tax/global-employer-services/
compensation-consulting

Survey Overview

This is a Health Insurance Industry specific Sales Compensation Survey designed to assist companies by providing high-quality, industry-specific competitive sales compensation, pay levels and incentive plan design information. This survey covers multiple position levels within the sales job family.

Survey Editor

Judy Canavan, jcanavan@bdo.com
(215) 636-5635

General Information

Industries Covered

Health Insurance

Survey Specifications

Range of Revenue of Reporting Companies . . . . (Left Blank)
Frequency of Survey Updates . . . . Annual/Specific Date
Annual Publication Date . . . . September
First Year of Publication. 2013
Restrictions . . . . Industry
Data Delivery Methods . . . . Electronic/Soft Copy
Non-Participant Report Available . . . . No
Custom Reporting. . . . . Standard Reporting
Data from World Regions . . . . (Left Blank)
Number of Companies. . . . . 25+
Number of Sales Jobs 45
Data Submitted . . . . Incumbent Level
Sales Volume by Job Title. . . . . Yes

Practices

Plan Performance Metrics...................... Yes
Formula Mechanics .... Yes
Benefits.................................... No
Allowances (e.g., Car, Mobile Devices, Internet) ... Yes
Contests/Spiffs.............................. Yes
Long-Term Incentives (e.g., Stock, RSU).......... Yes

Compensation Data

	Base Salary	Incentive Earnings	Total Compensation
Target	Yes	Yes	Yes
Actual	Yes	Yes	Yes

Major Sales/Customer Contact Job Families Featured in the Survey

New Sales Executives, Account Managers (renewals), Major/National/Large Group/ Small Group/Individual/FEP/Self Insured, Sales Management, Inside Sales, Sales Support

Culpepper and Associates, Inc.

Culpepper Sales Compensation Survey
3780 Mansell Road, Suite T-40, Alpharetta, GA 30022
(770) 641-5400
https://www.culpepper.com/Surveys/Compensation/Sales/

Survey Overview

The *Culpepper Sales Compensation Survey* provides global market data to benchmark the compensation of your organization's sales talent. It includes 48 job families covering sales executives, sales management, sales representatives, sales engineering, and sales operations & administration.

Survey Editor

Leigh Culpepper, leigh@culpepper.com
(770) 641-5446

General Information

Industries Covered

Technology, IT, Digital Media/Advertising, Engineering, Life Sciences, Medical & Health Care and General Industry

Survey Specifications

Range of Revenue of Reporting Companies . . . . $5M–$10B+
Frequency of Survey Updates . . . . Evergreen
Annual Publication Date . . . . Monthly updates with ability to view historical data by effective date
First Year of Publication. 1981
Restrictions . . . . None
Data Delivery Methods . . . . Electronic/Soft Copy, Online
Non-Participant Report Available . . . . No
Custom Reporting. . . . . Online Access/User Defined
Data from World Regions . . . . North America, Europe, Asia, Middle East, Other Americas, Africa
Number of Companies. . . . . 830+ Participating Companies
Number of Sales Jobs . . . . 48 Sales Job Families
Data Submitted . . . . Incumbent Level
Sales Volume by Job Title. . . . . Yes

Practices

Plan Performance Metrics . . . . No
Formula Mechanics . . . . No
Benefits . . . . No
Allowances (e.g., Car, Mobile Devices, Internet) . . . Yes
Contests/Spiffs . . . . No
Long-Term Incentives (e.g., Stock, RSU) . . . . Yes

Compensation Data

	Base Salary	Incentive Earnings	Total Compensation
Target	Yes	Yes	Yes
Actual	Yes	Yes	Yes

Major Sales/Customer Contact Job Families Featured in the Survey

Sales Executives: Top Sales Executive, Sales & Marketing Executive, Product Market/Segment/Channel Sales Executive, Sales Operations Executive, Sales Support Executive, Contracts Executive, Commercialization Executive, Product Management Executive

Sales Management: Sales & Professional Services Management, Inside & Outside Sales Management, Outside Sales Management, Inside Sales Management, Telesales Management, Renewal Sales Management, Strategic/Key Account Sales Management, Product Specialty Sales Management

Sales Representatives: Outside Sales Reps—New Business, Outside Sales Account Managers, Inside Sales Reps—New Business, Inside Sales Account Managers, Telesales Reps—Outbound, Telesales Reps—Inbound, Renewal Sales Reps, Strategic/Key Sales Account Managers, Product Sales Specialists

Sales Planning and Analysis: Sales Operations & Planning Management, Sales Commission Analysts, Sales Operations Analysts, Sales Force Effectiveness Analysts, Sales Planning Support Specialists

Sales Operations and Administration: Sales Administration Management, Sales Administrative Assistants, Order Processors

Contracts, Bids and Proposals: Contract Operations Management, Contract Specialists, Bid/Proposal Management, Bid/Proposal Specialists, Quote Coordinators

Sales Development: Sales Development Management, Sales Development Specialists, Telemarketing Representatives

Sales Engineering: Sales Engineering Management, Pre-Sales Engineering, Post-Sales Engineering, Pre- and Post-Sales Engineering, Sales Engineering Support Specialists

Sales Training: Sales Training Management, Sales Trainers

Related Jobs: Business Development and Marketing jobs are in the *Culpepper Operations Compensation Survey* and the *Culpepper Digital Marketing & Media Compensation Survey*

Post-Sales Client Engagement: Engagement jobs, including Client Relationship and Customer Success, are in the *Culpepper Operations Compensation Survey*

DGL Consultants, LLC

**Defined Contribution (401k, 403b and 457 Plans)
Retirement Plan Sales Compensation Survey:
Large Plan Markets**
3492 Hill Circle, Colorado Springs, CO 80904
(719) 634-7041
www.dglconsultants.com

DGL CONSULTANTS
compensation

Survey Overview

This custom survey benchmarks the compensation levels for six key retirement plan sales and service roles. Distribution is primarily through plan sponsors, intermediaries and consultants in the large plan retirement markets.

Findings include:

- Drivers of Compensation
- Fixed and Variable Compensation
- Ranges and Dispersion of Compensation Paid
- Measure of Overall Productivity
- Cost of Sales in Basis Points
- Pay Progression Analysis
- Production Progression Analysis
- Tenure Distribution

Survey Editor

Donald Lariviere, don@dglconsultants.com
(719) 634-7041

General Information

Industries Covered

Financial Services

Survey Specifications

Range of Revenue of Reporting Companies . . . . (Left Blank)
Frequency of Survey Updates . . . . (Left Blank)
Annual Publication Date . . . . June, Biennial publication
First Year of Publication. 2016
Restrictions . . . . Industry
Data Delivery Methods . . . . Electronic/Soft Copy
Non-Participant Report Available . . . . Yes
Custom Reporting. . . . . Standard Reporting
Data from World Regions . . . . North America

Number of Companies.........................(Left Blank)
Number of Sales Jobs 6
Data Submitted .... Averages/Percentiles,
                                            Incumbent Level
Sales Volume by Job Title...................... Yes

Practices

Plan Performance Metrics...................... Yes
Formula Mechanics .... Yes
Benefits..................................... No
Allowances (e.g., Car, Mobile Devices, Internet) ... Yes
Contests/Spiffs............................... Yes
Long-Term Incentives (e.g., Stock, RSU).......... Yes

Compensation Data

	Base Salary	Incentive Earnings	Total Compensation
Target	Yes	Yes	Yes
Actual	Yes	Yes	Yes

Major Sales/Customer Contact Job Families Featured in the Survey

Institutional Sales, Internal Sales Support, Relationship Manager/Client Service, Sales Desk Manager, Divisional Sales Manager, National Sales Manager

DGL Consultants, LLC

**Defined Contribution (401k, 403b and 457 Plans)
Retirement Plan Sales Compensation Survey:
Small to Midsize Plan Markets**

DGL CONSULTANTS
compensation

3492 Hill Circle, Colorado Springs, CO 80904
(719) 634-7041
www.dglconsultants.com

Survey Overview

This custom survey benchmarks the compensation levels for six key retirement plan sales and service roles. Distribution is primarily through financial advisors (registered reps, RIA's, consultants, etc.) that sell retirement plans, investment only products and record-keeping services to small and mid-sized companies.

Findings include:

- Drivers of Compensation
- Fixed and Variable Compensation
- Ranges and Dispersion of Compensation Paid
- Measure of Overall Productivity
- Cost of Sales in Basis Points
- Pay Progression Analysis
- Production Progression Analysis
- Tenure Distribution

Survey Editor

Donald Lariviere, don@dglconsultants.com
(719) 634-7041

General Information

Industries Covered

Financial Services

Survey Specifications

Range of Revenue of Reporting Companies . . . . (Left Blank)
Frequency of Survey Updates . . . . (Left Blank)
Annual Publication Date . . . . June, Biennial publication
First Year of Publication. 2006
Restrictions . . . . Industry
Data Delivery Methods . . . . Electronic/Soft Copy
Non-Participant Report Available . . . . Yes
Custom Reporting. . . . . Standard Reporting

Data from World Regions . . . . North America
Number of Companies . . . . (Left Blank)
Number of Sales Jobs 6
Data Submitted . . . . Averages/Percentiles,
Incumbent Level
Sales Volume by Job Title . . . . Yes

Practices

Plan Performance Metrics . . . . Yes
Formula Mechanics . . . . Yes
Benefits . . . . No
Allowances (e.g., Car, Mobile Devices, Internet) . . . Yes
Contests/Spiffs . . . . Yes
Long-Term Incentives (e.g., Stock, RSU) . . . . Yes

Compensation Data

	Base Salary	Incentive Earnings	Total Compensation
Target	Yes	Yes	Yes
Actual	Yes	Yes	Yes

Major Sales/Customer Contact Job Families Featured in the Survey

External Wholesaler/Regional Pension Consultant, Internal Wholesaler/Inside Sales, Relationship Manager/Client Service/Enroller, National Accounts Manager/Channel Development & Implementation Manager, Regional Sales Manager, Divisional or National Sales Manager

Economic Research Institute (ERI)

Sales and Marketing Salary Survey
111 Academy Drive, Suite 270, Irvine, CA 92617
(800) 627-3697
www.erieri.com

Survey Overview

The *Sales and Marketing Salary Survey* documents market-based pay data for 183 benchmark jobs from up to three databases: digitized public sources, ERI Assessor Series data and direct participants. The following information is reported for each job title (salary data are shown in means, medians and percentile cuts): Annual Salary; Incentive/Variable Pay; Total Direct Annual Compensation; Job Description; and Selected Characteristics of the Occupation (SCO). Data collection begins October 1 and ends on March 31. Survey results are published annually in July, with an effective date of March 31 of the given survey year.

Survey Editor

Katherine Stewart, katherine.stewart@erieri.com
(800) 627-3697, ext. 300

General Information

Industries Covered

All Industries

Survey Specifications

Range of Revenue of Reporting Companies . . . . All Revenues
Frequency of Survey Updates . . . . Annual/Specific Date
Annual Publication Date . . . . July 1
First Year of Publication. 2007
Restrictions . . . . None
Data Delivery Methods . . . . Online
Non-Participant Report Available . . . . Yes
Custom Reporting. . . . . No
Data from World Regions . . . . North America
Number of Companies. . . . . (Left Blank)
Number of Sales Jobs 183
Data Submitted . . . . Averages/Percentiles
Sales Volume by Job Title. . . . . No

Practices

Plan Performance Metrics . . . . No
Formula Mechanics . . . . No
Benefits . . . . No
Allowances (e.g., Car, Mobile Devices, Internet) . . . No
Contests/Spiffs . . . . No
Long-Term Incentives (e.g., Stock, RSU) . . . . (Left Blank)

Compensation Data

	Base Salary	Incentive Earnings	Total Compensation
Target	(Left Blank)	(Left Blank)	(Left Blank)
Actual	Yes	Yes	Yes

Major Sales/Customer Contact Job Families Featured in the Survey

Advertising, Marketing, Promotions, Public Relations and Sales Managers, Operations Specialties Managers, Other Sales and Related Workers, Retail Sales Workers, Sales Representatives, Services Sales Representatives, Wholesale and Manufacturing Supervisors of Sales Workers

Employer Associations of America

National Sales Compensation Survey
N19 W24400 Riverwood Drive, Waukesha, WI 53188
(262) 696-3384
www.eaahub.org/surveysdata

Survey Overview

This annual national survey reports on compensation throughout the U.S. covering 15 positions spanning a full (typical) sales force from executive to inside sales. This year's report contains 838 organizations representing 1,809 locations. Each job contains multiple compensation strategies (three types of strategies, plus combined compensation, which summarizes all three types).

Survey Editor

Cindy Mixon, cindy.mixon@mranet.org
(262) 696-3384

General Information

Industries Covered

Natural Resources/Mining, Utilities, Construction, Non-Durable Goods Manufacturing, Durable Goods Manufacturing, Retail Trade, Wholesale Trade, Transportation/Warehousing, Information (Communication and Broadcasting), Financial Activities, Professional/Business Services, Education Services, Health Services, Social Services, Leisure/Hospitality Services, Services not elsewhere classified

Survey Specifications

Range of Revenue of Reporting Companies . . . . $0–$250M+
Frequency of Survey Updates . . . . Annual/Specific Date
Annual Publication Date . . . . November
First Year of Publication. . . . . (Left Blank)
Restrictions . . . . None
Data Delivery Methods . . . . Electronic/Soft Copy, Online
Non-Participant Report Available . . . . Yes
Custom Reporting. . . . . No
Data from World Regions . . . . North America
Number of Companies. 720
Number of Sales Jobs 15
Data Submitted . . . . Incumbent Level
Sales Volume by Job Title. . . . . Yes

Practices

Plan Performance Metrics . . . . No
Formula Mechanics . . . . No
Benefits . . . . No
Allowances (e.g., Car, Mobile Devices, Internet) . . . No
Contests/Spiffs . . . . No
Long-Term Incentives (e.g., Stock, RSU) . . . . No

Compensation Data

	Base Salary	Incentive Earnings	Total Compensation
Target	No	No	No
Actual	Yes	Yes	Yes

Major Sales/Customer Contact Job Families Featured in the Survey

Top Sales & Marketing Executive, Top Sales Executive, Top International Sales Executive, General Sales Manager, Sales Manager, Sales Trainer, National Accounts Manager, International Sales Representative/Account Executive, Senior Outside Sales Representative/Account Executive, Outside Sales Representative/Account Executive, Junior Outside Sales Representative, Inside Sales Representative, Senior Inside Sales Representative, Order Processing Supervisor, Route Sales Representative

Additional Data on: Independent Sales Representatives

Fitzgerald's Compensation Consulting Services, Inc.

2020 Agency/Brokerage Insurance Positions Survey
619 N. Park Drive, Salisbury, MD 21804
(443) 736-7753
https://fitzgeralds-surveys.com/home

Survey Overview

The purpose of this report is to provide insurance organizations with current benchmark position compensation levels for use by participating organizations in their program planning. The data contained in this report focuses on total direct compensation, including Annual Base Salary, Annual Incentive Awards and expected value of recent long-term incentive grants or awards.

Survey Editor

Allan Fitzgerald, afitzgerald@ccs-consultants.com
(443) 736-7753

General Information

Industries Covered

Brokerage

Survey Specifications

Range of Revenue of Reporting Companies . . . . $25M–$6B
Frequency of Survey Updates . . . . Annual/Specific Date
Annual Publication Date . . . . Early September
First Year of Publication. 2004
Restrictions . . . . None
Data Delivery Methods . . . . Paper, Electronic/Soft Copy, Online
Non-Participant Report Available . . . . Yes
Custom Reporting. . . . . Standard Reporting
Data from World Regions . . . . North America
Number of Companies. 8
Total Number of Survey Jobs 63
Number of Sales Jobs 11
Data Submitted . . . . Incumbent Level
Sales Volume by Job Title. . . . . No

Practices

Plan Performance Metrics......................No
Formula Mechanics ....No
Benefits.....................................No
Allowances (e.g., Car, Mobile Devices, Internet)... Yes
Contests/Spiffs..............................No
Long-Term Incentives (e.g., Stock, RSU).......... Yes

Compensation Data

	Base Salary	Incentive Earnings	Total Compensation
Target	No	Yes	Yes
Actual	Yes	Yes	Yes

Major Sales/Customer Contact Job Families Featured in the Survey

Account Executive, Claims, Loss Control, Miscellaneous, Placement, Profit Center Management, Sales, Sales/Account Executive, Services, Technical Assistants, Top Insurance Management

Fitzgerald's Compensation Consulting Services, Inc.

2020 Call Center Insurance Positions Survey
619 N. Park Drive, Salisbury, MD 21804
(443) 736-7753
https://fitzgeralds-surveys.com/home

Survey Overview

This statistical report presents the results from the 2020 Center Survey, which focuses on the pay elements of Total Cash Compensation (base salary, incentives and other cash compensation). Identifies and provides general information about the survey, survey participants, company characteristics, call center practices and geographic regions.

Survey Editor

Allan Fitzgerald, afitzgerald@ccs-consultants.com
(443) 736-7753

General Information

Industries Covered

Property Casualty Insurance Centers

Survey Specifications

Range of Revenue of Reporting Companies . . . . $700M–$14B
Frequency of Survey Updates . . . . Annual/Specific Date
Annual Publication Date . . . . Mid-August
First Year of Publication. 2000
Restrictions . . . . None
Data Delivery Methods . . . . Paper, Electronic/Soft Copy,
                                                        Online
Non-Participant Report Available . . . . Yes, and by Job
Custom Reporting. . . . . Standard Reporting
Data from World Regions . . . . North America
Number of Companies. 22
Total Number of Survey Jobs 65
Number of Sales Jobs 16
Data Submitted . . . . Incumbent Level
Sales Volume by Job Title. . . . . No

Practices

Plan Performance Metrics . . . . No
Formula Mechanics . . . . No
Benefits . . . . No
Allowances (e.g., Car, Mobile Devices, Internet) . . . Yes
Contests/Spiffs . . . . No
Long-Term Incentives (e.g., Stock, RSU) . . . . No

Compensation Data

	Base Salary	Incentive Earnings	Total Compensation
Target	No	Yes	No
Actual	Yes	Yes	Yes

Major Sales/Customer Contact Job Families Featured in the Survey

Claim Centers, Cross Centers Positions, Human Resource Service Centers, Insurance Telesales Centers, Processing Centers, Underwriting Centers

Fitzgerald's Compensation Consulting Services, Inc.

2020 Executive Insurance Positions Survey
619 N. Park Drive, Salisbury, MD 21804
(443) 736-7753
https://fitzgeralds-surveys.com/home

Survey Overview

Survey of executive roles in the insurance industry.

Survey Editor

Allan Fitzgerald, afitzgerald@ccs-consultants.com
(443) 736-7753

General Information

Industries Covered

P&C, Health and Specialty Lines Insurance

Survey Specifications

Range of Revenue of Reporting Companies . . . . $53M–$19.8B
Frequency of Survey Updates . . . . Annual/Specific Date
Annual Publication Date . . . . Early August
First Year of Publication. 2012
Restrictions . . . . Industry
Data Delivery Methods . . . . Paper, Electronic/Soft Copy,
                                                              Online
Non-Participant Report Available . . . . Yes
Custom Reporting. . . . . Standard Reporting
Data from World Regions . . . . North America
Number of Companies Represented 13
Total Number of Jobs 178
Number of Sales Jobs 6
Data Submitted . . . . Incumbent Level
Sales Volume by Job Title. . . . . No

Practices

Plan Performance Metrics. . . . . No
Formula Mechanics . . . . No
Benefits . . . . No
Allowances (e.g., Car, Mobile Devices, Internet) . . . Yes
Contests/Spiffs. . . . . No
Long-Term Incentives (e.g., Stock, RSU) . . . . Yes

Compensation Data

	Base Salary	Incentive Earnings	Total Compensation
Target	(Left Blank)	Yes	Yes
Actual	Yes	Yes	Yes

Major Sales/Customer Contact Job Families Featured in the Survey

Top Sales & Marketing, Top Sales, Top Marketing, Top National Accounts, Top Field Sales, Regional Field Sales, Top Claims

Fitzgerald's Compensation Consulting Services, Inc.

2020 Health Insurance Positions Survey
619 N. Park Drive, Salisbury, MD 21804
(443) 736-7753
https://fitzgeralds-surveys.com/home

Survey Overview

Fitzgerald's Compensation Consulting Services presents the results from the *2020 Health Insurance Positions Survey*, which focuses on cash compensation, pay practices and benefits. Competitive pay practices and information have been submitted from 22 health insurance companies participating in this year's survey.

Survey Editor

Allan Fitzgerald, afitzgerald@ccs-consultants.com
(443) 736-7753

General Information

Industries Covered

Accident, Claims, Dental, Disability, Health Care, Health Benefits, Health Care plus Life, Medical, Pharmaceutical, TPA, Vision

Survey Specifications

Range of Revenue of Reporting Companies . . . . $1.75M–$42B
Frequency of Survey Updates . . . . Annual/Specific Date
Annual Publication Date . . . . Late June to Early July
First Year of Publication. 2006
Restrictions . . . . None
Data Delivery Methods . . . . Paper, Electronic/Soft Copy,
                                                                                       Online
Non-Participant Report Available . . . . Yes, by Job Available
Custom Reporting. . . . . Standard & Custom Reporting
Data from World Regions . . . . North America
Number of Companies Represented 56
Total Number of Jobs 408
Number of Sales Jobs 40
Data Submitted . . . . Incumbent Level
Sales Volume by Job Title. . . . . No

Practices

Plan Performance Metrics . . . . No
Formula Mechanics . . . . No
Benefits . . . . No
Allowances (e.g., Car, Mobile Devices, Internet) . . . Yes
Contests/Spiffs . . . . No
Long-Term Incentives (e.g., Stock, RSU) . . . . No

Compensation Data

	Base Salary	Incentive Earnings	Total Compensation
Target	No	Yes	No
Actual	Yes	Yes	Yes

Major Sales/Customer Contact Job Families Featured in the Survey

Accreditation, Actuarial, Appeals, Audit/Reimbursement, Behavioral Health, Business Change, Claims, Clinical Products & Programs, Community Health, Compliance, Congressional, Contracts, Credentialing, Customer Service, Dental/Vision, Direct Sales, Disease Management, EDI, Enrollment & Billing, Fraud Investigation, Media Communications, Medical Directors, Medical Policy, National Networks, Operations, Pharmacy, Provider Data, Provider Networks, Quality Initiatives, Recovery/Refunds, Review and Case Management, Sales & Sales Support, Underwriting

MedReps.com

MedReps 2020 Medical Sales Salary Report
2655 Northwinds Pkwy, Alpharetta, GA 30009
(866) 619-1629
https://www.medreps.com/medical-sales-careers/2020-medical-sales-salary-report

Survey Overview

The *2020 Medical Sales Salary Report* looks at the year-over-year income growth of medical sales professionals, and analyzes how income is affected by product sold, company size, age, experience, gender and other influential factors. Reports specific to each of the main product types—medical device, pharmaceutical, medical equipment and biopharma/biotech—are also available.

Survey Editor

Robyn Melhuish, rmelhuish@hcstaffingtech.com
(866) 619-1629

General Information

Industries Covered

Medical device, Medical Equipment, Pharmaceutical, Biotech

Survey Specifications

Range of Revenue of Reporting Companies . . . . (Left Blank)
Frequency of Survey Updates . . . . Annual/Specific Date
Annual Publication Date . . . . June
First Year of Publication. 2011
Restrictions . . . . Industry
Data Delivery Methods . . . . Online
Non-Participant Report Available . . . . Yes
Custom Reporting. . . . . No
Data from World Regions . . . . North America
Number of Companies. . . . . (Left Blank)
Number of Sales Jobs . . . . (Left Blank)
Data Submitted . . . . Average/Percentiles
Sales Volume by Job Title. . . . . Yes

Practices

Plan Performance Metrics . . . . No
Formula Mechanics . . . . No
Benefits . . . . Yes
Allowances (e.g., Car, Mobile Devices, Internet) . . . Yes
Contests/Spiffs . . . . No
Long-Term Incentives (e.g., Stock, RSU) . . . . Yes

Compensation Data

	Base Salary	Incentive Earnings	Total Compensation
Target	(Left Blank)	(Left Blank)	(Left Blank)
Actual	Yes	Yes	Yes

Major Sales/Customer Contact Job Families Featured in the Survey

Field Sales, Sales Manager, Sales Director/VP

Mercer

Canadian Mercer Life Sciences Compensation Survey
400 West Market Street, Suite 700, Louisville, KY 40202
(800) 333-3070
www.imercer.com

Survey Overview

The *Canadian Mercer Life Sciences (MLS) Compensation Survey* is a valuable resource providing companies with need-to-know information about compensation practices in the life sciences industry to attract and retain top talent. The survey covers a broad selection of benchmark positions relevant to the industry ranging from pre-clinical and clinical research, medical affairs, sales, marketing, production and administration, as well as the full range of general infrastructure/support functions. Online and interactive report delivery through Mercer WIN® enables fully customized reporting with statistics and data elements according to your individual needs, including instant comparisons of your organization's data against the market.

Survey Editor

Matthew Kreger, matthew.kreger@mercer.com
(212) 345-7720

General Information

Industries Covered

Life Sciences

Survey Specifications

Range of Revenue of Reporting Companies	CAD$61M–CAD$1,040M (Interquartile Range)
Frequency of Survey Updates	Annual/Specific Date
Annual Publication Date	September
First Year of Publication	2011
Restrictions	Industry
Data Delivery Methods	Electronic/Soft Copy
Non-Participant Report Available	Yes
Custom Reporting	Online Access/User Defined
Data from World Regions	North America, Canada only
Number of Companies	118
Number of Sales Jobs	33 jobs reportable (each job has multiple levels)/209 reportable jobs + level combinations
Data Submitted	Incumbent Level
Sales Volume by Job Title	No

Practices

Plan Performance Metrics . . . . No
Formula Mechanics . . . . No
Benefits . . . . No
Allowances (e.g., Car, Mobile Devices, Internet) . . . Yes
Contests/Spiffs . . . . No
Long-Term Incentives (e.g., Stock, RSU) . . . . Yes

Compensation Data

	Base Salary	Incentive Earnings	Total Compensation
Target	No	Yes	Yes
Actual	Yes	Yes	Yes

Major Sales/Customer Contact Job Families Featured in the Survey

Sales Management, Sales Representatives, Technical Sales, Key Accounts, Sales Training, Sales Administration, Clinical Education, Customer Service

Mercer

US Mercer SIRS® Medical Device Sales Compensation Survey

400 West Market Street, Suite 700, Louisville, KY 40202
(800) 333-3070
www.imercer.com

Survey Overview

The *US Mercer SIRS® Medical Device Sales Compensation Survey* presents competitive compensation data for a select group of sales benchmark jobs in the medical device industry with the ability to analyze the data by primary product line, secondary product line, sales volume and sales quota. It focuses on compensation-related information and is delivered in both PDF and Excel format. This survey is very valuable for organizations that manage sales compensation by product line or would like to understand variation in compensation practices based on type or specialty of device being sold.

Primary product lines include Airway Management, Cardiac Rhythm Management & Valves, Clinical Chemistry & Diagnostic Products, Cosmetic Devices, Gastroenterology and Urology, General & Hospital Supplies, Ophthalmic Products, Orthopedic Products, Perfusion Systems/Cardiovascular Surgical Tools & Systems, Specialty Surgery and Vascular Devices. Secondary product lines include Capital Equipment, Consumables/Disposables, Durable Goods and Implantable Devices.

Survey Editor

Matthew Kreger, matthew.kreger@mercer.com
(212) 345-7720

General Information

Industries Covered

Life Sciences—Medical Devices

Survey Specifications

Range of Revenue of Reporting Companies . . . . $52.3M–$20,147M
Frequency of Survey Updates . . . . Annual/Specific Date
Annual Publication Date . . . . September
First Year of Publication. 2000
Restrictions . . . . Industry, Must Participate in
                                                                SIRS® Benchmark Survey

Data Delivery Methods . . . . Electronic/Soft Copy
Non-Participant Report Available . . . . No
Custom Reporting. . . . . Online Access/User Defined
Data from World Regions . . . . North America
Number of Companies. 125
Number of Sales Jobs 53
Data Submitted . . . . Incumbent Level
Sales Volume by Job Title. Yes

Practices

Plan Performance Metrics. No
Formula Mechanics . . . . No
Benefits . . . . No
Allowances (e.g., Car, Mobile Devices, Internet) . . . No
Contests/Spiffs. . . . . No
Long-Term Incentives (e.g., Stock, RSU) . . . . Yes

Compensation Data

	Base Salary	Incentive Earnings	Total Compensation
Target	No	Yes	Yes
Actual	Yes	Yes	Yes

Major Sales/Customer Contact Job Families Featured in the Survey

Sales – Medical Devices, Sales – National Accounts, Inside Sales, Training – Sales, Clinical Education, Engineering – Field, Technician – Field

Mercer | Comptryx

Mercer | Comptryx
17 Main Street, Hopkinton, MA 01748
(508) 435-3999
www.imercer.com/products/comptryx

Survey Overview

Mercer | Comptryx is a dynamic Global Salary Survey for the technology industry that uniquely reports both pay and on-demand workforce analytics market data. The survey covers virtually all jobs, all levels, all functions (including sales) and all standard compensation elements (base, allowances, STI, LTI, benefit fringe rates). Our state-of-the-art-reporting system provides in-depth workforce analysis using a menu of organizational metrics. Unlike simple salary surveys, which only let you price jobs, *Mercer | Comptryx* also helps you find the optimal size, shape, mix and cost for your company or sales organization.

Survey Editor

Roger Sturtevant, roger.sturtevant@mercer.com
(508) 435-3999, ext. 50

General Information

Industries Covered

Tech Sector, Aerospace and Defense

Survey Specifications

Range of Revenue of Reporting Companies	$100M–$125B
Frequency of Survey Updates	Evergreen
Annual Publication Date	(Left Blank)
First Year of Publication	2011
Restrictions	Industry
Data Delivery Methods	Electronic/Soft Copy
Non-Participant Report Available	No
Custom Reporting	Online Access/User Defined
Data from World Regions	North America, Europe, Asia, Middle East, Other Americas, Africa
Number of Companies	400+
Number of Sales Jobs	1,600
Data Submitted	Incumbent Level
Sales Volume by Job Title	No

Practices

Plan Performance Metrics . . . . No
Formula Mechanics . . . . No
Benefits . . . . Yes
Allowances (e.g., Car, Mobile Devices, Internet) . . . Yes
Contests/Spiffs . . . . (Left Blank)
Long-Term Incentives (e.g., Stock, RSU) . . . . Yes

Compensation Data

	Base Salary	Incentive Earnings	Total Compensation
Target	Yes	Yes	Yes
Actual	Yes	Yes	Yes

Major Sales/Customer Contact Job Families Featured in the Survey

Service Contract, Distributor, Retail, Government, Territory, Key Account, Internet, Professional Services, Contract Renewal, OEM/VAR, Inside/Telesales

MRA—The Management Association

Benchmark Compensation Survey
N19 W24400 Riverwood Drive, Waukesha, WI 53188
(262) 696-3508
www.mranet.org

Survey Overview

This annual survey reports on compensation for employees across the U.S. and includes separate breakout sections for Illinois, Iowa, Minnesota, and Wisconsin covering 457 core jobs in key business areas from staff level through leadership across 18 job families. This year's report contains 1,225 organizations reporting on over 53,000 employees.

Survey Editor

Kelly Greinke, kelly.greinke@mranet.org
(262) 696-3448

General Information

Industries Covered

Manufacturing—Union, Manufacturing—Non-Union, Services (Includes Retail Trade, Wholesale Trade, Transportation/Warehousing, Information/Communication/Broadcasting, Professional/Business Services, Education Services, Social Services, Leisure/Hospitality Services, Public Administration, and Services not elsewhere classified), Financial Activities, Health Care/Health Services, Goods Producing, Non-Manufacturing (Includes Natural Resources/Mining, Utilities and Construction)

Survey Specifications

Range of Revenue of Reporting Companies	$0–$250M+
Frequency of Survey Updates	Annual/Specific Date
Annual Publication Date	July
First Year of Publication	1901
Restrictions	None
Data Delivery Methods	Electronic/Soft Copy, Online
Non-Participant Report Available	Yes
Custom Reporting	Online Access/User Defined
Data from World Regions	North America
Number of Companies	1,225
Number of Sales Jobs	32
Data Submitted	Incumbent Level
Sales Volume by Job Title	Yes

Practices

Plan Performance Metrics . . . . No
Formula Mechanics . . . . No
Benefits . . . . No
Allowances (e.g., Car, Mobile Devices, Internet) . . . No
Contests/Spiffs . . . . No
Long-Term Incentives (e.g., Stock, RSU) . . . . No

Compensation Data

	Base Salary	Incentive Earnings	Total Compensation
Target	No	Yes	No
Actual	Yes	Yes	Yes

Major Sales/Customer Contact Job Families Featured in the Survey

Marketing Director, Marketing and Sales Senior Manager, Assistant Sales Manager, Sales Manager (Regional Administration), Sales Manager (Export), Government Accounts Manager, Marketing Manager, Marketing Generalist III (Advanced), Marketing Generalist II (Experienced), Marketing Generalist I (Entry), Public Relations Manager, Public Relations Representative II, Market Research Manager, Market Research Analyst III (Advanced), Market Research Analyst II (Experienced), Market Research Analyst I (Entry), Telemarketing Supervisor, Customer Service Director, Customer Service Manager, Customer Service Supervisor, Customer Service Representative I (Entry), Customer Service Representative II (Experienced), Customer Service Representative III (Advanced), Sales/Marketing Assistant, Order Processing Supervisor, Order Clerk, Sales Correspondent Senior, Sales Correspondent, Sales Representative - Telemarketing, Telemarketing Supervisor, Telephone Order Processing Representative, and Sales Representative - Inside Sales

Pearl Meyer

CHiPS One World
93 Worcester Street, Wellesley, MA 02481
(508) 460-9600
www.pearlmeyer.com

Pearl Meyer

Survey Overview

A comprehensive, global, total compensation survey focusing on technology firms and other firms with large technology populations.

Survey Editor

Rebecca Toman, rebecca.toman@pearlmeyer.com
(508) 630-1475

General Information

Industries Covered

A broad range of jobs from engineering to administrative functions to sales

Survey Specifications

Range of Revenue of Reporting Companies . . . . Small to Really Big
Frequency of Survey Updates . . . . Annual/Specific Date
Annual Publication Date . . . . First Week of July
First Year of Publication. 1989
Restrictions . . . . Industry
Data Delivery Methods . . . . Electronic/Soft Copy, Online
Non-Participant Report Available . . . . No
Custom Reporting. . . . . Standard Reporting
Data from World Regions . . . . North America, Europe, Asia, Middle East, Other Americas, Africa
Number of Companies. . . . . 100+
Number of Sales Jobs . . . . 100+
Data Submitted . . . . Averages/Percentiles
Sales Volume by Job Title. (Left Blank)

Practices

Plan Performance Metrics. (Left Blank)
Formula Mechanics . . . . (Left Blank)
Benefits . . . . (Left Blank)
Allowances (e.g., Car, Mobile Devices, Internet) . . . (Left Blank)
Contests/Spiffs. . . . . (Left Blank)
Long-Term Incentives (e.g., Stock, RSU) . . . . (Left Blank)

Compensation Data

	Base Salary	Incentive Earnings	Total Compensation
Target	(Left Blank)	Yes	Yes
Actual	Yes	Yes	Yes

Major Sales/Customer Contact Job Families Featured in the Survey

Field Sales - Direct - Commercial, Field Sales - Direct - Government, Field Sales - Direct - Combination, Field Sales - Direct Roll-Up, Field Sales - Indirect OEM, Field Sales - Indirect VAR, Field Sales - Indirect Distributor, Field Sales - Indirect Retail, Field Sales - Indirect Multiple Channels, Field Sales - Indirect Roll-Up, Field Sales - Direct and Indirect Combination, Field Sales - Direct and Indirect Roll-Up, Product/Service Sales Specialist (Overlay), Strategic Client Management, Global Account Management, National (Domestic) Account Management, Maintenance Contract Sales, Retail - Sales (Store), Inside Sales Representative - Consumer, Inside Sales Representative - B2B Supplies, Consumables, Packaged Offerings, Inside Sales Representative - B2B Product/Service/Solutions, Inside Sales Roll-Up

Pearl Meyer

Forest Products Industry Compensation Survey
93 Worcester Street, Wellesley, MA 02481
(508) 460-9600
www.pearlmeyer.com

Pearl Meyer

Survey Overview

The Forest Products Industry Compensation Association (FPICA) is comprised of approximately 40 forest products companies doing business in the United States. The FPICA members participate in a survey with respect to compensation matters. The survey is for the sole and exclusive use of participating members. An administrative consultant coordinates the administration of the survey and is the contact person for the survey provider with respect to matters relating to the conduct of the survey.

Survey Editor

Andrew Guigno, andrew.guigno@pearlmeyer.com
(508) 630-1508

General Information

Industries Covered

Forest Products Industry

Survey Specifications

Range of Revenue of Reporting Companies	Small to Really Big
Frequency of Survey Updates	Annual/Specific Date
Annual Publication Date	August 1
First Year of Publication	11 Years Ago
Restrictions	Industry
Data Delivery Methods	Electronic/Soft Copy, Online
Non-Participant Report Available	No
Custom Reporting	Standard Reporting
Data from World Regions	(Left Blank)
Number of Companies	40+
Number of Sales Jobs	18
Data Submitted	Averages/Percentiles
Sales Volume by Job Title	(Left Blank)

Practices

Plan Performance Metrics......................(Left Blank)
Formula Mechanics ....(Left Blank)
Benefits....................................(Left Blank)
Allowances (e.g., Car, Mobile Devices, Internet)...(Left Blank)
Contests/Spiffs...............................(Left Blank)
Long-Term Incentives (e.g., Stock, RSU)..........(Left Blank)

Compensation Data

	Base Salary	Incentive Earnings	Total Compensation
Target	(Left Blank)	Yes	Yes
Actual	Yes	Yes	Yes

Major Sales/Customer Contact Job Families Featured in the Survey

Division Sales and Marketing Manager, Level II Sales Representative, Level III Sales Representative, Level IV National Account Executive, Regional Sales Manager, Inside Sales Representative I, Inside Sales Representative II, Inside Sales Representative III, Sales Manager, Sales Service Manager, Customer/Sales Service Representative, National/Divisional Sales Manager, Sales Supervisor/Manager, Customer Sales Service Manager, Customer/Sales Service Representative, Inside Sales/Customer Service Representative

Pearl Meyer

HR Alliance Compensation Survey
93 Worcester Street, Wellesley, MA 02481
(508) 460-9600
www.pearlmeyer.com

Pearl Meyer

Survey Overview

HR Alliance's (formerly WTPF) Compensation Survey is the most stable and reliable source of competitive regional pay information for human resources professionals supporting the government contracting, technology and professional services communities in the Washington, D.C., area. The survey has been conducted each year since 1989. In 2010, WTPF joined forces with the SAIC Security Cleared Federal Contracting Personnel Survey and now also gathers information on security clearances—at both the incumbent and policy level.

Survey Editor

Rebecca Toman, rebecca.toman@pearlmeyer.com
(508) 630-1475

General Information

Industries Covered

Geographic: Washington, D.C., only with a high proportion of government contracting organizations

Survey Specifications

Range of Revenue of Reporting Companies . . . . Small to Very Large
Frequency of Survey Updates . . . . Annual/Specific Date
Annual Publication Date . . . . Late August
First Year of Publication. . . . . 10+ Years Ago
Restrictions . . . . Geography
Data Delivery Methods . . . . Electronic/Soft Copy, Online
Non-Participant Report Available . . . . No
Custom Reporting. . . . . Standard Reporting
Data from World Regions . . . . (Left Blank)
Number of Companies. . . . . 50+
Number of Sales Jobs . . . . 20+
Data Submitted . . . . Averages/Percentiles
Sales Volume by Job Title. . . . . (Left Blank)

Practices

Plan Performance Metrics . . . . (Left Blank)
Formula Mechanics . . . . (Left Blank)
Benefits . . . . (Left Blank)
Allowances (e.g., Car, Mobile Devices, Internet) . . . (Left Blank)
Contests/Spiffs . . . . (Left Blank)
Long-Term Incentives (e.g., Stock, RSU) . . . . (Left Blank)

Compensation Data

	Base Salary	Incentive Earnings	Total Compensation
Target	(Left Blank)	Yes	Yes
Actual	Yes	Yes	Yes

Major Sales/Customer Contact Job Families Featured in the Survey

Account Management, Business Development, Sales Engineering, Marketing, Marketing Communications, Customer Relationship Management, Customer Relationship Delivery Management, Delivery Management, Sales Management

Pearl Meyer

National Engineering and Construction Salary Survey   **Pearl Meyer**
93 Worcester Street, Wellesley, MA 02481
(508) 460-9600
www.pearlmeyer.com

Survey Overview

The *National Engineering and Construction Salary Survey (NECSS)* is a compensation information source specifically focused on engineering and construction/construction management companies with significant operations in both areas, primarily in the power, petrochemical, civil, environmental, transportation and/or mining and metals industries. The survey covers approximately 18 job families (109 jobs) and provides policy and practice information in areas of salary administration, turnover, overtime, college recruiting and hiring rates, as well as variable pay plans.

Survey Editor

Rebecca Toman, rebecca.toman@pearlmeyer.com
(508) 630-1475

General Information

Industries Covered

Engineering and Construction

Survey Specifications

Range of Revenue of Reporting Companies . . . . Large to Very Large
Frequency of Survey Updates . . . . Annual/Specific Date
Annual Publication Date . . . . August 15
First Year of Publication. . . . . 25+ Years Ago
Restrictions . . . . Industry
Data Delivery Methods . . . . Electronic/Soft Copy, Online
Non-Participant Report Available . . . . No
Custom Reporting. . . . . Standard Reporting
Data from World Regions . . . . (Left Blank)
Number of Companies. . . . . 35+
Number of Sales Jobs 5
Data Submitted . . . . Averages/Percentiles
Sales Volume by Job Title. . . . . (Left Blank)

Practices

Plan Performance Metrics...................... (Left Blank)
Formula Mechanics .... (Left Blank)
Benefits..................................... (Left Blank)
Allowances (e.g., Car, Mobile Devices, Internet)... (Left Blank)
Contests/Spiffs.............................. (Left Blank)
Long-Term Incentives (e.g., Stock, RSU).......... (Left Blank)

Compensation Data

	Base Salary	Incentive Earnings	Total Compensation
Target	(Left Blank)	Yes	Yes
Actual	Yes	Yes	Yes

Major Sales/Customer Contact Job Families Featured in the Survey

Business Development Job Family – 5 levels – Variable Compensation Reported

Pearl Meyer

The Executive Compensation and Benchmarking Survey
93 Worcester Street, Wellesley, MA 02481
(508) 460-9600
www.pearlmeyer.com

Pearl Meyer

Survey Overview

The report covers the complete top two layers of a firm's management team including over 70 executive positions. In addition to a traditional competitive pay summary by benchmark position, the report also gives data for non-benchmark positions (e.g., direct report to CEO, not matched elsewhere) allowing you to determine an appropriate survey match for each one of your top executives, even those with a unique range of responsibilities.

Survey Editor

Rebecca Toman, rebecca.toman@pearlmeyer.com
(508) 630-1475

General Information

Industries Covered

Broad Range

Survey Specifications

Range of Revenue of Reporting Companies . . . . Medium to Very Large
Frequency of Survey Updates . . . . Annual/Specific Date
Annual Publication Date . . . . Early July
First Year of Publication. . . . . 20+ Years Ago
Restrictions . . . . Industry
Data Delivery Methods . . . . Electronic/Soft Copy, Online
Non-Participant Report Available . . . . No
Custom Reporting. . . . . Standard Reporting
Data from World Regions . . . . (Left Blank)
Number of Companies. . . . . 600+
Number of Sales Jobs . . . . (Left Blank)
Data Submitted . . . . Averages/Percentiles
Sales Volume by Job Title. . . . . (Left Blank)

Practices

Plan Performance Metrics . . . . (Left Blank)
Formula Mechanics . . . . (Left Blank)
Benefits . . . . (Left Blank)
Allowances (e.g., Car, Mobile Devices, Internet) . . . (Left Blank)
Contests/Spiffs . . . . (Left Blank)
Long-Term Incentives (e.g., Stock, RSU) . . . . (Left Blank)

Compensation Data

	Base Salary	Incentive Earnings	Total Compensation
Target	(Left Blank)	Yes	Yes
Actual	Yes	Yes	Yes

Major Sales/Customer Contact Job Families Featured in the Survey

Top Sales, Top Marketing and Sales, Direct Report to Top Sales, Direct Report to Top Marketing and Sales

Radford
An Aon Company

**Radford Global Compensation Database—
Sales Roles Job Module**
2570 North First Street, Suite 500, San Jose, CA 95131
(408) 321-2500
https://radford.aon.com

Survey Overview

Sales professionals across sectors share a unique challenge: selling innovation. Meeting this mandate requires top talent, flexible incentives and intelligent sales targets. Our sales data and practices offering is designed to address these issues across multiple sales channels and industries. The sales compensation and practices data in the Radford Global Compensation Platform provides human resources and compensation professionals with access to rewards and sales plan design insights covering technology, life sciences, medical devices, retail and e-commerce, manufacturing, media and gaming, private markets and a host of other industry verticals on a global survey platform, using a global job architecture.

Survey Editor

Julie Mills, jmills@radford.com
(408) 321-2540

General Information

Industries Covered

Technology, Life Sciences, Medical Devices, Retail and e-Commerce, Manufacturing, Energy, Media and Gaming, Private Markets, General Industry, and many more

Survey Specifications

Range of Revenue of Reporting Companies . . . . Less than $0–$10B+
Frequency of Survey Updates . . . . Evergreen
Annual Publication Date . . . . Quarterly
First Year of Publication 1986
Restrictions . . . . Industry
Data Delivery Methods . . . . Online
Non-Participant Report Available . . . . No
Custom Reporting . . . . Standard Reporting, Online
                                                                    Access/User Defined
Data from World Regions . . . . North America, Europe, Asia,
                                                                    Middle East, Other Americas,
                                                                    Africa

Number of Companies. . . . . 1,800+
Number of Sales Jobs . . . . 400+
Data Submitted . . . . Incumbent Level
Sales Volume by Job Title. Yes

Practices

Plan Performance Metrics. Yes
Formula Mechanics . . . . Yes
Benefits. . . . . Yes
Allowances (e.g., Car, Mobile Devices, Internet) . . . Yes
Contests/Spiffs. . . . . Yes
Long-Term Incentives (e.g., Stock, RSU) . . . . Yes

Compensation Data

	Base Salary	Incentive Earnings	Total Compensation
Target	Yes	Yes	Yes
Actual	Yes	Yes	Yes

Major Sales/Customer Contact Job Families Featured in the Survey

Alliances & Partnerships, Contract Management & Renewal, Consulting Services, Customer Success, Field Sales (Direct, Retail, OEM/VAR, Multi-Channel), Global & Regional Sales Leadership, Global & National Strategic Account Management, Inside/ Telesales, Internet Ad Sales, Leasing & Finance Sales, Maintenance/Services, Managed Care, Medical Device Sales (Implantable, Non-Implantable), Pharmaceutical Sales (Hospital Pharma, Specialty/Non-Specialty Pharma, Oncology, Vaccine, Rare Disease), Life Sciences Sales (Diagnostics, Animal Health, Life Sciences Products/Services), Relationship Management, Sales Administration & Support, Sales Engineering (Pre- & Post-Sale), Sales Executives, Sales Operations (Deal Desk, Commissions Analyst, Operations Analyst, Order Process Management), Sales Training, Salesforce Effectiveness/Sales Enablement, Telemarketing/Lead Development

Salary.com

IPAS® Global Benchmark Survey
610 Lincoln Street North Building, Suite 200,
Waltham, MA 02451
(781) 989-9488
www.salary.com

Survey Overview

IPAS® Global Benchmark Survey gives you access to salaries for over 2,200 benchmark jobs across all global industries. This unique single data source allows you to search and filter data by organization size and geographic location. We offer a straightforward and consistent approach for comparing your benchmark jobs around the world, at all levels, to your competitors. Results for key data elements are delivered via our easy-to-use online web tool and results are updated quarterly.

Survey Editor

Tricia Mulkeen, tricia.mulkeen@salary.com

General Information

Industries Covered

Not listed

Survey Specifications

Range of Revenue of Reporting Companies	<$50M–>$10B
Frequency of Survey Updates	Evergreen (Open All Year)
Annual Publication Date	N/A
First Year of Publication	2020
Restrictions	None
Data Delivery Methods	Online
Non-Participant Report Available	Yes
Custom Reporting	Standard Reporting, Online Access/User Defined
Data from World Regions	North America, Europe, Asia, Middle East, Other Americas, Africa
Number of Companies	360 companies
Number of Sales Jobs	318 Sales Job Function/Job Level Combinations
Data Submitted	Incumbent Level
Sales Volume by Job Title	No

Practices

Plan Performance Metrics . . . . No (For retail positions only)
Formula Mechanics . . . . No
Benefits . . . . No
Allowances (e.g., Car, Mobile Devices, Internet) . . . Yes
Contests/Spiffs . . . . No
Long-Term Incentives (e.g., Stock, RSU) . . . . No

Compensation Data

	Base Salary	Incentive Earnings	Total Compensation
Target	No	Yes	Yes
Actual	Yes	Yes	Yes

Major Sales/Customer Contact Job Families Featured in the Survey

Sales: Advertising Sales, Federal Government Sales, Field Account/Territory Sales Management, Channel Sales (Distributor/Retail), Sales & Marketing, Product Leasing Sales, Key/Major Account Management, Contract Renewal Sales, OEM/VAR Sales, Partner Sales, Client Relationship Management, Services/Support Sales, Outbound Telesales

Sales Operations: Engagement/Bid Proposal, CRM Administration, Ad Campaign Support, Systems Engineering, Sales Forecasting & Analysis, Sales Operations, Inbound Telesales, Sales Order Administration/Processing, Sales Program Management, Sales Training, Telemarketing, Sales Support

Technical Support/Customer Service: Customer/Product Support, Field Service Dispatch, Technical Support Engineering, Field Customer Engineering, Customer/Technical Service Support Management, Call Center Scheduling, Program Management, Customer Support/Call Center Quality, Product Repair, Account Support Management, Customer Service (General)

Job Levels Reported (if applicable and/or when sufficient data):
8 Management Levels–Supervisor to Executive
8 Professional Levels–Entry to Fellow
5 Support Levels–Entry to Expert

Salary.com

IPAS® Global Consumer Industry Survey
610 Lincoln Street North Building, Suite 200,
Waltham, MA 02451
(781) 989-9488
www.salary.com

Survey Overview

Since 1996, we have offered several U.S. surveys, which opened the door to the world of pay and benefits in the consumer industry. In 2012, we combined three of our consumer surveys (Apparel & Footwear, Specialty Retail and Luxury Goods) into one comprehensive, global product. The *IPAS® Global Consumer Industry Survey* creates a single, comprehensive source of reliable market intelligence. In 2012, the survey expanded from U.S. only to Global and we are currently reporting jobs in 9 countries.

Survey Editor

Tricia Mulkeen, tricia.mulkeen@salary.com

General Information

Industries Covered

Apparel, Footwear, Luxury Goods, Consumer Goods

Survey Specifications

Range of Revenue of Reporting Companies . . . . $150M–$10B (typical range)
Frequency of Survey Updates . . . . Annual/Specific Date
Annual Publication Date . . . . September
First Year of Publication. 1996
Restrictions . . . . Industry
Data Delivery Methods . . . . Online
Non-Participant Report Available . . . . Yes
Custom Reporting. . . . . Standard Reporting, Online
Access/User Defined
Data from World Regions . . . . North America, Europe,
Asia (Mainly USA, recently
expanded to global, 9 countries
available in 2020 for certain jobs
only)
Number of Companies. . . . . 33 companies in 2020 (71
unique/premier brands)
Number of Sales Jobs . . . . 59 Sales Job Function/Job Level
Combinations (wholesale) plus
retail/store sales associates

Data Submitted . . . . Incumbent Level
Sales Volume by Job Title. . . . . No

Practices

Plan Performance Metrics. . . . . No (For retail positions only)
Formula Mechanics . . . . No
Benefits . . . . No
Allowances (e.g., Car, Mobile Devices, Internet) . . . No
Contests/Spiffs. . . . . No
Long-Term Incentives (e.g., Stock, RSU) . . . . Yes (Eligibility and general
information only, actual LTI
values not collected)

Compensation Data

	Base Salary	Incentive Earnings	Total Compensation
Target	No	Yes	Yes
Actual	Yes	Yes	Yes

Major Sales/Customer Contact Job Families Featured in the Survey

Sales (Corporate/Wholesale): Dealer/Customer Relations, Key Account Sales, Sample Management, Sales & Marketing, Sales Planning/Analysis, Sales Support, Field Sales, Inside Sales Store Sales Associate and Lead Store Sales Associate

Store Management: Department Managers, Assistant Store Managers, Associate Store Managers, Store Managers

Salary.com

IPAS® Global High Technology Compensation Salary Survey

610 Lincoln Street North Building, Suite 200,
Waltham, MA 02451
(781) 989-9488
www.salary.com

Survey Overview

IPAS® is a unique single source of global market data focusing on the high-technology industry. It allows participants to price jobs around the world and compare jobs in various countries using the same methodology, participants, currency and system.

Global compensation data is collected from the most prestigious firms in the industry and validated by a team of experts, so participants can be certain that they have the highest quality information available to build their compensation programs around the world.

Input requirements are kept minimal by focusing on key data elements and results are delivered via our web tool, easily accessible any time. Data is collected throughout the year based upon participants' focal review effective dates. Survey results are updated quarterly.

Survey Editor

Tricia Mulkeen, tricia.mulkeen@salary.com

General Information

Industries Covered

High-technology (Computer Systems/Peripherals, Software, Electronics, Semiconductor/Chip Manufacturing, Tele-communications, Networking, Web/Internet, Professional Services/Consulting). Expanding to other industries such as Manufacturing and Aerospace & Defense

Survey Specifications

Range of Revenue of Reporting Companies . . . . <$50M–>$10B
Frequency of Survey Updates . . . . Evergreen
Annual Publication Date . . . . Survey results updated quarterly
First Year of Publication. 1998
Restrictions . . . . Industry
Data Delivery Methods . . . . Online
Non-Participant Report Available . . . . Yes
Custom Reporting. . . . . Standard Reporting, Online
                                                       Access/User Defined

Data from World Regions . . . . North America, Europe, Asia, Middle East, Other Americas, Africa

Number of Companies. . . . . 370 companies in 2020

Number of Sales Jobs . . . . 548 Sales Job Function/Job Level Combinations

Data Submitted . . . . Incumbent Level

Sales Volume by Job Title. . . . . No

Practices

Plan Performance Metrics. No

Formula Mechanics . . . . No

Benefits . . . . No

Allowances (e.g., Car, Mobile Devices, Internet) . . . Yes

Contests/Spiffs. . . . . No

Long-Term Incentives (e.g., Stock, RSU) . . . . Yes*

* Long-Term Incentive eligibility only

Compensation Data

	Base Salary	Incentive Earnings	Total Compensation
Target	No	Yes	Yes
Actual	Yes	Yes	Yes

Major Sales/Customer Contact Job Families Featured in the Survey

Sales: Advertising Sales, Federal Government Sales, Field Account/Territory Sales Management, Channel Sales (Distributor/Retail), Sales & Marketing, Product Leasing Sales, Key/Major Account Management, Contract Renewal Sales, OEM/ VAR Sales, Professional Services/Outsourcing Sales, Partner Sales, Client Relationship Management, Services/Support Sales, Outbound Telesales

Sales Operations: Engagement/Bid Proposal, CRM Administration, Ad Campaign Support, Systems Engineering, Sales Forecasting & Analysis, Sales Operations, Inbound Telesales, Sales Order Administration/Processing, Sales Program Management, Sales Training, Telemarketing, Sales Support

Technical Support/Customer Service: Customer/Product Support, Technical Support Engineering, Field Customer Engineering, Customer/Technical Service Support Management, Call Center Scheduling, Program Management, Customer Support/Call Center Quality, Product Repair, Account Support Management, Customer Service (General)

Job Levels Reported (if applicable and/or when sufficient data):
8 Management Levels–Supervisor to Executive
8 Professional Levels–Entry to Fellow
5 Support Levels–Entry to Expert

The Croner Company

C2HR Content Developers Compensation Survey
55 Shaver Street, San Rafael, CA 94901
(415) 485-5530
www.croner.biz

Survey Overview

The *C2HR Content Developers Compensation Survey* is a participant-only compensation survey conducted annually to provide cable programmers, broadcast networks, digital and other media companies with up-to-date, market competitive compensation data.

Participant companies include all five national broadcast networks and all of the leading cable programmers, as well as companies that create content for internet channels.

Survey Editor

Hali Croner, (415) 485-5530

General Information

Industries Covered

Broadcast Networks, Cable Programming

Survey Specifications

Range of Revenue of Reporting Companies . . . . (Left Blank)
Frequency of Survey Updates . . . . Annual/Specific Date
Annual Publication Date . . . . September
First Year of Publication. 2001
Restrictions . . . . None
Data Delivery Methods . . . . Electronic/Soft Copy, Online
Non-Participant Report Available . . . . Yes
Custom Reporting. . . . . Standard Reporting, Online
Access/User Defined
Data from World Regions . . . . North America
Number of Companies. 47
Number of Sales Jobs 78
Data Submitted . . . . Averages/Percentiles
Sales Volume by Job Title. . . . . Yes

Practices

Plan Performance Metrics . . . . Yes
Formula Mechanics . . . . Yes
Benefits . . . . No
Allowances (e.g., Car, Mobile Devices, Internet) . . . No
Contests/Spiffs . . . . (Left Blank)
Long-Term Incentives (e.g., Stock, RSU) . . . . Yes

Compensation Data

	Base Salary	Incentive Earnings	Total Compensation
Target	Yes	Yes	Yes
Actual	Yes	Yes	Yes

Major Sales/Customer Contact Job Families Featured in the Survey

Advertising Sales, Advertising Sales Analysis, Affiliate Marketing, Affiliate Sales, Integrated Sales and Marketing, International Sales, Sales Operations, Syndication Sales

The Croner Company

C2HR Content Providers Compensation Survey
55 Shaver Street, San Rafael, CA 94901
(415) 485-5530
www.croner.biz

Survey Overview

The *C2HR Content Providers Compensation Survey* is a highly industry specific survey. Conducted annually to provide multiple systems operators (MSOs) with up-to-date, market competitive compensation data.

The participants in the survey include the large MSOs, as well as smaller, regional companies and satellite operators, telecommunications companies and home security companies.

Survey Editor

Hali Croner, (415) 485-5530

General Information

Industries Covered

Cable TV and Satellite Multiple System Operators

Survey Specifications

Range of Revenue of Reporting Companies . . . . (Left Blank)
Frequency of Survey Updates . . . . Annual/Specific Date
Annual Publication Date . . . . September
First Year of Publication. 2001
Restrictions . . . . Industry
Data Delivery Methods . . . . Electronic/Soft Copy, Online
Non-Participant Report Available . . . . Yes
Custom Reporting. . . . . Standard Reporting, Online
                                                                Access/User Defined
Data from World Regions . . . . North America
Number of Companies. 14
Number of Sales Jobs 94
Data Submitted . . . . Averages/Percentiles
Sales Volume by Job Title. . . . . Yes

Practices

Plan Performance Metrics . . . . Yes
Formula Mechanics . . . . Yes
Benefits . . . . No
Allowances (e.g., Car, Mobile Devices, Internet) . . . No
Contests/Spiffs . . . . (Left Blank)
Long-Term Incentives (e.g., Stock, RSU) . . . . Yes

Compensation Data

	Base Salary	Incentive Earnings	Total Compensation
Target	Yes	Yes	Yes
Actual	Yes	Yes	Yes

Major Sales/Customer Contact Job Families Featured in the Survey

Carrier Sales, Channel Sales, Commercial Inside Sales, Commercial Sales Account Management, Commercial Sales Engineering, Commercial Sales Support, Direct Sales, Embedded Retail Sales, Home Security Sales, Inbound Sales, MDU Sales, MDU Sales Account Management, Major Account/Enterprise Commercial Sales, Small-to-Medium Business Commercial Sales, Outbound Sales, Regional Retail Sales, Sales Operations, Store Retail Sales, Third-Party Sales

The Croner Company

Croner Digital Content and Technology Survey
55 Shaver Street, San Rafael, CA 94901
(415) 485-5530
www.croner.biz

Survey Overview

The *Croner Digital Content and Technology Survey* is conducted annually to provide up-to-date market compensation data to companies conducting a material part of their business via online and mobile platforms. The report is designed specifically for companies that develop and publish frequently updated internet content and/or provide consumers and businesses with online and mobile transactions and services.

Participant companies in the *Croner Digital Content and Technology Survey* span multiple industry segments, including digital advertising services, e-commerce retail, e-commerce transactions, media and entertainment, food and beverage, online/mobile gaming, publishing, search/social networks, web publishing and business products/services. Positions reported in the survey are specific to digital organizations or to digital units within a larger organization.

Survey Editor

Hali Croner, (415) 485-5530

General Information

Industries Covered

All Companies with Internet/Mobile Presence

Survey Specifications

Range of Revenue of Reporting Companies . . . . (Left Blank)
Frequency of Survey Updates . . . . Annual/Specific Date
Annual Publication Date . . . . August
First Year of Publication. 1996
Restrictions . . . . None
Data Delivery Methods . . . . Electronic/Soft Copy, Online
Non-Participant Report Available . . . . Yes
Custom Reporting. . . . . Standard Reporting, Online
                                                              Access/User Defined
Data from World Regions . . . . North America, United
                                                              Kingdom, China, France,
                                                              Germany and Spain
Number of Companies. 100
Number of Sales Jobs 105

Data Submitted . . . . Averages/Percentiles
Sales Volume by Job Title. . . . . Yes

Practices

Plan Performance Metrics. . . . . Yes
Formula Mechanics . . . . Yes
Benefits. . . . . No
Allowances (e.g., Car, Mobile Devices, Internet) . . . No
Contests/Spiffs. . . . . No
Long-Term Incentives (e.g., Stock, RSU) . . . . Yes

Compensation Data

	Base Salary	Incentive Earnings	Total Compensation
Target	Yes	Yes	Yes
Actual	Yes	Yes	Yes

Major Sales/Customer Contact Job Families Featured in the Survey

Ad Producing, Ad Inventory Management, Advertising Traffic, Advertising Operations, Advertising Solutions, Digital Product Sales, Field Advertising Sales, Inside Advertising Sales, Lead Generation Administrations, Local Advertising Sales, Offers Sales, Pre-Sales, Programmatic Sales, Sales Account Services, Sales Analysis, Sales Marketing, Sales Operations, Sales Strategy and Planning, Sales Training, Yield Analytics

The Croner Company

Croner Entertainment Survey
55 Shaver Street, San Rafael, CA 94901
(415) 485-5530
www.croner.biz

Survey Overview

The *Croner Entertainment Survey* is an industry-specific survey conducted annually to serve as a comprehensive compensation resource for benchmark positions in the film, television, music and digital entertainment industries. It includes positions at all organizational levels, from executive to hourly, across a broad range of job families.

Survey Editor

Hali Croner, (415) 485-5530

General Information

Industries Covered

Theatrical, Television and Music Production/Post-Production, Distribution & Sales

Survey Specifications

Range of Revenue of Reporting Companies . . . . (Left Blank)
Frequency of Survey Updates . . . . Annual/Specific Date
Annual Publication Date . . . . November
First Year of Publication. 2013
Restrictions . . . . Industry
Data Delivery Methods . . . . Electronic/Soft Copy, Online
Non-Participant Report Available . . . . Yes
Custom Reporting. . . . . Standard Reporting, Online
                                                                                 Access/User Defined
Data from World Regions . . . . North America
Number of Companies. 37
Number of Sales Jobs 75
Data Submitted . . . . Averages/Percentiles
Sales Volume by Job Title. . . . . Yes

Practices

Plan Performance Metrics. . . . . No
Formula Mechanics . . . . No
Benefits . . . . No
Allowances (e.g., Car, Mobile Devices, Internet) . . . Yes
Contests/Spiffs. . . . . (Left Blank)
Long-Term Incentives (e.g., Stock, RSU) . . . . Yes

Compensation Data

	Base Salary	Incentive Earnings	Total Compensation
Target	Yes	Yes	Yes
Actual	Yes	Yes	Yes

Major Sales/Customer Contact Job Families Featured in the Survey

Distribution Sales, International Sales/Distribution, Digital Sales/Distribution, Integrated Sales and Marketing, Sales Planning, Sales Operations, Retail Development/ Sales, Retail Store, Sales/Distribution - International

The Croner Company

Croner Local Media Survey
55 Shaver Street, San Rafael, CA 94901
(415) 485-5530
www.croner.biz

Survey Overview

The *Croner Local Media Survey* is an industry-specific survey conducted annually to provide local advertising sales compensation, advertising sales plan design features and compensation for local television and radio station programming and operations across multiple industries, including cable, television, radio and digital media.

Survey Editor

Hali Croner, (415) 485-5530

General Information

Industries Covered

Cable, Television, Radio and Digital (Online and Mobile Media)

Survey Specifications

Range of Revenue of Reporting Companies . . . . (Left Blank)
Frequency of Survey Updates . . . . Annual/Specific Date
Annual Publication Date . . . . September
First Year of Publication. 2010
Restrictions . . . . Industry
Data Delivery Methods . . . . Electronic/Soft Copy
Non-Participant Report Available . . . . Yes
Custom Reporting. . . . . Standard Reporting
Data from World Regions . . . . North America
Number of Companies. 14
Number of Sales Jobs 33
Data Submitted . . . . Averages/Percentiles
Sales Volume by Job Title. . . . . Yes

Practices

Plan Performance Metrics. . . . . Yes
Formula Mechanics . . . . Yes
Benefits . . . . No
Allowances (e.g., Car, Mobile Devices, Internet) . . . No
Contests/Spiffs. . . . . No
Long-Term Incentives (e.g., Stock, RSU) . . . . Yes

Compensation Data

	Base Salary	Incentive Earnings	Total Compensation
Target	Yes	No	Yes
Actual	Yes	No	Yes

Major Sales/Customer Contact Job Families Featured in the Survey

Digital Sales, Local National Sales, Integrated Sales and Marketing, Sales Planning, Sales Operations, Sales Account Service Management

The Croner Company

Croner Software Games Survey
55 Shaver Street, San Rafael, CA 94901
(415) 485-5530
www.croner.biz

Survey Overview

The *Croner Software Games Survey* is the benchmark survey of the entertainment software industry. This leading-edge report provides compensation data for jobs in all gaming platform types, including mobile, social, console, PC, handheld, MMO, cloud, VR and casino games. The survey has provided market data about positions in companies that publish and/or develop software for entertainment and education in the U.S. and Canada since 1990, its scope and content evolving each year casino gaming industry.

The North America Survey reports data and policies and practices such as bonus plans and selected benefits for companies and includes positions and cuts specific to mobile and social gaming. The International Supplement reports data for selected positions in the U.K and Europe.

Survey Editor

Hali Croner, (415) 485-5530

General Information

Industries Covered

Software Games: Including Entertainment, Educational and Casino

Survey Specifications

Range of Revenue of Reporting Companies	(Left Blank)
Frequency of Survey Updates	Annual/Specific Date
Annual Publication Date	December
First Year of Publication	1990
Restrictions	Industry
Data Delivery Methods	Electronic/Soft Copy, Online
Non-Participant Report Available	Yes
Custom Reporting	Standard Reporting, Online Access/User Defined
Data from World Regions	North America, United Kingdom
Number of Companies	52
Number of Sales Jobs	36
Data Submitted	Averages/Percentiles
Sales Volume by Job Title	Yes

Practices

Plan Performance Metrics......................Yes
Formula Mechanics ....Yes
Benefits.....................................Yes
Allowances (e.g., Car, Mobile Devices, Internet)...Yes
Contests/Spiffs..............................No
Long-Term Incentives (e.g., Stock, RSU)..........Yes

Compensation Data

	Base Salary	Incentive Earnings	Total Compensation
Target	Yes	Yes	Yes
Actual	Yes	Yes	Yes

Major Sales/Customer Contact Job Families Featured in the Survey

Advertising Sales, Field Sales-Regional, Programmatic Sales, Sales Administration, Sales Analysis, Sales Management, Sales Marketing

Western Compensation & Benefits Consultants

Marketing & Sales Compensation Survey
595 Howe Street, Suite 502,
Vancouver, BC, V6C 2T5 Canada
(604) 683-9155
www.wcbc.ca

Survey Overview

WCBC's *Marketing & Sales Compensation Survey,* conducted annually, provides salary and incentive data for over 80 positions. The survey covers a broad range of Canadian organizations in all sectors of the economy.

Survey Editor

Linda Reid, linda_reid@wcbc.ca
(604) 683-9155

General Information

Industries Covered

Professional, Scientific & Technical Services, Retail Trade, Educational Services, Health Care & Social Assistance, Associations & Regulatory Bodies, Finance & Insurance, Agriculture, Forestry, Fishing & Hunting, Mining, Quarrying and Oil & Gas Extraction, Manufacturing, Transportation & Warehousing, Arts, Entertainment, Recreation, Tourism, Hospitality, Wholesale Trade, Other

Survey Specifications

Range of Revenue of Reporting Companies . . . . $50M–>$100M
Frequency of Survey Updates . . . . Annual/Specific Date
Annual Publication Date . . . . September
First Year of Publication. 1985
Restrictions . . . . None
Data Delivery Methods . . . . Paper, Electronic/Soft Copy, Online
Non-Participant Report Available . . . . Yes
Custom Reporting. . . . . Online Access/User Defined
Data from World Regions . . . . North America
Number of Companies. . . . . 150+
Number of Sales Jobs . . . . 80+
Data Submitted . . . . Incumbent Level
Sales Volume by Job Title. . . . . No

Practices

Plan Performance Metrics . . . . No
Formula Mechanics . . . . No
Benefits . . . . No
Allowances (e.g., Car, Mobile Devices, Internet) . . . No
Contests/Spiffs . . . . No
Long-Term Incentives (e.g., Stock, RSU) . . . . No

Compensation Data

	Base Salary	Incentive Earnings	Total Compensation
Target	No	No	No
Actual	Yes	Yes	Yes

Major Sales/Customer Contact Job Families Featured in the Survey

General Operations, Marketing/Media, Sales/Merchandising/Advertising, Art/Design/Media, Communications/Events/Community Relations, Customer Services/Technical Service/Call Centre, Retail, Member Relations/Fundraising, Business Development

Western Management Group

Retail Sales Compensation Survey
237 West Main Street, Los Gatos, CA 95030
(408) 399-4900
www.wmgnet.com

Survey Overview

This survey includes multiple levels for jobs in the Retail industry, and additional positions specific to the restaurant and grocery sectors. For each job, we collect Base Salary, Sales Incentives, Non-Sales Incentives and Targeted Incentive Compensation. Store type/channel, product category and geographic breakouts available.

Survey Editor

DeLynn Gentile, delynn@wmgnet.com
(408) 399-4900, ext. 227

General Information

Industries Covered

Retail Sales

Survey Specifications

Range of Revenue of Reporting Companies . . . . $25M–$150B
Frequency of Survey Updates . . . . Annual/Specific Date
Annual Publication Date . . . . July
First Year of Publication 2004
Restrictions . . . . None
Data Delivery Methods . . . . Paper, Electronic/Soft Copy, Online
Non-Participant Report Available . . . . No
Custom Reporting . . . . Standard Reporting, Online Access/User Defined
Data from World Regions . . . . North America, Europe
Number of Companies 101
Number of Sales Jobs 315
Data Submitted . . . . Incumbent Level
Sales Volume by Job Title . . . . No

Practices

Plan Performance Metrics . . . . No
Formula Mechanics . . . . Yes
Benefits . . . . Yes
Allowances (e.g., Car, Mobile Devices, Internet) . . . Yes
Contests/Spiffs . . . . Yes
Long-Term Incentives (e.g., Stock, RSU) . . . . Yes

Compensation Data

	Base Salary	Incentive Earnings	Total Compensation
Target	Yes	Yes	Yes
Actual	Yes	Yes	Yes

Major Sales/Customer Contact Job Families Featured in the Survey

Store and Sales Management, Visual Merchandising/Presentation, Merchandising Processing, Warehousing/Distribution/Transportation, Inventory/Logistics/Planning, Purchasing, Customer Service, Market/Advertising/Promotion, Indirect/Online/Internet Sales, Finance/Risk Management, Loss Prevention/Security, Human Resources, Facilities Support and Real Estate, Administration-Store Level, Franchise Sales/Operations, IT Systems, Store Operations/Communications, Executive/Senior Management, Pharmacy, Photography, Beauty/Fragrance, Optical, Grocery and Restaurant

Western Management Group

Sales and Service Compensation Survey
237 West Main Street, Los Gatos, CA 95030
(408) 399-4900
www.wmgnet.com

Survey Overview

The survey collects data for key Sales and Service positions in the Consumer Products, High-Technology Commercial and Media industries. Jobs include sales forces directly to end-users or retailers, business-to-business or indirectly through channels. Media industry and sales support jobs for companies that sell as space have been added to the survey. Data collected includes Total Cash Compensation in the form of Actual earned and Targeted Base Pay, Sales Incentives and Non-Sales Variable Pay for the previous and current sales plan. Industry product and revenue level breakouts are available.

Survey Editor

Toni McGrath, toni@wmgnet.com
(408) 399-4900, ext. 229

General Information

Industries Covered

Consumer Products, High-Technology, Commercial and Media Industries

Survey Specifications

Range of Revenue of Reporting Companies . . . . $33M–$163B
Frequency of Survey Updates . . . . Annual/Specific Date
Annual Publication Date . . . . July
First Year of Publication. 1985
Restrictions . . . . None
Data Delivery Methods . . . . Paper, Electronic/Soft Copy, Online
Non-Participant Report Available . . . . No
Custom Reporting. . . . . Standard Reporting, Online Access/User Defined
Data from World Regions . . . . North America
Number of Companies. 194
Number of Sales Jobs 120
Data Submitted . . . . Incumbent Level
Sales Volume by Job Title. . . . . No

Practices

Plan Performance Metrics . . . . No
Formula Mechanics . . . . Yes
Benefits . . . . Yes
Allowances (e.g., Car, Mobile Devices, Internet) . . . Yes
Contests/Spiffs . . . . Yes
Long-Term Incentives (e.g., Stock, RSU) . . . . Yes

Compensation Data

	Base Salary	Incentive Earnings	Total Compensation
Target	Yes	Yes	Yes
Actual	Yes	Yes	Yes

Major Sales/Customer Contact Job Families Featured in the Survey

General Sales, Product Specialty Sales, Retail Account Management, Government Sales, Business Development, Inside Sales, Media Sales, Sales Administration, Sales Automation, Sales Forecasting, Remote Support, Field Service, Education and Systems Engineering

Willis Towers Watson

**2020 Sales Compensation and
    Design Survey – U.S.**
44 South Broadway, 13th Floor,
White Plains, New York 10601
(800) 645-5771
www.wtwdataservices.com

WillisTowersWatson **I.I'I'I.I**

Survey Overview

Our *Sales Compensation and Design Survey – U.S.* focuses exclusively on jobs that are directly involved in the sales process. This survey is ideal for organizations searching for data on the "hunter," the "farmer" and hybrid roles—those tasked with pursuing and closing new sales opportunities, as well as those responsible for retaining and growing existing client relationships.

Use data from this survey report to:

- Gauge the competitiveness of your overall sales compensation package in the external market.
- Ensure your high performers are keeping up with other high performers in the market.
- See how your organization's sales incentive design practices compare against the market.

The survey report offers:

- Robust data on pay levels, including sales incentive plans and corporate performance bonus plans for key benchmark sales positions
- Insightful information on sales incentive design practices and trends, including performance measures and payout mechanisms
- Simplified job structure and incentive data reporting requirements
- Enhanced reporting that further supports the specific requirements of sales compensation managers

Data elements are reported on:

- Base salary
- Variable compensation, including:
  - o All forms of sales compensation (including commissions and target-based quota bonuses)
  - o Participation in any companywide annual incentive plans
  - o Information collected on target and actual values
- Total annual compensation (target and actual)
- Pay mix between fixed and variable compensation (target and actual)
- Company car benefits
- Long-term incentive eligibility

Survey Contact

Client Care, wtwusdata@willistowerswatson.com
(800) 645-5771

General Information

Industries Covered

Banking and Finance, Durable Goods, Energy, Health Care, Insurance, Nondurable Goods, Retail and Wholesale Trade, Services

Survey Specifications

Range of Revenue of Reporting Companies . . . . $20M–$280B
Frequency of Survey Updates . . . . Annual/Specific Date
Annual Publication Date . . . . September
First Year of Publication. 2019
Restrictions . . . . None
Data Delivery Methods . . . . Online
Non-Participant Report Available . . . . No
Custom Reporting. . . . . Standard Reporting, Online
                                                                                      Access/User Defined
Data from World Regions . . . . North America
Number of Companies. 460
Number of Sales Jobs . . . . More than 120 Discipline/Level
                                                                                      combinations
Data Submitted . . . . Incumbent Level
Sales Volume by Job Title. . . . . No

Practices

Plan Performance Metrics. . . . . Yes
Formula Mechanics . . . . Yes
Benefits . . . . No
Allowances (e.g., Car, Mobile Devices, Internet) . . . Yes
Contests/Spiffs. . . . . Yes
Long-Term Incentives (e.g., Stock, RSU) . . . . Yes

Compensation Data

	Base Salary	Incentive Earnings	Total Compensation
Target	Yes	Yes	Yes
Actual	Yes	Yes	Yes

Major Sales/Customer Contact Job Families Featured in the Survey

Account/Relationship Management, Channel Sales, Direct Sales, Large Deal Acquisition Sales, New Account Acquisition Sales, Remote Sales, Retail Store Sales and Operations, Sales, Technical Sales Support

SALES
COMPENSATION
ADMINISTRATION
VENDORS GUIDE

SALES COMPENSATION ALMANAC • 2022

SALES COMPENSATION ADMINISTRATION VENDORS GUIDE

Sales compensation administration software and service providers use powerful administration tools to track, report and model sales compensation transactions. Use this list of vendors to locate and assess the right administration software to help manage your pay program. Vendors are continually upgrading their offerings; contact them for a demonstration of how their software solutions can manage your payout calculations.

IN THIS SECTION
- Vendors Listing
- Other SPM Vendors

Notes

Sales Performance Management (SPM) is a growing market with more companies adopting an application specific solution. Many companies are retiring their desktop, spreadsheet administration tools in favor of a professional SPM application.

SPM solutions are expanding to serve various purposes, including goal setting, incentive design tools and territory planning.

This listing does not constitute an endorsement or recommendation of any listed vendors.

Founded in 2006
1,900+ Employees
447M+ in Revenue

San Francisco
(415) 742-8199
anaplan.com

Global enterprises use Anaplan's solutions to design their go-to-market strategy, streamline sales performance and drive revenue growth. For the 5th consecutive year, Anaplan is positioned as a Leader in the 2020 Gartner Magic Quadrant for Sales Performance Management (SPM) report. Anaplan for Sales delivers core capabilities across sales planning, sales incentives and sales insights, which enable business leaders to navigate the need for rapid scenario-based planning and the urgency around pivoting, course correcting and transforming their revenue objectives amid market disruptions. Delivered on a platform built on a single code base, Anaplan connects your go-to-market strategy with your financial plans, workforce strategies, marketing operations, revenue plans and end-to-end supply chain processes, through its Connected Planning offering.

Licensing Structure

--

Delivery Model

SaaS

Training

Online classes/certification

Support

Live chat, email and phone

SPM Products/Solutions

Sales Incentives • Territory Planning • Quota Planning • Sales Capacity Planning • Sales Forecasting • Pipeline Optimization • Account Segmentation

Primary Industries

Banking & Capital Markets • Consumer Products • Insurance • Life Sciences & Healthcare • Retail • Technology • Telecommunications

Sample Customers

HP • Zillow • LegalZoom • Cox Automotive • DocuSign • VMware • Tableau • Hitachi Automotive

Integration With Other Systems

The Anaplan platform integrates with enterprise systems, including Salesforce, Informatica, MuleSoft, Dell Boomi, SnapLogic, Tableau and DocuSign.

Machine Learning/AI Capabilities

30+ Predictive Capabilities with Optimizer Engine that includes heuristic algorithms for prescriptive actions for quota, territory and incentives.

Predictive Insights continuously gathers thousands of insights and buying signals on millions of businesses worldwide to segment accounts, align territories and optimize pipeline health.

PlanIQ™ with Amazon Forecast drives accurate decisions with seamlessly integrated ML-based forecasting.

Additional Offerings

Corporate FP&A • Business Unit FP&A • Workforce Planning • Demand Management • Marketing Planning

Founded in 2017

90+ Employees

Not reported

San Francisco, CA

–

captivateiq.com

CaptivateIQ is a software company headquartered in San Francisco specializing in commission tracking to ensure teams are aligned, efficient and productive to maximize revenue. Its SPM solution allows integration from a variety of sources, so that companies can incorporate other software and data. Users can design comp plans, customize territories and quotas, and watch the changes in real-time. CaptivateIQ's technology takes sales compensation out of the IT organization and gives control back to business users, who can access performance data to motivate sales teams and drive real ROI in the compensation program.

Licensing Structure

Annual subscription based on # of payees

Delivery Model

SaaS

Training

Onboarding and training provided regularly online

Support

Live chat, email and phone

SPM Products/Solutions

Territory and Quota Management • Reporting • Sales Capacity Planning

Primary Industries

Technology, Business Services, Financial Services, Healthcare, Manufacturing

Sample Customers

Gong • Harness • Intercom • OneLogin • Plaid • TripActions • Newfront Insurance

Integration With Other Systems

CaptivateIQ's SPM solution integrates with dozens of data sources including Salesforce, Microsoft Dynamics, Workday, BambooHR, NetSuite, Intacct, Stripe, QuickBooks, Snowflake, Redshift, SQL databases, and SFTP.

Machine Learning/AI Capabilities

--

Additional Offerings

Advanced Reporting • Dashboard • Email Statements • Plan Management • Inquiries • ASC606 • SSO • Approvals • Audit Log

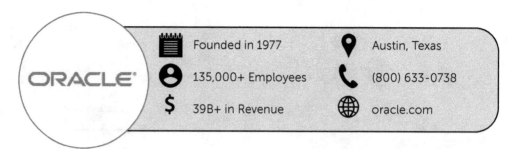

Oracle provides a range of tools for managing business data, supporting business operations and facilitating collaboration and application development. For the 5th year, Oracle is positioned as a Leader in the 2020 Gartner Magic Quadrant for Sales Performance Management (SPM) report, moving up from Challengers. Oracle's SPM has the capability to process complex incentive compensation packages, allowing executives and managers to deploy their sales, territory, and quota plans. Oracle SPM streamlines the rollout of new plan initiatives, provides productivity tools, generates intelligence-based plans, and presents business insights to drive sales performance.

Licensing Structure

--

Delivery Model

SaaS/On-premise

Training

Oracle University, multiple courses for targeted training with over 180 million + digital minutes watched

Support

Phone, email, knowledge base and community engagement

SPM Products/Solutions

Sales Planning • Quota and Territory Management • Incentive Compensation • Forecasting • Estimation Wizards for CPQ

Primary Industries

Automotive • Communications • Construction and Engineering • Consumer Goods • Financial Services • Food and Beverage • Healthcare • High Technology • Hospitality • Industrial Manufacturing • Life Sciences • Media and Entertainment • Public Sector • Retail • Utilities

Sample Customers

Mazda • AFG • General Electric • Motorola • Arrow • McAfee • Equifax • Parker Hannifan • Ricoh

Integration With Other Systems

Oracle invests in integration with other Oracle products, but it requires customers to purchase Integration Cloud Service to connect to non-Oracle applications.

Machine Learning/AI Capabilities

Oracle has made investments in machine learning and advanced analytics. These include a connection to sales forecasting, bots for dispute resolution, and use of its DataFox acquisition to improve the overall SPM and customer experience processes. Predictions exist for capabilities such as segmenting populations, attribute importance and anomaly detection.

Additional Offerings

Oracle HCM • Taleo • Oracle ERP • Oracle Sales

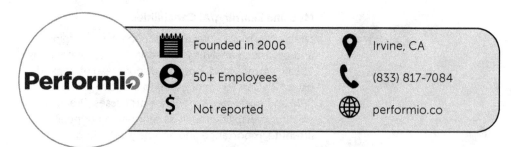

Founded in 2006

50+ Employees

Not reported

Irvine, CA

(833) 817-7084

performio.co

Performio is incentive compensation management software that combines enterprise functionality with the ease of use required of modern software applications. Performio is featured as a Niche Player in the 2020 Gartner Magic Quadrant for Sales Performance Management (SPM) report. Over the past year, Performio has made updates to its SPM product, including upgrades to UI and their territory and quota management solutions.

Licensing Structure

Per user annual license fee

Delivery Model

SaaS

Training

Performio offers hands-on training, as well as an online support hub for technical training and support with experts

Support

Phone, email, mobile app and online support portal

SPM Products/Solutions

API • Commission Overrides and Tables • Dashboards • Forecasting • ICM • Reporting • Systems Integration

Primary Industries

Automotive • Banking • Business Services • Financial Services • Manufacturing • Marketing & Advertising • Media • Medical Device • Pharmaceuticals • Retail • Software • Telecommunications • Wholesale

Sample Customers

AstraZeneca • Boehringer Ingelheim • Grubhub • Hudl • Johnson & Johnson • Optus • Service Express • Validity • Vodafone • Wedbush Securities • WP Engine

Integration With Other Systems

Performio's SPM has an open systems approach that allows companies to integrate with Salesforce, NetSuite, and any other systems using REST API.

Machine Learning/AI Capabilities

--

Additional Offerings

Dedicated Database • Virtual Product Clusters • Sandbox

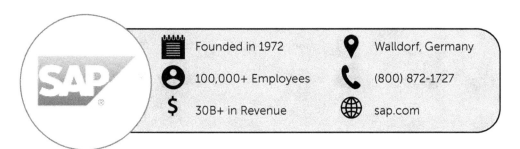

Founded in 1972

100,000+ Employees

30B+ in Revenue

Walldorf, Germany

(800) 872-1727

sap.com

SAP is a market leader in enterprise application software, helping companies of all sizes and in all industries run across many operational areas. For the 7th consecutive year, SAP is positioned as a Leader in the 2020 Gartner Magic Quadrant for Sales Performance Management (SPM) report. SAP delivers their SPM offering to a range of buyers from midmarket to large enterprises with global deployments. The SPM solutions are designed to work with other customers' existing technology investments both SAP and otherwise.

Licensing Structure

Tiered user model

Delivery Model

SaaS

Training

E-learning, virtual instructor-led, on-site are available with classes and certification

Support

Phone, email, live chat

SPM Products/Solutions

ICM • Territory and Quota Planning and Management • Distribution Management • Licensing and Appointment Administration and Management (US Insurance) • Augmented Intelligence • Advanced Analytics • Variable Compensation • Compensation

Primary Industries

Financial Services • Telecommunication • Healthcare • Retail • Consumer Industries • Discrete Industries • Service Industries

Sample Customers

Haven Life • Toyota • Aetna • Exide Life • MSC Industrial • Expedia • HD Supply • Maui Jim • Honeywell • BBVA Compass • Independence Blue Cross • BJ's Wholesale

Integration With Other Systems

SAP offers seamless integration with their hierarchy of hundreds of enterprise software, such as SFDC, Workday, legacy on-premise and others.

Machine Learning/AI Capabilities

SAP's SPM solution includes analytics with machine learning that increases operational efficiency and planning effectiveness, which in turn helps turn sales professionals into profitable contributors of the organization.

Additional Offerings

HR and People Engagement • Employee Experience Management • Business Technology Platform • ERP and Finance • Network and Spend Management • Supply Chain Management • CRM and Customer Experience

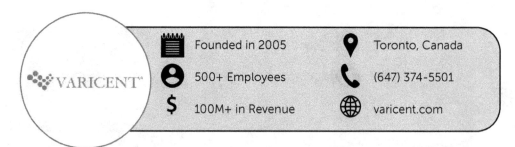

At the end of 2019, Varicent purchased IBM's SPM solution and, in the last year, the company experienced significant revenue and customer growth. For the 2nd year, Varicent is positioned as a Leader in the 2020 Gartner Magic Quadrant for Sales Performance Management (SPM) report. With the additions of their Symon.AI, Territory and Quota Planning and Lead to Revenue solutions, Varicent offers a broad suite of capabilities. Varicent has capabilities for handling large transaction volumes and complex compensation packages, while providing advanced analytics through AI and machine learning.

Licensing Structure

Tracked payees

Delivery Model

SaaS or On-premise

Training

Courses offered through: web-based, instructor-led, self-paced virtual

Support

InApp, phone, email, video conference, free Ask the Expert consulting hours

SPM Products/Solutions

ICM • Territory and Quota Planning • Modeling • Workflow Management • Dashboards and Reporting

Primary Industries

High-Tech • Financial Services • Medical Devices • Pharmaceuticals • Telecommunications • Hospitality • Media • Entertainment • Transport

Sample Customers

Carnival • DXL • Getty Images • HughesNet • Moody's Analytics • Siemens • Shopify • Thermo Fisher Scientific • T-Mobile • Quantum

Integration With Other Systems

Varicent consumes data from any number of disparate data sources, integrating that data directly into an organization's existing infrastructure. Compensation results and commission statements can also be exported directly to downstream systems.

Machine Learning/AI Capabilities

Varicent offers NLP based data connectors, data prep, data shape and data visualization through its Symon.AI platform which comes with a suite of storytelling apps, sales performance management blueprints and the ability to run in embedded mode from directly within Varicent ICM.

Additional Offerings

Lead to Revenue • Symon.AI

Founded in 2005

San Jose, California

600+ Employees

(408) 977-3132

Not reported

xactlycorp.com

Xactly is a privately held, pure-play SaaS company, which provides cloud-based enterprise services for small businesses all the way up to global enterprises. For the 7th year, Xactly is positioned as a Leader in the 2020 Gartner Magic Quadrant for Sales Performance Management (SPM) report. Xactly offers two different products: Incent and AlignStar that have different delivery models, SaaS and Hybrid with the administrator function on-premises, respectively. Both products utilize Xactly's experience in the cloud, AI, and advanced analytics to optimize performance. Xactly offers a range of products, listed below, that complement and add additional features to their SPM offerings, allowing businesses to Plan, Manage, Integrate, Incent, and Analyze the sales organization.

Licensing Structure

--

Delivery Model

SaaS/Hybrid

Training

Xactly University, multiple courses for targeted training: tracks, on-sites, pop-ups, instructor led, on demand, eLearning

Support

Phone, email, video conference

SPM Products/Solutions

Enterprise Performance Management • Insights • Forecasting • Incentive Compensation Management • Commission Expense Accounting • Territory Management and Planning • Sales Performance Analytics

Primary Industries

Business Services • Financial Services • High-Tech • Manufacturing & Wholesale • Retail • Telecommunications

Sample Customers

Carestream • Cascade • Cox Automotive • DocuSign • Hyatt • Interxion • Qlik • Rosetta Stone • TIBCO • Western Union

Integration With Other Systems

Xactly has REST API integration, estimator APIs, out-of-the-box connections to Salesforce and Microsoft Dynamics, as well as estimator widgets for Salesforce and PROS CPQ.

Machine Learning/AI Capabilities

Xactly's sales performance AI platform is backed by more than 14 years of aggregated and anonymized sales pay and performance insights from hundreds of thousands of subscribers.

Additional Offerings

Xactly Benchmarking • Xactly Sales Planning •
Advanced Quota Planning • Xactly Objective • Xactly
Insights • Xactly Forecasting • Xactly SimplyComp •
Commission Expense Accounting • Xactly Connect

Other SPM Vendors

beqom
https://www.beqom.com/
Nyon, Switzerland

CellarStone: QCommission
https://www.qcommission.com/
Half Moon Bay, CA

Core Commissions
https://corecommissions.com/
Vancouver, WA

Iconixx
https://iconixx.com/
Austin, TX

Incentive Solutions
https://www.incentivesolutions.com/
Atlanta, GA

NetCommissions
http://www.netcommissions.com/
Wakefield, MA

Nice
https://www.nice.com/
Hoboken, New Jersey

Optymyze
https://optymyze.com/
London, United Kingdom

ZS Associates
https://www.zs.com/
Evanston, IL

SALES
COMPENSATION
EDUCATION
RESOURCES

SALES COMPENSATION ALMANAC • 2022

EDUCATIONAL RESOURCES

Sales compensation is a constantly evolving topic. Use these resources to help learn and expand your knowledge about sales compensation concepts and principles.

IN THIS SECTION

- Courses
- Webinars
- Books
- Alexander Group's Sales Compensation Resource Center

SALES COMPENSATION EDUCATION RESOURCES
(*Our Recommendations)

COURSES

WorldatWork (WorldatWork.org)
AMC: Advancing Your Modeling Capabilities With Excel
CPI: Analyzing & Automating Rewards Data With Excel
Hello Excel Power Query, My New BFF
*Redesigning Sales Compensation Plans
WSF: Working Smarter & Faster With Excel

WEBINARS

WorldatWork (WorldatWork.org)
Best Practices for Making the Shift to Modern Leadership
How to Create SPIFs with Guaranteed ROI

BOOKS
*2022 Sales Compensation Almanac, David J. Cichelli, 2021, AGI Press, ISBN:
    978-1-7358646-4-8
*Compensating the Sales Force, (Third edition), David J. Cichelli, 2017,
    McGraw-Hill, ISBN: 9781260026818
Designing a Sales Compensation Plan; How to create an effective incentives
    program for your sales force, Vangelis Sakelliou, 2019, Nielsen, ISBN:
    1838161627
Designing Sales Compensation Plans: Fundamentals for the HR Professional,
    Jerry Colletti, David Cichelli, 2013, WorldatWork Press, ISBN:
    9781579632939
Dianne Auld's Excel Tips: Featuring Compensation & Benefits Formulas,
    Third Edition, Dianne Auld, 2020, WorldatWork Press, ISBN:
    9781579633912
Quotas!: Design Thinking to Solve Your Biggest Sales Challenge, Mark
    Donnolo, 2019, Association for Talent Development, ISBN 1950496236
Sales Compensation Math, Jerry Colletti, Mary Fiss, J. Mark Davis, 2008,
    WorldatWork Press, ISBN: 9781579631864

Sales Compensation Perspectives, The Alexander Group, 2020, AGI Press, ISBN: 9781735864600

Sales Compensation Solutions, Andris Zoltners, Prabhakant Sinha, Chad Albrecht, Steve Marley, Sally Lorimer, ZS Associates, Inc., ISBN: 9780998934709

The Complete Guide to Sales Force Incentive Compensation, Andris A. Zoltners, Prabhakant Sinha, Sally E. Lorimer, 2006, AMACOM, ISBN: 100814473245

The Future of Sales Compensation Hardcover, Chad Albrecht, Steve Marley, 2016, ZS Associates, Inc., ISBN: 0985343656

What Your CEO Needs to Know About Sales Compensation: Connecting the Corner Office to the Front Line, Mark Donnolo, 2013, AMACOM, ISBN: 9780814432273

*ALEXANDER GROUP'S SALES COMPENSATION RESOURCE CENTER

Access Alexander Group's sales compensation articles, videos, surveys and more at https://www.alexandergroup.com/sales-compensation-resource-center/

CASE STUDIES

SALES COMPENSATION ALMANAC • 2022

SALES COMPENSATION CASE STUDIES

Learn how other companies examine and update their sales compensation practices with case studies from the Alexander Group's client engagements. Our mid-career consultants prepare these case studies; they add to our catalog of hundreds to thousands of client engagements.

IN THIS SECTION

This year's case studies include:

- Distribution (2)
- Healthcare
- Internet Security
- Record and Information Management
- Technology (3)

Industry: Distribution

ELECTRICAL DISTRIBUTION COMPANY REDESIGNS SALES ORGANIZATION

By Kelly Rue

Project Identification

The Company was purchased by a private equity firm just prior to the Alexander Group's (AGI) engagement. The private equity firm noted the stagnancy of the business and an opportunity for additional revenue and profit growth. The private equity firm had plans to make big changes at the Company as a whole, but it saw the clearest opportunities within the electrical division.

The Company is comprised of three divisions: cable, electrical and fabrication. The electrical division sells electrical, electronic, and apparatus repair products to electrical OEM (original equipment manufacturer) and repair customers, and electrical equipment manufacturers. This division employs more than 40 sellers.

The Alexander Group performed a detailed diagnostic for the electrical division. Following the diagnostic, our team prepared a full program design and detailed design road map to outline requirements for this division to exist as a stand-alone commercial organization. In addition, AGI created a change adoption road map and provided implementation support. The overall project included:

- Sales coverage model (including digital engagement portal and tools)
- Buyer journey mapping
- Job design
- Opportunity modeling
- Account segmentation
- Sizing
- Service levels creation
- Territory design
- Sales compensation design

Primary objectives of the project included:
- Refinement of total addressable market data
- Evaluation of current headcount levels compared to market opportunity and benchmarks
- Improved sales effectiveness

- Evaluation of e-commerce and digital presence
- Redesign of sales compensation
- Assessment of management practices

Through the assessment, AGI determined that the electrical division's lagging growth stemmed from a generalist field solutions representative (FSR) role, which was not properly enabled with opportunity and account targeting information. Sellers reported spending almost 40% of their time on expansion efforts; however, year-over-year expansion was only 10% with 17% year-over-year churn. Lack of consistent record-keeping and CRM system created little continuity in the account planning process. Sellers had strong customer relationships but were self-managed and individually prioritized accounts. Sales were primarily closed on relationship and price. Sellers were performing low-value tasks and indicated that resource levels were ineffective. However, headcount benchmarks reflected appropriate, if not, over-investment in sales coverage resources. This caused sellers to feel under-supported in resources, such as talent, training, and skills, tools, and process, and/or role definition and execution.

Historic account segmentation relied solely on existing revenue, and tasked FSRs with managing accounts with over $50,000 in revenue. Upon assessment, AGI uncovered that through "management exceptions," 40% of accounts managed by FSRs fell below that $50,000 revenue threshold. AGI learned that the commission compensation plan was partially to blame, because FSRs were keen of grabbing and holding accounts to maximize their sales compensation earnings.

The sales compensation program's inability to motivate sellers compounded the electrical division's retention-focused strategy and structure. Minimal pay differentiation between high and low performers resulted in a lack of seller motivation. Pay mix was overly conservative (75/25) compared to benchmark, and leverage was lower than benchmark. Additionally, most sellers did not understand how their performance correlated to incentive pay outs.

Industry Profile
The electrical equipment wholesaling industry experienced annual growth of .6% from 2015 to 2019, with a declining profit margin. Since the overall market experienced low growth, business growth for the electrical division needed to come from stealing market share from competitors rather than tracking with market growth. Key industry trends include selling a wide variety of products to a variety of end markets. The Electrical division works with many vendors to service their customers in the electrical OEM, motor apparatus repair and

assembly markets. The electrical division provides over 100,000 products to customers. Market opportunity relies heavily on manufacturing and production and, ultimately, ties to consumer spending levels. Construction activity and electric power consumption are also strong indicators of demand. Barriers to entry in the market are low and players experience high levels of competition.

Products, Customers, Coverage, and List of Jobs

The Company was a value-added distributor of equipment and repair parts to OEMs, apparatus repair professionals and contract manufacturers. Customers were primarily segmented by size and span with national, key and field account segments. Managers were player/coaches with responsibility for assigned accounts and people management. The coverage model included field solutions representatives (outside sellers), account specialists (inside sellers) and customer care representatives (customer service). Although the Company was a mature business operating in a mature market, its specialization was low, and the business had not effectively evolved to adapt to the changing market and to manage and maintain its growth.

Customers ranged from large, national OEMs, to small motor repair shops. In the sales model, sellers and customer service personnel treated all customers the same, even though these different customers required unique levels of service. Motor repair customers required in-depth product knowledge and expertise from FSRs, whereas most OEM customers, who might purchase at a higher volume, had more straightforward needs and ordered stock items on a recurring basis. The Company designed some tools and systems, which benefitted its large OEM customers, such as the Company's proprietary inventory management system to help customers automatically reorder stock items when personal inventory levels got low. No formal segmentation existed by end market, and while there were informal specialists throughout the organization, each seller covered a variety of different types of accounts. Through AGI's design, the organization rolled out new outside and inside end market specialist roles specifically to cover the motor repair customer segment. The new coverage model also introduced lead generation representative roles to identify and qualify new customers. During interviews, customers communicated an opportunity to reduce the number of field seller visits if the Company continued to meet its needs from a technical, inventory and delivery perspective. As a result, AGI introduced a senior account specialist role to manage high-level core accounts and reduce the organization's field presence.

Title	Job Abstract	Performance Metrics
National Account Manager	• Proactively develops and maintains relationships with national accounts • Regularly communicates to share the Company's value propositions and opportunities • Establishes customer trust by engaging in solution selling • Conducts QBRs to help identify expansion opportunities • Manages goals and expectations for accounts as well as field/inside seller(s) • Establishes and maintains trust with suppliers	• Gross margin dollars • MBO (sales milestones)
Field Solutions Representative	• Proactively develops and maintains strategic and key account relationships • Regularly communicates to share the Company's value propositions and close future opportunities • Conducts QBRs to help identify expansion opportunities • Promotes new products and campaigns to support corporate and vendor marketing • Engages vendor reps to identify and spec in solutions	• Gross margin dollars • Accelerator and decelerator tied to new logo conversion rate
Senior Account Specialist	• Proactively develops and maintains relationships with core (high) segment • Manages accounts in a structured inside sales environment and engages with customers throughout the sales process • Communicates with customers to share the Company's value propositions and opportunities • Promotes new products and campaign support by product management/marketing • Engages with suppliers and supplier product specialists to identify/spec solutions • Pursues leads from lead generation team and works on customer quote and bid packages	• Gross margin dollars

Account Specialist	• Proactively develops and maintains relationships with core (high) segment • Manages accounts in a structured inside sales environment and engages with customers throughout the sales process • Pursues leads from lead gen team and works on customer quote and bid packages • Regularly communicates to share the Company's value propositions and opportunities • Promotes new products and campaigns supported by product management/marketing • Develops strong relationships with core vendors and leverages them as part of the solution presentation (and possible lead generation)	• Gross margin dollars • New customer gross margin dollars
Lead Generation Representative	• Identifies leads via outbound calls, emails, and other digital mediums • Qualifies leads from web-based inquiries, lapsed customer lists and cold leads • Identifies the needs and challenges of prospective customers • Meets and exceeds daily outreach quotas through a consistent process • Well-versed and participates in the Company's marketing campaigns • Engages with suppliers regularly regarding core and new product development	• N/A
Outside End Market Specialist	• Provides in-person and/or remote end market technical expertise about the Company's solutions during persuasion phase of the sales process • Leverages relationships with core vendors as part of the solution presentation (and possibly lead generation) • Promotes new products and campaigns supported by product management/marketing	• End market gross margin dollars

Inside End Market Specialist	• Provides remote end market technical expertise about the Company's solutions during persuasion phase of the sales process • Develops strong relationships with core vendors and leverages them as part of the solution presentation (and possibly lead generation) • Promotes new products and campaigns to support corporate and vendor marketing • Selectively provides online support for web-based technical inquiries	• End market gross margin dollars

Project Solution and Outcome

The project included designing new sales compensation plans for the national account manager, field solutions representative, account specialist, and newly created senior account specialist, outside end market specialist, and inside end market specialist roles. The goal of the new plans was to align sales compensation with sales growth objectives and grow sales revenue. It was critical that the new plans be clearly tied to performance as there had been a lot of informality in the previous compensation structure.

The new compensation plans were quota-based bonus structures with some form of gross margin dollar component. The new FSR compensation plan kept the previous gross margin measure, increased leverage, and added a new customer conversion accelerator to promote conversion and growth. The senior account specialist plan mirrored the FSR plan with a slightly lower excellence point.

As part of the redesign, AGI resegmented accounts to consider current revenue and incremental opportunity when determining coverage. Under the new coverage model, the account specialist role was responsible for the accounts qualified and passed on by the lead generation representative. For this reason, rather than have the new customer conversion accelerator, the account specialist compensation plan had a separate measure for new customer gross margin dollars in addition to total gross margin dollars. The inside and outside end market specialist roles were designed to assist field solutions representatives and account specialists with closing additional business when expert product/technical knowledge was required. Therefore, their compensation plans tied to overall end market gross margin dollars to encourage gross margin growth and increased sales in their respective end markets.

Performance Metrics

Metric	Definition of Metric, Importance and Unique Issues
Gross Margin Dollars	As a distributor, gross margin dollars are imperative to ensure profitability of sales.
New Logo Conversion	Number of new customers (have not purchased from the Company in the past three years) who complete their first purchase with the Company.
New Customer Gross Margin Dollars	As a distributor, gross margin dollars are imperative to ensure profitability of sales. New customer gross margin dollars promote conversion.
End Market Gross Margin Dollars	As a distributor, gross margin dollars are imperative to ensure profitability of sales. Total end market gross margin dollars are the most accurate way to measure the impact of an end market specialist since this role is to leverage expertise to assist any sales as needed to customers in their end market.

Kelly Rue is a manager at the Alexander Group.

Industry: Distribution

FACILITIES SUPPLY GO-TO-MARKET TRANSFORMATION

By Kelly Rue

Project Identification

The Alexander Group's (AGI) engagement was with a facilities segment, a newly established business of an industry leading company. As a new business, the organization had substantial growth goals of 30% sales growth with 30% margins, and 30% strategic products mix in the next three years.

Prior to AGI's engagement, the Company acquired two janitorial and sanitation (JanSan) suppliers. All three divisions operated as independent organizations with different target markets, different primary products sold, and different compensation plans. Despite these differences, commonalities existed across divisions: The job portfolios were primarily field-based sales representatives with only service-oriented inside resources, and the outside sales reps' sales compensation plans were driven by commission. The Company's future growth strategy focused on conversion and penetration in multifamily, long-term care, and hospitality customer segments; however, the newly acquired divisions historically sold to building service contractors, education facilities, and healthcare customer segments. At the newly acquired divisions, commission was calculated on gross profit dollars, whereas at the historic division, commission was calculated on sales revenue dollars.

Scale and increased U.S. market share were dependent on a fully integrated one organizational approach including inside sales and overall go-to-market structure and strategy. The Company sought to develop an optimal go-to-market model, and build programs, processes and tools that were consistent, scalable, and flexible to future strategies. AGI's role was to assess the organization's current sales model to prioritize changes. The work included creating a ready-to-launch sales model, which would align strategic growth goals with tactical programs and establish a forward-looking coverage model that matched the right resources against the best target opportunities. This sales model was to properly "size the prize" to assist the team in prioritizing opportunities, organize coverage and jobs for success, effectively size and deploy these roles, and align pay with performance to empower the sales team.

Industry Profile

The highly fragmented maintenance, repair and operations (MRO) and janitorial supplies market did not have a dominant competitor. The overall janitorial and facilities maintenance supply industry was in the decline phase of its life cycle with low revenue volatility.

The market was largely tied to downstream demand trends and levels of disposable income. However, lower levels of disposal income were expected to be partially offset by aging population growth, which would increase hospital visit rates and lower vacancy rates in elder care institutions. Although the overall growth in the market was low, there was still significant growth opportunity for individual competitors.

The market experienced a stronger presence of national accounts and buyer groups changing the purchasing trends of the industry. The Company has a well-known brand-name but is a new player in the facilities supply market. Initial brand recognition helped to get sellers in the door; however, the organization had an opportunity to earn customer support as a viable MRO/janitorial and sanitation supplier. Additionally, market players were shifting from outside sales to inside sales focus based on customer buying patterns.

Products, Customers, Coverage, and List of Jobs

The Company's go-forward focus was to improve organic sales and margin growth, national scale, and strategic products and initiatives. The organization sought to grow its position in the market through both organic growth and acquisition.

The facilities division distributes products to support facilities maintenance across the multifamily, government, hospitality, education, and healthcare industries. The division's most commonly sold products include janitorial supplies, door and cabinet hardware, appliances, lighting, and paint equipment.

At the onset of the project, outside sales reps covered all types and sizes of accounts. Overlay renovation specialists supported major renovations, and inside support resources assisted with order entry, order tracking and quoting.

Outside sales reps were "income producers" with strong customer relationships, who were largely self-managed. Outside sales reps were solely optimized geographically, and individually dictated their sales process, including which accounts they targeted and prioritized. Sellers had tools available to identify opportunities, but no system for quantifying or prioritizing opportunities. Additionally, seller adoption of available tools was low.

After the acquisitions, there was a push for sellers from all three divisions to sell the full basket of products equally. However, the newly acquired division sellers traditionally sold janitorial and paper products, whereas, historic division sellers sold broadly across the product portfolio, with appliances and tools receiving the greatest attention. The significant variance in historic product focus across divisions effectively led to deployment of different types of sales reps across different regions of the United States.

As part of the project, the Company created a product specialist role to help the outside sales reps bridge gaps in product knowledge across the offering and better enable the outside sales reps to be successful.

AGI identified a long tail of accounts that bogged down outside sales reps, proving inefficient and increasing cost of sales. In addition, AGI determined that customers desired an omni-channel buying experience and wanted to interact with the organization on their own terms. To free up time for outside sales reps to focus on higher priority opportunities and increase omni-channel presence, AGI built out a new inside sales account manager role to cover down-market opportunities and cater to customers' different purchasing preferences. The inside sales account managers improved coverage of smaller accounts, while freeing up other resources to focus on support and service.

Further, AGI developed an opportunity and segmentation model to better direct outside sales reps to the highest priority accounts and align inside sales account managers to downstream opportunities. Additionally, AGI created an area sales manager playbook to provide the necessary tools and process for first-line sales managers to effectively coach and train their sellers. In the go-forward model, area sales managers will be able to guide individual sellers to the highest priority accounts, which will most efficiently help the organization meet its growth goals.

The Company created digital lead generation representatives to further enhance the organization's omni-channel presence through online offerings, creating a rich, interactive, virtual sales experience for prospects using web chats, video/web conferencing and other technology.

Title	Job Abstract	Performance Metrics
Outside Sales Representative	• Positioned as the "one-stop shop" for all offered products (MRO & JanSan) • Works on named accounts, with a loose geographic deployment • Works across all segments and industries • Teams with renovation specialists on applicable accounts/opportunities • Role is codified across all three divisions • Focuses exclusively on high-value accounts and opportunities	**Legacy Division** • Total revenue • Strategic products revenue • E-commerce revenue **New Divisions** • Gross profit dollars • Strategic products revenue • Lapsed accounts revenue
Renovation Specialist	• Expert on renovations and related products • Generally focused on multifamily or hospitality • Works with project manager to deliver renovation • May team with outside sales reps	• Total revenue • Gross profit dollars • Strategic products revenue
Product Specialist	• Specialist in specific product line • Overlay resource brought in by outside rep to assist in product selection and close sales • Generally, inside based, but occasionally in the field • Oriented towards MRO products for the new markets and JanSan products for the historic market • Also referred to as category specialists	• N/A (not sales compensation eligible)

Inside Sales Account Manager	• "Owns" down-market accounts and opportunities ("outside rep without a car")
	• 100% of activities are sales-oriented and customer-facing
	• Two types of calls
	  – Inbound order-taking from owned accounts, working to up-sell/cross-sell
	  – Outbound to own down-market accounts and works off of lead lists to make sales
		• Total revenue
		• Strategic products revenue
		• E-commerce revenue

Inside Support Rep Quotes	• 100% of activities are phone-based and support-oriented • Responsible for generating quotes based on inbound requests from customers and outside sales reps • Deployed by region (East and West) • While immediate scope may vary, in ideal end state, works exclusively with outside reps (inside account managers are self-sufficient) • Exclusively support-oriented • All sales opportunities routed to inside sales account manager or outside sales rep	• N/A (not sales compensation eligible)
Inside Support Rep Orders	• 100% of activities are phone-based and support-oriented • Two main activities, all inbound: order entry and order tracking • Deployed by region (East and West) • While immediate scope may vary, in ideal end state, works exclusively with outside reps (inside account managers are self-sufficient) • Exclusively support-oriented • All sales opportunities routed to inside sales account manager or outside sales rep	• N/A (not sales compensation eligible)
Lead Gen Rep	• Inside resource focused on generating and qualifying leads • Works off of web-generated leads, leads passed from outside sales rep, inside sales account manager, lapsed customers, or cold-calling • New role to generate and qualify leads and pass to the "right" sales resource	• Marketing qualified leads • Closed leads
Renovation Project Manager	• Overlay role managing renovation projects from point-of-sale to completion, acting as primary point of contact for customers • Involved in inventory and delivery tracking, ordering additional products as needed, and providing sales quotes to outside sales reps and customers	• N/A (not sales compensation eligible)
Big Accounts Project Manager	• 100% of activities are phone-based and support-oriented • Assigned to specific strategic accounts to provide dedicated customer service • Responsible for generating quotes, entering, ordering and resolving customer issues as they arise • Works closely with outside sales reps to provide exceptional customer service • Exclusively support-oriented • Manages an assigned list of accounts	• Total revenue • Gross profit dollars • Strategic products revenue

Project Solution and Outcome

AGI performed an assessment and full sales model transformation to promote retention of existing customers and encourage growth. AGI discovered misalignment in growth goals throughout the organization, and aligned strategic and tactical programs, including jobs, territories, management, and compensation. For sales compensation, outside sales reps moved from a commission to a quota-based structure to align rep payout with company objectives and performance. Further, AGI created a consistent archetype of plans to create continuity across divisions.

The project broke down siloes within the organization, designed a singular coverage model aligned to identify, land, adopt, expand, renew sales process (ILAER), and clearly defined job roles, responsibilities, and rules of engagement. The design reduced redundancy in roles, rightsized the headcount of the organization, and aligned compensation plans to drive new go-to-market strategy.

AGI developed an opportunity model, segmented accounts based on opportunity level, and redesigned jobs to align specific types of resources to different segments of accounts. Notably, AGI resized the inside support organization, which was stretched too thin to support outside sales reps and increased the number of product specialists to support outside sales reps more effectively with the wide variety of products they sell.

The future state centered on movement towards a single seller: outside sales rep. The outside sales representative sells products across the portfolio, covers similar client archetypes, and measures success on similar compensation plans. The team aligned on a single job profile for all outside sales reps and consistent opportunity identifiers for customer industries across all geographies and divisions.

When designing the new compensation plans, AGI's primary goal was to align these plans to the Company's go-forward growth strategy and management objectives. The new compensation plans also needed to be embraced by the sellers and implementable via the Company's systems. For the single outside sales rep role, AGI ultimately aligned on two different compensation plans that differed between legacy division and new divisions, as the Company did not think that the same plan would be implementable across divisions. The mechanics, pay curve, and pay and performance periods aligned across all outside sales reps; however, the measures and pay mix varied across divisions.

Historically, outside sales reps were on 100% commission plans. AGI moved outside sales reps from commission plans to a quota-based bonus structure, which pays sellers on performance-to-goal, breaking down today's income-producer mentality while driving accountability for performance. AGI adjusted the pay mix to install a base pay and move from "income producer" to professionalized "sales rep" model and developed a plan to build growth into sales goals and hold sellers accountable to those goals. In designing the new compensation plans, the team agreed to accelerate and decelerate rates based on performance-to-goal, increasing earning differentiation between high and low performers. Given the renovation specialist and product specialist overlay roles, AGI designed the plans to encourage collaboration between overlay and outside sales reps via double-crediting to goal.

For legacy division outside sales reps who were historically commissioned solely on sales revenue, the three measures designed in their new plans included: total revenue, strategic products revenue, and e-commerce revenue. While driving gross profit dollars was imperative, the design team thought that given historic operations, a shift to a quota-based bonus and to a gross profit dollars measure would not be implementable. For new division outside sales reps who were historically commissioned on gross profit dollars, the three measures designed in their new plans included: gross profit dollars, strategic products revenue, and lapsed accounts revenue. AGI designed the secondary measure of both plans to be strategic products revenue in order to encourage outside sales reps to sell the full basket of products across divisions.

Performance Metrics

Metric	Definition of Metric, Importance and Unique Issues
Total Revenue	Total revenue from assigned accounts
Gross Profit Dollars	Total gross profit dollars from assigned accounts
Strategic Products Revenue	Total revenue from specific product groups (specific strategic products to be determined by customer). Strategic products will differ by geography to encourage seller to promote products not most frequently sold today and have high potential
E-Commerce Revenue	Total revenue from assigned accounts from orders placed via the Company's website
Marketing Qualified Leads	Number of leads generated, qualified and passed to sales
Closed Leads	Number of leads generated that have placed their first sale at the Company

Glossary

ILAER: Sales process comprised of five steps: identify, land, adopt, expand, renew

JanSan: Janitorial and sanitation. Refers to the type of supplies or industry.

MRO: Maintenance, repair and operations. Supplies utilized in the production process (ultimately not seen as end products themselves).

Kelly Rue is a manager at the Alexander Group.

Industry: Healthcare

ORTHOPEDIC SALES COMPENSATION EVOLUTION

By Kelly Rue

Project Identification

The Company engaged the Alexander Group (AGI) to assist with coverage and compensation design for the orthopedics division, which has four offerings. The organization needed to reevaluate the compensation structure to address budget challenges and to better align sellers' efforts with the company's strategy. Historically, the organization was strongly resistant to change and therefore, the sales compensation plans did not evolve with the changing structure and market. Field sales representatives' performance and pay did not align with preferred organization results.

Core sales representatives aligned to four segments within orthopedics. Historically, core sales representatives from all four segments reported to a common manager; however, before the start of the project, the organization changed the reporting structure for core sales representatives to report to segment-focused management. The main focus of the compensation design was to focus on two of the segments (referred to as Segment A and Segment B) with the other two segments (referred to as Segment C and Segment D) being secondary.

Local field sales managers had autonomy in managing their reps, including the ability to change commission rates and set up cross-selling rates for their direct reports. Cross-selling varied across segments and territories. In certain segments and territories, core sales representatives found it easier and more lucrative to sell products from other segments. In Segment C, for example, 44% of reps cross-sold other segment products, and cross-sell earnings represented 22.3% of their overall earnings. Territories across the organization varied largely in terms of size and other factors. For small territories where there was limited sales coverage, cross-selling was necessary to service all customer segments and maintain their market presence. However, for core sales representatives in cross-selling, this was a distraction from core products and reduced specialization efficiencies.

Orthopedic medical device sales is a competitive industry and the Company hired talent from competitors. These competitive hires received a 12-month guarantee to entice them to work for the Company. These reps came to the Company under the assumption that they could bring a substantial portion of their business with them. However, they were not able to bring over as much of their prior business as hoped. They were expensive resources to employ. These expensive resources took a long time to make the level of sales necessary to offset their cost and the Company did not achieve the levels of growth anticipated with these investments.

Additionally, the organization adapted its sales coverage by bringing on additional fixed-cost resources to help grow sales. Corporate reserves funded these fixed base-salary support resources. Management did not ask core sales representatives to fund the support resources. The intention was for corporate to temporarily fund these resources to jump-start growth, and then pass the cost on to core sales representatives. The expected growth did not materialize. Core sales representatives used this additional support to better their quality of life rather than to grow their business. The go-forward goal was to proactively adjust the core sales representatives' compensation plans to pay for the support resources rather than to directly charge out the resources. AGI found through market research that most companies fund these support roles through a hybrid of seller and corporate funding.

Core sales representatives were historically on a commission rate structure. A couple years before the project, management reduced the flat 12.5% commission rate to 11%, added 7% (for a total rate of 18% commission) on growth dollars, and incorporated a 1% quota achievement bonus.

Feedback from sellers was that the current sales compensation plan was difficult to understand. The perceived level of importance of plan components was commission, then quota, then growth. Sales were declining. Participation in the growth component of the compensation plan was low—only 40% of core sales representatives were earning growth dollars, indicating that the component was ineffective. The growth incentive was confusing and was often realized as a windfall once sales grew over the previous year. With the growth incentive, the core sales representative earned a 1% commission retroactively compensating them from dollar one of annual sales. During one year, only 48% of Segment A territories achieved quota, the segment lost millions of dollars, but 40% of the segment's core sales representatives earned growth dollars associated with their sales compensation plan. The compensation plans were not driving the overall desired sales results and the Company needed to make a change. Notably, the growth and quota components of the current plans were not valued by the core sales representatives.

The Company measured core sales representatives on sales revenue; however, junior/associate sales representatives and clinical specialists were on base salaries. Clinical specialists received a corporate bonus tied to team or company revenue and results. The misalignment between plans for the core sales representatives and the junior/associate sales representatives caused a lack of teaming among colleagues.

Historically, the orthopedic division had seen 1% to 3% sales growth; however, growth was declining, while individual earnings were increasing. Additionally, the Company was at or above benchmark levels of investment in their compensation plans for each orthopedic segment.

Industry Profile

The orthopedics industry includes products that support, prevent or correct irregularities and improve the function of body parts. Key drivers of the industry were number of individuals aged 65 years and older, population participation in sports, and levels of disposable income. Orthopedic products are sold to hospitals, pharmacies and drug stores in the U.S. The Company sold orthopedic products for use in hospitals. The industry is highly concentrated with a few players owning the majority of the market share. Orthopedic products were a $10.6 billion industry but has experienced slow growth over the last five years. Management expects this shallow growth to continue over the next five years. Mergers and acquisitions are common as companies attempt to remain competitive.

Orthopedic sales organizations employed three different types of commercial sales models: paired model, team/pod model, and the team/pod model with dedicated case coverage. The paired model was the most simplistic, with a core sales representative owning direct sales and account maintenance activities and a junior/associate sales representative managing case coverage and assisting with account maintenance. The team/pod model was the most prevalent and involved a core sales representative, a junior sales representative, and a clinical specialist. The core sales representative conducted all of the direct selling activity and split case coverage responsibilities with a junior sales representative who conducted the account maintenance activity. The clinical specialist provided education and technical product expertise. The third type of coverage, team/pod model with dedicated case coverage, added an additional dedicated case coverage resource to the team/pod model who relieved the core sales representative and junior sales representative of their case coverage responsibilities. The Company employed the team/pod coverage model.

Sales representatives in the market with dedicated case coverage support indicated that their sales model was more effective than those without dedicated case coverage support. Sales representatives were able to cover, on average, 3.5 additional cases per week with the support of a dedicated case coverage resource than they were without the same level of support.

Career progression typically started with entry-level case coverage associates who progressed to junior/associate sales representatives, then clinical specialists, and finally to the core sales representative position.

Industry trends included smaller, more dedicated coverage, and better strategic alignment.

Products, Customers, Coverage, and List of Jobs

The organization employed a team/pod model (without direct dedicated case coverage resources) across various segments. However, it employed 1099 contractors who backfilled sales needs, oftentimes picking up case coverage responsibilities. The team/pod model consisted of a core sales representative and a junior sales representative, who conducted selling, service, and case work while clinical resources provided education and technical product expertise. At the Company, junior sales reps and clinical specialists were internally funded, whereas at most competitors, these resources were field funded.

Title	Job Abstract	Performance Metrics
Regional Manager	• Controls the entire sales force—total autonomy on setting rates, reallocating rates, adjusting territories, setting up cross-selling rates • Responsible for enforcing sales strategy and managing core sales reps, junior sales reps, clinical specialists, and case coverage associates	• N/A
Core Sales Representative	• Direct seller assigned by geographic territory or to specific accounts • Sometimes paired with junior/associate sales reps in highly populated territories or high-volume accounts • There were four different segments of this job; these four roles all have the same responsibilities but with different orthopedic focus	• Sales revenue
Junior/Associate Sales Rep	• Entry level sales role • Paired with a more experienced, core sales rep • Responsible for case coverage and sales assistance	• N/A
Clinical Specialist	• Dedicated clinical specialist trained on highly technical products • Assisted with onboarding (internal and external) with a heavy educational component	• N/A

Contractor/1099	• Third-party contractors used to backfill sales force needs or to cover smaller markets • Often convert to full-time employees	• N/A

Project Solution and Outcome

As part of the project, AGI designed a new sales compensation plan for Segments A, B and C core sales representatives. The goal of the new plan was to align compensation incentives with sales growth, overall business performance, and company objectives. The new plans needed to be clear and understandable for managers and core sales representatives.

The newly designed plans moved from the aggressive current state, 100% variable pay model, to a 50/50 pay mix. The new 50/50 pay mix was in line with industry benchmarks and aimed to reduce the income producer mentality in the sales force.

AGI designed a plan that moved to a quota-based bonus structure to increase management's control of payouts and simplify the compensation plans. With the quota-based bonus structure, management could still drive growth by building in a growth component to individual core sales reps' quotas. The new mechanics of the plan focused sellers on quota attainment rather than a commission rate. The quota-based bonus also provided the flexibility to adjust the growth goal based on the opportunity available in a particular territory. AGI implemented a hard threshold at 70% of quota at the average level of recurring revenue year over year.

The new compensation plans aimed to increase correlation between pay and performance by providing greater opportunity for additional earnings to top performers and reducing the residual commission income that lower performers earned. The base commission in the old plans prevented the Company from properly leveraging the compensation model. The largest "fixed cost" of the old compensation plan was the base commission, which accounted for 90% of prior-year payouts.

Target total compensation varied by segment. AGI used a combination of industry benchmarks and historical averages to provide guidance on setting target total compensation levels for each segment. For example, target total compensation for Segment A sales representatives in the industry was notably higher than for Segment B sales representatives in the industry due to the complexity of the sale. AGI's recommendations incorporated this variance.

In addition to designing the new core sales representative plans, AGI made other preliminary compensation recommendations, such as phasing out the prevalent guarantees in place, and implementing a variable compensation component for junior sales reps who have the opportunity to grow expansion and renewal sales at existing clients.

Performance Metrics

Metric	Definition of Metric, Importance and Unique Issues
Total Revenue	Total revenue from accounts within the assigned geographic territory

Glossary

Pod: Group of cross-functional roles, dependently intertwined to service a single territory in a coordinated effort

Kelly Rue is a manager at the Alexander Group.

Industry: Internet Security

SIMPLIFYING COMPLEX MEASURES WITHIN THE PLAN

By Parker Hoffman

Project Identification

The Company is in the content delivery network (CDN), edge platform, and internet security markets. The Alexander Group's (AGI) engagement with the Company focused on the web division sales team. The Company's portfolio included a global content delivery network (CDN), cybersecurity, cloud services, web security, and internet security services. These products enable businesses to protect their websites and data centers and give users secure online experiences from any device, anywhere.

The Company attempted to implement a compensation structure that management rejected late in last year's planning cycle. The late-stage changes created significant rework for the compensation and operations teams, delayed the launch of the compensation program, and ultimately impinged on the ability of management to communicate the compensation program to field incumbents effectively. The metric created, lookback GMRR, the YTD net impact of monthly recurring revenue (MRR), is a non-industry standard measure and created payout confusion in both plan administration and commercial resources. Also, existing compensation plans did not effectively align organizational growth objectives with resultant sales behaviors. The Company sought to partner with AGI to develop a new sales compensation program, which will align with its go-to-market sales strategy and organizational structure.

AGI advised the Company to begin with a clear understanding of revenue strategies, job role design/expectations, and overall compensation philosophy. Applying the Alexander Group's proven design framework and process ensures buy-in from key stakeholders while building best-in-class plans. AGI suggested a project to 1) assess plans vis-à-vis the strategy/roles, philosophies/principles, and market practices, 2) confirm future sales strategy, job roles, and structure and 3) develop new sales compensation plans and select the right measures by job to enable rapid configuration of the administration environment.

The project objectives and deliverables included: 1) conducting a strategy, job role and pay-for-performance philosophy confirmation, 2) assessing the current plan and recommending preliminary measures, 3) creating simple, but effective sales compensation plans that align with the Company's future strategy and go-to-market model and 4) developing plans that drive desired sales behaviors and pay-for-performance culture.

Industry Profile

The Company resides within the internet cloud computing industry. Cloud computing consists of three primary services:

- Software as a Service (XaaS)
- Infrastructure as a Service (IaaS)
- Platform as a Service (PaaS)

The market for the Company's solutions is intensely competitive and characterized by rapidly changing technology, evolving industry standards, and frequent new product and service innovations. The Company expects competition for its offerings to increase both from existing competitors and new market entrants. The Company competes primarily based on the performance and reliability of their solutions, ROI and cost of savings, reduced infrastructure complexity, sophistication and functionality of their offerings, scalability, security, ease of implementation, and use of service, customer support, and price.

The Company competes with companies offering products and services that address internet performance problems, including companies that provide internet content delivery and hosting services, security solutions, technologies used by carriers to improve the efficiency of their systems, and streaming content delivery services.

Along with the competition, some challenges and risks have the potential to disrupt progress in this industry, compromise online experiences, and destroy value that took decades to build. Security threats are growing more sinister and advanced. Enterprise applications are moving from behind the firewall to the cloud. At the same time, employees increasingly demand remote access from a variety of devices, which the Company believes makes securing access harder to achieve with just traditional perimeter defenses. More consumers are "cutting the cord" and consuming entertainment over the internet rather than through traditional cable, and they are increasingly using mobile devices to view content and shop. Web pages are also vastly more complex than ever before with advertisements, videos, graphics, and other third-party content, causing speed and reliability to suffer.

Products, Customers, Coverage, and List of Jobs

The Company offers online solutions for the security, delivery and acceleration of websites and applications.

The Company provides services/software in the following areas:

1. **Cloud security solutions:** designed to defend websites, applications and data centers against a multitude of cyberattacks
2. **Enterprise security solutions:** designed to help customers move from a legacy perimeter-based approach to security to a Zero Trust security model
3. **Web and performance solutions:** enables dynamic websites and applications to have instant response times, no matter where the user is, what device or browser they are using, or how they are connected to the internet
4. **Media delivery solutions:** designed to enable enterprises to execute their digital media distribution strategies, not only by providing solutions to address their volume and global reach requirements but also improving the end-user experience
5. **Carrier solutions:** designed to help customers operate a cost-efficient network that capitalizes on traffic growth and new subscriber services by reducing the complexity of building a CDN and interconnecting access providers
6. **Services and support solutions:** designed to assist customers with integrating, configuring, optimizing, and managing core offerings

Go-to Market Strategy

The Company markets and sells its solutions globally through its direct sales and services organization and many channel partners. In addition to entering agreements with resellers, the Company has several other types of sales and marketing focused alliances with entities such as system integrators, application service providers, referral partners, and sales agents. The Company's sales and service and marketing professionals are located across the Americas, EMEA and Asia.

Title	Job Abstract	Performance Metrics
Account Executive (AE)	• Responsible for the strategic objective of maximizing revenue generation within their assigned territory through new customer acquisition that will help them become more successful and profitable online	• Revenue • Lookback GMRR
Account Manager (AM)	• Responsible for the strategic objective of increasing revenue generation by selling into the white space within their assigned territory through named existing accounts to enable their customers to become more successful and profitable online	• Revenue • Lookback GMRR
Partner AE	• Develop the region's indirect revenue by enabling and recruiting the right channels and alliances	• Channel revenue • Lookback GMRR
Solution Engineer	• Experienced sales engineering professionals, adept at defining solutions that meet the business and technical requirements of existing and prospective customers	• Revenue • Lookback GMRR
Product Specialist	• Quota carrying sales professional with in-depth industry knowledge. The primary goal of the product sales specialist is to partner with the direct sales force to increase their solution pipeline and overachieve targets in a defined territory	• (Product) Revenue • (Product) GMRR

Project Solution and Outcome

AGI's assessment of the Company's sales compensation plan design revealed several areas of improvement. The first area of improvement focused on the complexity of the lookback GMRR metric. The Company attempted to implement a compensation structure that management rejected late in last year's planning cycle. The metric created during this chaos, lookback GMRR, is a non-industry standard measure and has created some issues in both plan administration and in commercial resources understanding how the Company pays them. The lookback GMRR measure rewards for the "G" (growth) but does not account for other realities of managing accounts in the hunter/farmer hybrid model. The lookback GMRR quotas also directed focus away from protecting traffic revenue—both opportunities may be available for a given account.

The second area of improvement, similar to the first, focused on the non-traffic GMRR metric. This metric was taking the focus off preserving traffic GMRR. Non-traffic GMRR puts traffic revenue at risk without a control mechanism to limit write-downs of traffic with backfills of new solutions. The rigidness of either being on lookback GMRR (LB-GMRR) or non-traffic GMRR (NT-GMRR) assumes that account opportunity is binary; interview feedback suggested that little difference existed in rep behavior in those with different measures. Split plan types were also adding additional challenges when measuring managers who had reps on both plans.

Due to both these complicated measures, AGI recommended the Company prioritize controlling for downgrades in existing accounts and to pay for productive revenue "G" (growth). AGI designed a comp plan that focused around removing this complicated, non-industry standard measure, rewarding for maximizing renewals, and retaining as much price as possible on challenging renewals and balancing retaining at-risk revenue with driving net-new business. AGI and the Company agreed to pay on ACV and revenue for a few reasons. The first was to balance what it could control (booking new contracts and higher commits) but not at the expense of revenue (if measures adequately weighted). The second was that it would pay for the effort required on renewals as it triggered a new contract.

The third area of improvement focused on payout accuracy and transparency. The lookback nature of the plans created a moving baseline that limited reps' ability to quickly calculate anticipated payouts. The nature of the plan complicated an already complex contract landscape for the compensation and finance teams. Interview feedback revealed inaccurate incentive payments and incorrect account assignments. Due to this, AGI recommended that to manage the sales comp program performance and pay effectively, the Company must have the capabilities to track, measure and pay without as much manual involvement. AGI's shift from this complicated lookback metric to ACV and revenue would alleviate a lot of the manual processes and remove much tension on the tracking/payout processes.

The fourth area of improvement focused on performance distribution. There were stark differences in performance distributions between the LB-GMRR and the revenue measures. These differences indicated to AGI an issue with goal setting, performance or both. With the 70% weighting on LB-GMRR, this performance discrepancy could lead to more windfall payouts or turnover (as a result of pay below target). AGI also found that AE observed YTD leverage (upside) for top performers was at or below 2x; expected leverage should be 2.5x to 3x. Due to this, and in line with the previous AGI recommendations, the removal of the LB–GMRR and NT-GMRR measures alleviated the performance distributions discrepancies. AGI also revamped the AE leverage points to be more in line with industry center practice.

In addition to these four primary areas of improvement, when AGI conducted a "stoplight" (red, green, yellow) analysis of the entire compensation plan by component, AGI identified pay mixes as an additional area of improvement (along with the aforementioned leverage, mechanics and quotas/targets plan components). Pay mixes ranged from 50/50 to 70/30, and while most were in line with the benchmark, AGI worked with the Company to align all roles in scope to benchmarked pay mixes.

Performance Metrics

Metric	Definition of Metric, Importance and Unique Issues
Revenue Recognition	• Revenue recognition for a sales transaction is achieved when the Company recognizes revenue from that transaction in its quarterly SEC filings on forms 10Q and 10k
Revenue-Based Incentive	• For incentive calculations, revenue is the monthly revenue that the Company recognizes in its quarterly SEC reports. Revenue may include accruals, adjustments, credits, or other financial transactions. Revenue-based incentives may be earned by the participant who is actively servicing the account according to the earned incentive definition above and is typically considered earned at the time of payment unless revenue is restated before finally being recognized
Account/Product Monthly Recurring Revenue (GMRR)	• The GMRR is calculated as the net impact of MRR increases and decreases in account or products on any given sales transaction by account. GMRR incentive is determined using year-to-date (YTD) performance against annual quotas and calculated as a % of annual on-target variable. Plan participants are eligible to receive an accelerated commission rate when their annual attainment exceeds 100%
Total Customer Contract Value (TCCV)	• Incentives for carrier accounts with TCCV component will be calculated based on monthly recurring revenue multiplied by the contract term (up to 24 months) plus any related non-recurring revenue. Incentives are calculated the same as account/product GMRR and paid quarterly, two months in arrears
Management by Objective (MBO)	• For those with an MBO plan component, they are eligible for payouts based on specific goals agreed upon by them and their managers. The MBO achievement is calculated and paid either quarterly or annually. MBO payments are capped at 120% for quantitative measures, and 100% for subjective measures
ACV/TCV	• ACV = Total Contract Value/Contract Period in Years • TCV/ACV measures the contract over a duration of time • Gives credit for renewals, even downgrades, if TCV was added on to the original deal

ARR	• ARR = Monthly Recurring Revenue x 12 • ARR measures at a point in time and is impacted by revenue fluctuations including bursting • Only gives credit for net positive change to ARR; and does not recognize renewal activity absent of G

Parker Hoffman is a manager at the Alexander Group.

Industry: Record and Information Management (RIM)

SALES COMPENSATION IN A RECURRING REVENUE MODEL

By Parker Hoffman

Project Identification

The Company is a privately held records and information management (RIM) company. It provides records management storage and destruction services, as well as document management software. The Company is a multimillion-dollar firm with locations in the U.S., Canada, the Caribbean, Central America, and South America.

The Alexander Group's (AGI) engagement with the Company focused primarily on the hard copy sales team with a secondary focus on the software and conversion services teams. The Company's products enable businesses to secure and manage paper and digital documents in a cost-effective manner.

The Company was amid a sales transformation meant to jump-start revenue growth. The Company's sales roles were evolving as the Company moved from a purchase services approach to a subscription/recurring revenue/XaaS model. The new sales model will now include both the sale of records management and ongoing software solutions. The Company collaborated with AGI to develop a new sales compensation program to align with its new go-to-market sales strategy, organizational structure and revised sales roles.

AGI's approach was to ensure the sales compensation plans support revenue strategy, job role and incentive compensation philosophy. Applying the Alexander Group's proven design framework and process ensured buy-in from key stakeholders while building best-in-class plans. AGI suggested a consulting project to 1) confirm future sales strategy, job roles and structure; 2) develop new sales compensation plans; and 3) plan for successful implementation and rollout of new sales compensation plans.

The project objectives and deliverables included: 1) establishing market-competitive compensation levels, 2) defining most appropriate pay mix given changes to future job roles and responsibilities, 3) creating simple but effective sales compensation plans that align with the Company's future strategy and go-to-market model, and 4) developing plans that drive desired sales behaviors and serve the Company's pay-for-performance culture.

Industry Profile

The Company competes in the records and information management industry, which provides these services:

- Document management: collection, indexing and storage of physical documents and records, as well as digital information assets
- Data protection: protection and backup of computer data and other media
- Document destruction: secure destruction of information assets
- Digital solutions: includes active file management, document conversion, archiving, backup, and electronic litigation support (e-discovery) services

Larger market participants have higher safety and security standards with greater technical sophistication and efficiency. Smaller, local players generally compete on cost and offer a narrower range of services. The RIM market is highly fragmented. Offerings vary depending on location, services provided, security standards, efficiency and innovation, standardization, and price. There are thousands of storage and information management services providers around the world. Many organizations have their internal resources to manage documents.

Companies can outsource information management to a third party (known as vended) or performed wholly or partially in-house (known as unvended). The in-house or unvended portion represents most of the total information management market (65%). These in-house services offer a substantial opportunity for third-party RIM providers. Sales strategies include cross-selling and bundling services to existing customers, offering bundled products to new customers, and focusing on unvended to vended conversion. A large portion of the unvended market contains small and medium-sized enterprises. Future revenue growth from existing customers is declining in mature markets. Companies seek to grow services revenue among existing customers and convert unvended customers in the commercial mid-market and government sectors.

Products, Customers, Coverage, and List of Jobs

The Company's product offering includes the following types of services/software.

1. **Information governance:** everything having to do with the capture, formation, usage, storage, and deletion of information
2. **Off-site storage:** records centers and vaults offer advanced security and fire suppression technology and protection from natural disasters

3. **Scanning and conversion services:** turning paper files into digitalized documents
4. **Software for document management**
5. **Secure destruction:** proper destruction and disposal of sensitive paper documents, electronic media, and computer hard drives both off-site and on-site
6. **Data breach response:** preparation and response should a data breach occur

The Company has thousands of clients across many industries. Clients use the Company's services to comply with regulatory records management and disposition. The Company focuses on nine main verticals.

Title	Job Abstract	Performance Metrics
AVP	• Area vice president (AVP), sales, is responsible for managing sales executives and account managers selling the Company's core services within defined geography in the U.S.	• ARR bookings • NRR bookings
NAM	• National account manager (NAM) is responsible for managing an assigned portfolio of the Company's most significant and most strategic accounts	• ARR bookings • NRR bookings
NSE	• National sales executive (NSE) is responsible for the outside sales of multi-local, national new business, in any given territory, through the achievement of opportunity-based sales quotas	• ARR bookings • NRR bookings
RAM	• Regional account manager (RAM) develops and retains business from existing clients through the attainment of sales quotas and is responsible for maintaining key client relationships by understanding client objectives and strategy	• ARR bookings • NRR bookings
RSE	• Regional sales executive (RSE) is responsible for the outside sales of new business, in any given territory, through the achievement of opportunity-based sales quotas	• ARR bookings • NRR bookings
RSE, Conversion Services	• Digital sales executive markets and sells innovative conversion services solutions to midsized and large corporations	• ARR bookings • NRR bookings

SSE	• Software sales executive (SSE) markets and sells the innovative solution to midsized and large companies	• ARR bookings • NRR bookings

Project Solution and Outcome

AGI's assessment of the Company's sales compensation plan design revealed several areas of improvement. The first area of improvement focused on the complexity of the compensation plans. Multiple commission rate modifiers (five within the hard copy plan) drove complexity and distracted representatives from focus areas. The complexity also made it difficult for the operations team to track and calculate commission payouts. Due to this, AGI recommended one to two core measures in the plans to align with AGI's center practice of no more than three measures.

The second area of improvement focused on crediting events. Payment on invoiced revenue and multiple crediting events disconnected pay from persuasion. It also made it a challenge for sales operations to forecast and administer commissions and tough for representatives to track payments. These crediting events also created cash flow challenges due to ramp-up time. This ramp-up time reduced rep motivation and created "annuity" in future years. During the quantitative assessment, AGI found that 25% of the representatives with below goal performance and high TI% had spillover payments from the previous FY. Twenty percent of the representatives with high performance and low TI% had a large discrepancy between bookings and bookings paid/earned. With this limited correlation between pay and performance, and with a lag in commission payouts, representatives were exceeding goal and earning less than 100% of target incentive, repressing seller motivation. AGI recommended the Company pay as close as possible to the sales event to drive desired behavior. AGI utilized a past Alexander Group XaaS study figure of ~80% of XaaS companies, credit at booking to align the Company to center practice.

The third area of improvement focused on the distribution of performance for the representatives. AGI found a bimodal distribution of sales rep performance, e.g., most of the representatives were either underachieving (demotivating) or overachieving (potentially high payouts). Quotas seemed unreachable and were leading to increased turnover. Sellers' quotas did not align with market opportunity, resulting in excessive payouts for over performers. AGI recommended that the Company align its quota distribution to have ~2/3 of sales representatives meet or exceed their goal. AGI also recommended that the

Company review market opportunity within each territory and assign quotas to align with opportunity.

The fourth area of improvement focused on target total compensation (TTC) and pay level benchmarking. The Company's current pay levels were below market rates. AGI recommended that for the Company to attain its goal to hire and retain top talent, the Company needed to raise TTC levels.

The final area of improvement involved pay mixes. Most of the roles had adequate pay mixes, except for the account managers. The pay mix for the account managers did not align with the job role and responsibilities. The AM pay mix had more pay at risk, aligning more towards the sales executive role, even though the AM role had less emphasis on sales and persuasion activities. AGI recommended that the pay mix for this role be adjusted to align with the job's degree of persuasion and emphasize the relationship management focus with a more conservative pay mix (65/35-75/25).

Performance Metrics

Metric	Definition of Metric, Importance and Unique Issues
ARR Bookings	• Annual recurring revenue (ARR) refers to committed, regularly occurring payments for software and related services over a defined period • New customer (new logo) • Cross-sell to an existing customer • Up-sell to an existing customer
NRR Bookings	• Non-recurring revenue (NRR) refers to one-time, project-based services with a defined scope • New customer (new logo) • Cross-sell to an existing customer • Up-sell to an existing customer
NRR Modifier	• Credit multiplier
ARR Multiyear Contract	• Credit multiplier
ARR Portfolio Growth	• Annual recurring revenue (ARR) refers to committed, regularly occurring payments for software and related services over a defined period. Refers to sales to existing customers
NRR Portfolio Growth	• Non-recurring revenue (NRR) refers to one-time, project-based services with a defined scope. Refers to sales to existing customers

Parker Hoffman is a manager at the Alexander Group.

Industry: Technology

ALIGNING SALES COMPENSATION WITH AN EVOLVING COVERAGE MODEL

By Daniel Kravitz

Project Identification

The Company is a multimillion-dollar robotic process automation (RPA) company. It sells intelligent automation software to help organizations reduce costs and improve customer engagement. The Company combines RPA, capture, process orchestration, mobility and engagement, and analytics for its customers. It sells through direct and indirect channels.

Weak Q1 and Q2 performance led the Company to seek a thorough examination of its go-to-customer model. Further, recent integrations and proliferation of use cases disrupted priorities and decreased sales force effectiveness leading to below benchmark performance (revenue per rep) and lackluster customer lifetime value (high customer acquisition costs and churn). The Alexander Group (AGI) supported the Company driving solutions around sales force structure, coverage, job roles, sales compensation, and territory deployment to drive consistencies in the sales organization.

AGI analyzed sales time survey results, conversion, penetration and retention (CPR) analyses, pay for performance, and sales investment benchmarks. Interviews took place with the executive team, sales leadership and select sales representatives to understand the key issues facing the business, as well as to identify the organization's pain points. In addition, AGI held various design sessions with functional stakeholders to determine what future state "should and could" look like.

AGI's deliverables included an assessment of the Company's current sales operating model, including its sales compensation program, a blueprint of future state, coverage maps, job roles, a competency model, a workload model, full territory redesign, and new sales compensation designs. In addition, AGI worked with the Company's design team to define a communication plan to support the design.

Industry Profile

Business process automation (BPA) is the technology-enabled automation of complex business processes. BPA allows businesses to streamline manual tasks in order to expedite digital transformation, increase service quality, improve service delivery, and reduce costs. RPA is an emerging field within the BPA market.

The RPA market falls within the greater business process automation market. Synergies and efficiencies driven by RPA allow organizations to streamline IT and operations. In addition, RPA's ability to learn numerous skills with consistent execution should augment its demand in the future.

Over the coming years, RPA is anticipated to continue to see significant growth. The technology is in high demand by enterprises, which want to scale and execute more efficiently. RPA reduces the demand for human labor by processing workflow much quicker and more efficiently, thus reducing costs.

Most commonly, RPA companies sell direct to businesses or through indirect sales channels. The direct model deploys both hunters and farmers to cover each of the customer segments. The hunters focus on building relationships with accounts in their territory to drive new business volume. Once the Company lands an account, a service-oriented customer success representative is responsible for driving adoption of the software and expanding the current customer base and maintaining a recurring revenue stream. Sales engineers support the sales representatives with technical expertise and demos.

The indirect model leverages "off-the-shelf" software to sell through distributors, value-added resellers and system integrators. Different companies within the industry have different mixes of direct versus indirect sales. However, indirect has become more popular in new markets and when targeting accounts segments with lower opportunity to gain a breadth of coverage in a cost-effective manner.

Key Performance Metrics:
- Total software bookings
- Total service bookings
- Partner bookings

Products, Customers, Coverage, and List of Jobs

The Company offers two primary solutions, robotic process automation and capture.

- **Robotic Process Automation:** RPA is an efficient way for businesses to acquire and enhance information from various applications or data sources (including websites, portals, desktop applications, and enterprise systems) without any coding.
- **Capture:** Capture optimizes the way businesses capture, process and leverage documents and information virtually (i.e., through enhanced scanning, remotely with smartphones).

In addition to these solutions, the Company also offers other solutions; however, they only make up a small portion of sales, and were not the focus of the project.

The Company sells solutions to customers across all industries, but specifically focused on four primary verticals.

The Company uses a stratified coverage model to deploy named enterprise account executives (AEs), general territory AEs, inside territory representatives, and original equipment manufacturers (OEM) AEs. Named enterprise AEs and general territory AEs are deployed geographically (however, the enterprise AEs have an account list within their territories). The named enterprise AEs are responsible for hunting for new enterprise logos from a list of accounts and managing their current account base. The named enterprise AEs are supported by sales architects and engineers, pre-sales. General territory AEs support system integrators and value-added resellers in their region to hunt for new logos. General territory AEs manage current accounts directly without support from the channel. The inside sales representatives are supported by sales architects and engineers, pre-sales in the non-core market. Inside sales representatives' support system integrators and value-added resellers in region (non-core) to hunt for new logos. Inside sales representatives manage current accounts directly without support from the channel.

The Company segments customers based on sales footprint (i.e., ability to serve), current revenue and market opportunity. Accounts consist of the following three segments:

1. Enterprise
2. Core
3. Non-core

Initially, all countries are determined to be a core or non-core market. This determination was made in coordination with the project team based on opportunity within the country and the current ability to service the market by the Company's resources. For example, developing countries in Latin America, where the Company does not have outside resources were determined to be "non-core" markets, while the Company classified countries such as the U.S. and U.K. as core. Once the countries were determined to be core or non-core, AGI and the Company stratified accounts based on revenue and opportunity. The accounts with the highest opportunity and/or revenue were determined to be "enterprise." The Company classified the rest of the accounts as "general territory." Outside field resources primarily covered enterprise accounts. Core accounts (general territory) were covered primarily by partners but supported by outside resources. Non-core accounts were covered primarily by partners but supported by inside sales resources.

Title	Job Abstract	Performance Metrics
Enterprise/ BPO AE	• Pursues and lands new logos • Owns, persuades and closes sales opportunities with new enterprise or BPO logos • Manages existing enterprise or BPO customer relationships • Identifies, qualifies and closes up-sell and cross-sell opportunities • Supported by partner account managers on enterprise accounts • Collaborates with partners to increase mindshare and build partnerships	• SW bookings • Service bookings
General Territory AE	• Pursues and lands new logos • Works closely with partners to source, develop and close deals • Manages existing general territory customer and partner relationships • Supports partners with identification, qualification and closing of up-sell and cross-sell opportunities	• SW bookings
Inside Sales Rep	• Pursues and lands new logos • Supports partners with opportunity qualification, quoting, and sales processes • Manages existing general territory customer and partner relationships • Supports partners with identification, qualification and closing of up-sell and cross-sell opportunities	• SW bookings
OEM AE	• Identifies and builds new OEM partnerships • Conveys compelling value props and articulates joint business value to obtain design wins • Assesses and recommends shared vision on joint solution, including sales and profit goals	• Partner SW bookings
Partner Program Manager	• Regional point person who coordinates the partner team for enterprise, core and non-core territory markets • Supports field with non-sales partner administration, such as contracts, portal access, certifications, coordinating enablement, etc.	• N/A
Partner Recruitment Manager	• Identifies, recruits and onboards relationships with next generation partners • Onboards new partners • Enables partners to be sales ready	• MBOs

Partner Account Manager	• Drives/scales new and existing high value partnerships • Builds and maintains mindshare with high-value partners • Develops sales plans, including strategy, business goals, forecasts, and coverage plan • Shares strong technical knowledge with partners • Supports enterprise/general AEs	• Partner SW bookings • MBOs
Distribution Manager	• Recruits new and expands and retains existing distribution partners and business • Conveys compelling value props and articulates joint business value to distribution partners • Supports territory AE and inside sales reps for non-core products	• Distribution partner bookings
Distribution	• Recruits new and expands and retains existing distribution partners and business • Conveys compelling value props and articulates joint business value to distribution partners • Focuses on products for distribution	• Distribution partner bookings
Solutions Architect	• Articulates value propositions and how solutions meet buyer's needs, as well as general solution technical capabilities • Provides deep technical expertise and support during pre-sales process with new logos as well as during up-sell/cross-sell • Provides use case support and expertise	• Total bookings • Service bookings
Sales Engineer	• Provides technical expertise and support during pre-sales process with new logos as well as during up-sell/cross-sell • Able to articulate value propositions and how solutions meet buyer's needs, as well as general solution technical capabilities • Completes demos and POCs to validate how solutions meet customer's needs and business requirements	• Total SW bookings • Total service bookings
Sales Support Rep	• Processes orders • Supports less than 25K inbound partner transactions where no sales touch/influence is required	• N/A (not compensation eligible)
Customer Success Manager	• Guides select set of customers through successful onboarding and implementation • Supports customer success and drives usage, adoption, expansion, and renewal of the Company's solutions	• N/A (no current headcount, compensation plan not designed)

Renewal Rep	• Proactively closes maintenance and subscription renewal business with existing accounts (when everything stays the same)	• N/A (not compensation eligible)

Project Solution and Outcome

AGI assessed the Company's sales compensation program to inform its plan design. Key inputs into the assessment were:

1. Pay level benchmarks
2. Sales time survey
3. Field and executive interviews
4. Pay-for-performance analyses

Further, AGI aligned on the key strategic objectives for the Company, such as driving software booking growth and hitting EBIDA targets.

AGI identified three findings to consider in the sales compensation plan redesign:

1. Quota attainment
2. Paying for software growth
3. Communication

The first finding examined quota attainment. As part of the pay for performance, AGI reviewed the quota attainment of the sales representatives and sales managers. After discussion with management, and reviewing data, AGI learned that the Company over-allocated its sales goals by 35% to its sales team. This over-allocation led to low-quota attainment, below benchmark pay levels and high turnover. One of AGI's recommendations was to lower quotas, so that they were realistic for reps to hit. However, after significant discussions, AGI could not convince the Company to implement this change. The Company focused on hitting EBIDA targets and would not risk lower quotas (to overpay reps or have lower than expected earnings). Overall, this decision led to highly efficient reps (E/R), but also high turnover and low morale.

The second finding was paying for growth. A central theme for the Company was to grow software bookings (in order to hit the rule of 40).[1] AGI conducted field interviews and reviewed financial data and determined that the Company had low upside pay above goal and did not have a threshold below goal. This led the Company to bunch sales reps at similar pay levels and did not truly

---

1 The rule of 40% is nothing more than a rule of thumb to analyze the health of a software/SaaS business. It takes into consideration two of the most important metrics for a subscription company: growth and profit. Which means that your growth rate plus your profit should add up to 40%.

differentiate top performers from the pack. AGI proposed increasing upside to reward top performers, while adding a threshold as a funding mechanism. AGI believed that this would decrease turnover with the top performers (increasing fairness). At the same time, AGI was cognizant to maintain the simplicity of the compensation plan.

The third finding was communication. The Company had not rolled out many changes to the compensation plans in the past and was worried about the perception from the change. AGI supported the Company with the communication plan and messaging to the team. For example, AGI developed the content that the Company would roll out at the national sales meeting. Further, AGI outlined the meetings that would occur on the local level to communicate the plan, how it affects individual reps and how the reps would be paid.

AGI worked closely with the Company to address these issues in the redesign of the sales compensation plans. For the primary selling roles (enterprise account executive, general territory account executive), AGI recommended individual commission rates (ICRs). Although AGI assisted the Company to balance territories, the Company historically applied commission rates and wanted to move towards a quota-based bonus in the future. Therefore, AGI proposed implementing an ICR to begin the transition from a commission plan to a goal-based plan. The ICR plan (AEs) had the following measures:

1. Software bookings (85%)
2. Service bookings (15%)

AGI increased the rate above target (3x) to align incentive over-achievement. Further, AGI added a threshold at 50% (i.e., 0% rate below 50% of target), consistent with the recurring software business for the primary selling roles. The increased upside and threshold improved the pay-for-performance culture and redistributed earnings to top performers.

Performance Metrics

Metric	Definition of Metric, Importance and Unique Issues
Total Software Bookings	Total software bookings from assigned key accounts (up-sell/cross-sell) and new logo software bookings during the performance period
Service Bookings	Total service bookings from assigned key accounts during the performance period
Distribution Partner Bookings	Total distribution partner software bookings from assigned key accounts (up-sell/cross-sell) and new logo software bookings during the performance period

Partner Software Bookings	Total partner software bookings from assigned key accounts (up-sell/cross-sell) and new logo software bookings during the performance period
MBOs	Management business objectives (actual objectives vary by individual)—not defined by AGI
Non-Core Bookings	Total non-core software bookings from assigned accounts (up-sell/cross-sell) and new logo software bookings during the performance period
Team Software Bookings	Total team software bookings from assigned key accounts (up-sell/cross-sell) and new logo software bookings during the performance period
Team Service Bookings	Total team service bookings from assigned key accounts during the performance period

Glossary

EBIDA: Earnings before interest, depreciation, and amortization

OEM: Original equipment manufacturer

RPA: Robotic process automation

Rule of 40: Growth + EBIDA % > 40% annually

Daniel Kravitz is a director at the Alexander Group.

Industry: Technology

COMPENSATING MULTIYEAR SALES IN A SAAS WORLD

By Andrea Farinelli

Project Identification

The Company is a survey development software firm, which offers cloud-based software solutions for users worldwide ranging from individuals to large enterprises. It produces online survey creation software, as well as a variety of other tools, including marketing content creation, employee engagement tools and an online payment platform. All of the products are offered as a software as a solution (SaaS) with subscription-based payment options.

The Company experienced several business drivers that required a comprehensive assessment of its current sales compensation program. At the start of the project, a majority of the leadership team was new and needed a fresh perspective on the inner workings of the company. In addition, the Company was implementing a significant evolution of its business model and overall sales strategy, focusing on a sales-assisted route-to-market versus its traditional self-serve model. With this shift in strategy came mandatory and aggressive growth expectations in the sales-assisted market. In order to achieve these growth targets, the Company needed to shift towards account-based selling, as opposed to the product-based selling of the past. These changes required an optimized sales coverage model and an investment in additional headcount. It also required a deep understanding of the appropriate sales compensation levers to motivate the new desired behaviors.

The Alexander Group's (AGI) focus was on the United States sales teams. The project consisted of three phases: detailed coverage and job confirmation, sales compensation program assessment, and a comprehensive sales compensation design phase. In the first and second phases, AGI conducted interviews, gathered documents on the Company's strategy and go-to-customer plans, and focused on its sales compensation philosophy. The second phase included design sessions, working towards complete plan designs and, ultimately, costing out those plans. The main deliverables for this project included a detailed compensation assessment, plan design benchmarking, plan designs for the next fiscal year, and compensation program cost modeling

Industry Profile

Software technology companies can focus on SaaS, on-premise technology, or a combination of both. The Company is a purely SaaS company. The world of SaaS is ever-changing, with new challenges, roadblocks and innovative thinking elevating the industry to the next level. With the introduction of SaaS subscription selling, technology companies have had to overhaul their business and selling practices. Mainly, there is a significant need to drive customer lifetime value (CLV) after the initial sale. It is common for the initial sale in a SaaS business to be low in revenue dollars. The most critical success factor for growth is the customer continuing to renew its subscription with little company investment, thus driving a significantly higher CLV than on-premise solutions. This has driven the need for additional sales resources to drive the customer's adoption of the software, and ultimate success, and resulted in industry deployment of customer success managers (CSMs) or other adoption-based sales roles.

With the introduction of CSMs, coupled with the main seller, account executive and/or account manager, concerns around sales crediting become a significant issue. In SaaS technology companies, bookings and monthly recurring revenue metrics drive performance. Management needs to clarify who receives credit for each sale, as well as who owns accounts, and for how long. In addition, management needs to focus sellers on the preferred type of business, such as new logos, length of contract, renewal, up-sell, and cross-sell, all driving CLV.

Products, Customers, Coverage, and List of Jobs

The Company uses a direct sales model, focusing its sales-assisted efforts on mid-market and enterprise-sized companies. While it offers products to smaller companies, the Company largely sells these products as self-serve products and can be purchased online or downloaded for free.

Title	Job Abstract	Job Goals
Business Development Reps—Outbound	Develop sales qualified leads for sellers	• Qualify customer leads through outbound call activity • Pass leads to account executives to drive higher account contract value (ACV) for the team
Sales Development Reps—Inbound	Qualify inbound sales leads and pass to the sellers	• Pass leads to account executives to drive higher ACV for the team
Enterprise Account Executives	Develop and close ACV business within the enterprise space, focusing on new logo deals	• Consult customer on product needs • Drive ACV
Mid-Market Account Executives	Develop and close ACV business within the mid-market space, focusing on new logo deals	• Consult customer on product needs • Drive ACV
Account Executives	Develop and close ACV business through sales	• Consult customer on product needs • Drive ACV

Account Managers	Drive ACV expansion within current set of accounts	• Drive up-sell and cross-sell activities within book of business
Sales Engineers	Provide technical support to sellers in order to close ACV business	• Provide technical expertise to sellers and customers during pre-sales activities
Customer Success Managers	Drive customer adoption and value realization, which leads to expansion and renewal opportunities	• Drive expansion and renewals within book of business • Maintain or increase monthly recurring revenue

Project Solution and Outcome

AGI conducted a full sales compensation assessment, which showed four main areas of improvement, including out-year payments, management by objectives (MBO) usage, rules of engagement, and policies and procedures.

Out-Year Payments. Account executives received their main commission payments on the ACV, i.e., they received credit on total revenue dollars received by the company in the first year of the contract. In addition, they received a flat percentage commission rate on all out-year revenue on the contract. While in theory this is an acceptable practice, the execution was not working. The account executives received very low leverage on their main measure (ACV) and making it up on the out-year commission payments. However, the out-year commission payments were unpredictable and very challenging to monitor, model and control.

AGI addressed this by removing the out-year payments from account executives' plans. The new plan designed utilized a multiyear credit uplift to when the contract was signed for more than one year. For example, if a $300,000, three-year deal closes, the sales representative would normally receive credit for $100,000 (one year's worth). However, since it is a three-year deal, the representative would receive credit of $120,000, a 1.2x uplift. This allows for predictable costs and a motivational sales plan.

MBO Usage. AGI found an unproductive use of MBO measures in the sales compensation plans. For a wide variety of roles, outside of account executives, the Company used MBOs to incent for a variety of activities. However, the Company based the achievement of each MBO on management discretion and non-quantifiable results. This resulted in "phantom base," meaning only a small percentage of individuals ever received less than 100% of their MBO payout, effectively making it a guarantee.

In order to create a more objective program, MBOs were removed for a majority of the sales roles. In exchange, measureable behaviors, or true ACV sales quotas, replaced the MBOs. One role that continued with an MBO was the sales engineer role. However, even for this role, the MBO changed to a clearly measurable, subjective activity that the operations team (not the managers) monitored.

Rules of Engagement. AGI also reviewed the rules of engagement between account executives, account managers and CSMs. This resulted in channel and crediting conflict on post-initial sale add-on and up-sell opportunities. AGI emphasized that even with the best sales compensation design, the plan would fail if the crediting rules and quotas were not designed appropriately for these roles.

Significant effort went into designing swim lanes, outlining likely crediting scenarios for these roles, who receives credit when, and pointing out the areas that lacked coverage. AGI ultimately recommended that quotas and crediting take into account all roles involved and ensured team work where needed.

Policies and Procedures. The last area of improvement during the assessment phase was around policies and procedures in the sales compensation program. The first issue discovered was that incentive pay was distributed inaccurately on several occasions. AGI hypothesized this was a result of manual processes where automation is really necessary. Related to this was the second issue around the use of draws. Due to the inability to pay out on a quarter-to-date basis, the Company made draws each month to stabilize cash flow. However, market practice indicates that paying out monthly on quarter-to-date achievement is the best way to motivate sellers and align rewards to efforts.

AGI recommended switching to a more effective program, likely including an automation system. The Company was already in the progress of onboarding one such program, which will allow for all recommendations to be executed upon implementation.

Andrea Farinelli is a manager at the Alexander Group.

Industry: Technology

DESIGNING SALES COMPENSATION TO BOOST STAGNATING GROWTH

By Daniel Kravitz

Project Identification

The Company is a multimillion-dollar business intelligence and data integrity company. It has been a leading player in the industry for many years and boasts an experienced sales team with strong customer relationships. The Company's primary products are business intelligence and data management.

However, with the entrance of new competitors, the Company has seen a decline in brand awareness and market share, leading to stagnating new logo sales and silos within the organization. For example, each sales office operates as a branch. The branches do not share best practices, plays or strategic techniques (segmentation, account targeting, etc.), because it's not in the branch's best interest and fear it could erode their account base. Further, the sales compensation program did not support the goal of increasing software bookings. Sales representatives were paid on a one-size-fits all plan that was overly complex. The Company engaged the Alexander Group (AGI) to help break down internal barriers (i.e., lack of communication and collaboration between regions, different sales roles, etc.), create a go-to customer strategy that drives growth, and develop a best-in-class sales compensation program.

To accomplish these objectives, AGI analyzed sales time survey results, conversion, penetration and retention (CPR) analyses, pay for performance, and sales investment benchmarks. In addition, AGI interviewed the executive team, sales leadership and a select set of sales representatives to understand what key issues the business faced and identify pain points for the organization. AGI held various design sessions that drove to consensus of what future state should and could look like.

The deliverables of the project included an assessment of the Company's current sales operating model, including its sales compensation program, a blueprint of future state, an account targeting model, a competency model, a workload model, full territory redesign, new sales compensation designs, and an implementation road map. AGI worked with the Company's leadership team to define a communication plan.

Industry Profile

The business intelligence (BI) industry refers to technologies, applications and practices for the collection, integration, analysis, and presentation of data. BI enables businesses to collect data, run queries and rapidly prepare reports to optimize decision making in real time. This can lead to improved efficiency, better inventory management, new revenue opportunities, better account messaging, and identify insights to make accurate and timely business decisions.

Most commonly, BI companies sell direct to businesses or through indirect sales channels. The direct model deploys a traditional bifurcated hunter/farmer model to cover each of the customer segments. The hunters focus on building relationships with accounts in their territory to drive new business volume. Once an account is landed, a service-oriented customer success representative is responsible for driving adoption of the software and expanding the current customer base. This role helps increase renewal rates. Sales engineers support the sales representatives with technical expertise and demos.

The indirect model leverages off-the-shelf software to sell through distributors, value-added resellers and system integrators. Different companies within the industry have different mixes of direct versus indirect sales. However, indirect has become more popular in new markets and when targeting accounts segments with lower opportunity in order to gain a breadth of coverage in a cost-effective manner.

Key Performance Metrics:
- Total software bookings
- Total service bookings
- Renewal bookings
- Qualified leads

Products, Customers, Coverage, and List of Jobs

The Company sells solutions to customers across all verticals. The Company uses a stratified coverage model to deploy strategic account managers, account executives and inside account executives to cover accounts based on geography and customer segment. The strategic account managers are responsible for retaining and growing a small list of the Company's most important accounts (five accounts per rep). Account executives are responsible for hunting for new business and managing accounts within designated geographic territories. The inside account executives are responsible for hunting for new business and managing current accounts in the "rest of market" segment. Sales engineers and sales architects provide sales representatives with technical expertise pre-sale (new logos) and during expansion activities. Technical account managers support sales representatives during implementation driving adoption of the technology.

The Company segments customers based on current revenue and market opportunity. Accounts are divided into the following segments:

1. Strategic
2. Named
3. Rest of market

Named accounts are further broken out between standard named, state and local, and healthcare.

Title	Job Abstract	Performance Metrics
Account Executive	• Pursues and lands qualified leads identified by sales development reps • Hunts for new opportunities from a list of named account targets (key accounts) • Manages and grows relationships and drives expansion and renewals across all solutions within assigned key accounts	• Total software bookings • Service bookings
Strategic Account Manager	• Manages and grows relationships with highly strategic accounts • Responsible for adoption, cross and up-sell, and renewal efforts in strategically important accounts • Coordinates with internal teams to deliver full company value	• Total software bookings • Service bookings • Renewal bookings
Inside Sales Rep	• Pursues and lands qualified leads identified by sales development reps; hunts for new opportunities from a list of named (regular accounts) account targets across all solutions in "rest of market" • Manages and grows relationships and drives expansion and renewals across all solutions within assigned regular accounts	• Total software bookings
Sales Development Rep	• Identifies, qualifies and delivers sales leads within all segments through outbound and inbound lead activities • Builds and harvests communities of social interest online via multiple forums; uses social media presence to generate opportunities in addition to list dialing their personal production goals and region production and profitability goals	• Number of qualified leads • Total software bookings (from leads)

Technical Account Manager	• Responsible for customer success for newly acquired key accounts during implementation and strategic accounts • Provides technical expertise and confirms installation/implementation success • Discusses enhancement options with newly onboarded accounts • Provides account executive and strategic account manager valuable insights to expand and renew accounts	• Total team software bookings • Customer Excellence KPIs: • (1) Transactional NPS • (2) Relational NPS
System Engineer	• BI product specialist who assists account executives and account managers with new logo sales, up-sales and cross-sales • Provides product demos and key technical support during pre-sales process	• Total software bookings • Team software bookings
Solution Architect	• Data management product specialist who assists account executives and account managers with new logo sales, up-sales and cross-sales • Provides product demos and key technical support during pre-sales process	• Total software bookings • Team software bookings
Business Development Manager	• Scopes professional service related to new logo sales and up-sell/cross-sell opportunities • Collaborates with account executives and strategic account managers	• N/A (not eligible)
Implementation Manager; Consulting	• Drives and project manages all implementation activities required to bring a new client or solution live • Advises account executive, inside sales representative and strategic account manager as needed for key issues related to implementation issues, concerns and timing	• N/A (not eligible)

Project Solution and Outcome

AGI assessed the Company's sales compensation program to inform its plan design for the next year. Key inputs into the assessment were:

1. Pay level benchmarks
2. Field and executive interviews
3. Pay-for-performance analyses

Further, AGI aligned on the key strategic objectives for the Company for the next year, such as driving revenue growth at all costs, to inform its recommendation.

AGI identified three findings to consider in the sales compensation plan redesign:

1. Fairness
2. Complexity
3. Communication

The first finding was fairness. The Company employed a one-size-fits-all commission plan. The plan paid the same commission tiers to all sales reps, regardless of assigned territory and overall opportunity. Some representatives inherited territories with significant opportunity and were able to landlord accounts (renewals and new bookings) and were compensated the same way. This drove a culture of protecting account bases at the expense of hunting for new logos. Further, new reps, with less rich territories, were not able to earn enough incentive pay, leading to above benchmark turnover (25%).

The second finding was complexity. AGI received feedback from the field, through ride-alongs and interviews, that the sales compensation plan was too complex, and representatives did not understand how they were being paid. AGI reviewed the Company's sales compensation plans and noted that the sales compensation plan (one plan for all reps) had multiple measures, various modifiers (i.e., data management product), and bonuses (new logo, quarterly, annual, new department). Further, representatives were not provided with examples of how they were paid or incentive calculators. This created confusion among the sales force and led to discontent when commissions were paid out.

The third finding was communication. The Company lacked a true sales operations function and was slow to roll out new incentive plans, commission payments or changes within the sales organization. Further, representatives were generally not kept in the loop to changes as significant siloes existed between corporate and the field. This lack of communication created a culture of distrust among the sales force.

AGI worked closely with the Company to address the issues in the redesign of the sales compensation plans. AGI's most important consideration was to create one sales compensation plan per role, reduce the complexity of the plan and align pay with relative effort. Further, AGI aligned the compensation plan with the business objective of expanding current accounts and driving new logos.

For the primary selling roles (account executives), AGI recommended transitioning from a ramped commission plan to a quota-based bonus plan with two measures:

1. Total software bookings (80%)
2. Total service bookings (20%)

AGI removed many of the bonuses but increased upside above goal (3x) to align incentive with actual performance. Further, AGI shifted the more strategic accounts from the account executive (to the strategic account managers) to focus the role on driving new business (and reducing the need to call out renewals separately).

In addition, AGI worked with sales leadership to maintain the pay levels for top performers. The Company's top performers represented a significant portion of overall sales. Therefore, an important tenet of the design process was to not "break the system." This was done through providing lower quotas in year one (and planning to ramp over time). Although this was not AGI's preferred solution, it was one that the Company felt most comfortable with.

After designing the structural changes to the program, AGI worked with the Company to outline a communication plan. One key finding from the assessment was that representatives felt out of the loop. Therefore, AGI outlined a plan to proactively share changes in the compensation plan at the national meeting and explain what was changing and why. AGI then created coaching cadence frameworks for first-line sales managers to explain individual impacts and confirm plan enrollment through plan documents. Overall, the communication plan was designed to rebuild trust between management and the field.

Performance Metrics

Metric	Definition of Metric, Importance and Unique Issues
Total Software Bookings	Total software bookings (TCV) from assigned key accounts (up-sell/cross-sell) and new logo software bookings during the performance period
Service Bookings	Total service bookings from assigned key accounts during the performance period
Renewal Bookings	Total software bookings (TCV) from assigned strategic accounts (renewals) during the performance period

Number of Qualified Leads	The total number of qualified leads during the performance period
Number of Meetings	The total number of meetings set up with assigned strategic accounts
Total Team Software Bookings	Total team software bookings (TCV) from assigned key accounts (up-sell/cross-sell) and new logo software bookings during the performance period
Team Service Bookings	Total service team bookings from assigned key accounts during the performance period
Team Renewal Bookings	Total team software bookings (TCV) from assigned strategic accounts (renewals) during the performance period
KPIs	Customer Excellence KPIs: (1) Transactional NPS (2) Relational NPS

Daniel Kravitz is a director at the Alexander Group.

WHITEPAPERS

SALES COMPENSATION ALMANAC • 2022

WHITEPAPERS

The Alexander Group encourages our consultants to share their experiences, formulate new ideas and contribute to the profession. In this section, explore select topics authored by the Alexander Group's consultants.

IN THIS SECTION

This year's whitepapers feature the following topics:

- How to Compensate Customer Success Roles in High-Growth Software Companies
- How to Use Spiffs to Reward Sellers
- Sales Compensation: How to Reduce Base Pay and Increase Pay at Risk
- Sales Compensation: Rewarding Team Selling
- Sales Compensation Cost Modeling: Determining Methodology and Components

HOW TO COMPENSATE CUSTOMER SUCCESS ROLES IN HIGH-GROWTH SOFTWARE COMPANIES

By Daniel Kravitz

Software companies are transitioning from a perpetual to a recurring revenue model. As they transition, sales management is deploying new roles to maximize customer lifetime value. Post-contract signing efforts have now become more critical to success. Profitable sales can now take multiple years. Sales management must create new sales roles and compensate them to support these long-horizon revenue opportunities. The "customer success" role helps drive continuing revenue post-sale.

Sales Process and Growth Phases Provide Job Design Foundation

The transition from perpetual software licenses to a recurring revenue model has led companies to redefine the sales process. Different sales roles play in different parts of the sales process. The sales process can be broken down into five phases: Identify, Land, Adopt, Expand, and Renew (ILAER).

The ILAER sales process provides the foundation for job design. However, deploying the ILAER model differs by the phase of growth: Phase 1: Start-Up (Top-Line Growth); Phase 2: Volume Growth (Revenue Management); Phase 3: Re-Evaluation (Margin Management); and Phase 4: Optimization (Segment Growth) (see the following figure).

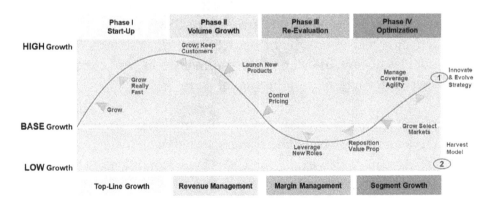

As companies move through the phases of growth, they have differing strategic objectives and sales roles. This whitepaper focuses on phase 1, start-up companies.

Job Definition Drives Sales Compensation Design

Sales compensation design depends on the company's phase of growth and the individual job responsibilities. The customer success manager (CSM) role is primarily responsible for driving technology adoption, penetrating accounts and increasing renewal rates (post-sale). However, various types of the CSM role exist. Companies employ CSM roles based on a continuum of service focus to sales focus. As CSM roles move left on the continuum, more of their job scope is technical, training and usage focused. As customer success roles move right on the continuum, more of their job scope is penetration and renewal focused.

Although there are infinite iterations of the job, most companies will implement one of these three CSM roles:

1. Service CSM
2. Expansion CSM (sales only)
3. Hybrid CSM (both service and sales)

Service CSM. Service CSMs tend to be highly technical. They play a substantive role training and onboarding customers. Service CSMs are much less focused on sales activities, such as up-sell or cross-sell, and help customers realize value from solutions/software. They are more common in mature companies that have distinct ownership splits in the sales process.

Expansion CSM. Expansion CSMs function like traditional farmers. They grow recurring revenue through high renewal rates, including up-selling/cross-selling. In high-growth companies, expansion CSMs are becoming more common as a way to further penetrate existing customers.

Hybrid CSM. Hybrid CSMs balance responsibilities of a service CSM and an expansion CSM. They play a substantive role in training and onboarding of customers, but as a means to drive renewals. These CSMs proactively engage with customers. Hybrid CSMs are common in start-up companies where employees are expected to wear multiple hats.

Each CSM role has different responsibilities and strategic objectives. Therefore, each role commands different sales compensation plans when used by a start-up company.

Sales Compensation Design

Management designs sales roles to drive the objectives of each growth phase. For start-ups, job roles typically focus on the following objectives.

1. Improving market share
2. Increasing brand loyalty
3. Creating profitable business

Appropriate sales compensation plans depend on the job's mix of sales and service accountabilities. Most companies compensate CSMs on a corporate plan. However, there is a trend to move CSMs to variable plans to reward adoption/persuasion outcomes. In start-up companies, investments are lean, and companies need to maximize every dollar. This creates a greater need to get sales compensation correct.

When designing sales compensation for CSM roles, companies must determine if the role is eligible for sales compensation. If the role is eligible for sales compensation, the next steps of the design process are to determine:

- **Target Total Compensation (TTC):** base salary plus target incentive (TI).
- **Pay Mix:** split between salary and incentive; expressed as percent of TTC (e.g., 60/40).
- **Leverage:** percent of TI that top performers (90th percentile) are expected to earn at excellence (design point where top 10% of sellers earn full upside).
- **Measures:** individual components (tied to weights) of TI (i.e., software bookings).
- **Mechanics:** how sales compensation is paid (i.e., commissions, quotas, etc.).

Service CSMs

In order to be eligible for sales compensation, a sales role must have:

1. Significant customer contact
2. Ability to persuade the customer
3. High level of sales process involvement
4. Clear and quantifiable sales objectives

The service CSM does not spend a significant amount of time persuading customers to buy additional products. In addition, they do not have a significant level of sales process involvement. Therefore, service CSMs are generally not eligible for sales compensation plans. They are generally compensated on corporate plans, with bonus opportunities between 10% to 20% of base salary.

Expansion CSMs

Expansion CSMs are focused on persuading customers to renew contracts and purchase additional products (post-sale). They have significant customer contact and have the ability to persuade the customer. Therefore, the expansion CSM should be sales compensation eligible.

The next step is to select the TTC for the expansion CSM. When designing TTC, companies should create:

- Competitive pay levels aligned to both internal and external comparable roles
- Compensation programs that meet fiscal requirements

Start-up companies often pay below the median TTC market benchmark for expansion CSMs. Management provides additional compensation in the form of equity and/or additional perks (free meals, flexibility, fitness, etc.). Although this is not a rule, start-up companies generally have less cash on hand to invest in employees and require employees to do more with less.

Pay mix for expansion CSMs in start-up companies is more aggressive than in mature companies. Pay mix reflects the job's degree of individual influence. Sales jobs with the most influence on the purchasing decision will have the most aggressive pay mix. Expansion CSMs generally have pay mixes between 70/30 and 80/20. However, start-up companies tend to have more aggressive pay mixes. It is not uncommon for start-up expansion CSMs to have a pay mix between 60/40 and 70/30. By increasing the pay mix, start-up companies better align pay to performance. Further, leverage for an expansion CSM should be between 2x and 2.5x. Leverage reflects the job's degree of influence.

Measures and mechanics should reflect the realities of the job and the market. The measures for an expansion CSM should tie back to the goals of improving market share, increasing brand loyalty and creating a profitable business. Some common measures for expansion CSMs include the following.

1. Customer satisfaction (net promoter score)
2. Account bookings growth
3. Retention rate (or dollars)

4. Account penetration
5. Usage (if measurable)

When designing a compensation plan for an expansion CSM, start-up companies should choose a maximum of three measures. The most common payout mechanic for a start-up company is a commission rate. Start-up companies generally have trouble setting goals when there is a lot of market white space. Therefore, the risk of setting goals with incomplete information is high. Using a commission mechanic aligns the risk of the sales force with the business and creates a sink or swim mentality.

Role	Eligibility	TTC	Pay Mix	Mechanics	Measures	Leverage
Expansion CSM	Yes	Below 50th percentile of similar companies	60/40 to 70/30	Commission	• Customer satisfaction • Account bookings growth • Retention • Account penetration • Usage	2.5x

Hybrid CSMs

The hybrid CSM is not a typical sales role, but still has significant customer contact. Hybrid CSMs provide technical expertise post-sale, but as a means to create sticky relationships and maximize renewals long term. Therefore, they should be sales compensation eligible.

Compared to the expansion CSM, the TTC of a hybrid CSM tends to be higher. Hybrid CSMs have more technical expertise and are less sales-focused (more specialized skills tend to be more expensive). Hybrid CSMs generally have pay mixes between 80/20 and 90/10. However, start-up companies tend to have more aggressive pay mixes. It is not uncommon for start-up company hybrid CSMs to have a pay mix between 70/30 and 80/20. The higher than benchmark pay mix minimizes investment if the company misses its goals. Further, leverage for a hybrid CSM should be between 1.5x and 2x. In start-up companies, hybrid CSMs would have leverage closer to 2x.

The measures for a hybrid CSM should tie back to the goals of improving market share, increased brand loyalty and creating a profitable business. Some common measures for this role include:

1. Customer satisfaction (net promoter score)
2. Usage (if measurable)
3. Retention rate (or dollars)
4. MBOs (sales or service activities)

Role	Eligibility	TTC	Pay Mix	Mechanics	Measures	Leverage
Hybrid CSM	Yes	Below 50th percentile of similar companies	70/30 to 80/20	Commission	• Customer satisfaction • Usage • Retention • MBOs	2x

Conclusion

The CSM role has become more important as the recurring revenue model has become more prevalent. As such, it has become crucial to better define the CSM role. Sales compensation plans for CSMs must align with job responsibilities, strategic focus and growth phase.

Daniel Kravitz is a director at the Alexander Group.

HOW TO USE SPIFFS TO REWARD SELLERS

By Parker Hoffman

A company sought to reward sellers for revenue growth, plus numerous and changing short-term objectives. While management expected the sales compensation plan to reward revenue growth, the company realized the plan was not effective at addressing the various short-term objectives. Could spiffs help solve this challenge?

Spiffs, if used correctly, should complement the main sales compensation plan and not become an additive distraction.

So, what are spiffs? When should they be utilized? And how should they be communicated and implemented?

Spiffs are add-on rewards to drive short-term goals. They motivate, build culture, generate excitement, and reward outcomes. Spiffs require a clear objective and defined return on investment and should not undermine the sales compensation plan.

Frequency and Duration

Suboptimal revenue quota performance had become the norm over the past few years. Less than 40% of incumbents reached quota. Poor quota attainment leads to business underperformance and demotivated sales representatives. Additionally, the company had a recent problem with spiffs. In an attempt to offset the low earnings due to poor quota performance, the compensation team began providing add-on incentives such as spiffs. These add-on opportunities created sales effort misalignment between quota attainment and spiff objectives. Within the last 12 months, the company sponsored more than 40 spiffs, most of which were not strategic or targeted. Instead, the spiffs were acting as a band-aid for poor quota performance, helping representatives achieve their on-target earnings.

Benchmark data confirms that nearly 70% of companies use contests or spiffs. Those using contests/spiffs limit their use. Less than 20% of companies sponsor more than six contests/spiffs in a year.

Benchmark Practice: Spiff count should be less than five a year per job, and last no longer than one to three months.

Program Measures and Metrics

Many of the measures used in spiffs are similar, if not alike, to measures used in sales compensation, raising the question of redundancy. The key is to select criteria and metrics that do not compete with the standard compensation plan. In addition to role definition, organizational strategy and ongoing business issues may impact measure decisions.

Business Strategy & Considerations		
Observations	Details	Potential Spiff Implications
Incentive Growth	• A highly influential factor in measuring company results and performance each quarter	• Spiff on new customer revenue or new logo acquisition • Revenue penetration or number of products per account
All Products Are Not Created Equal	• Certain sales build the install base and open opportunity for service or software requirements • Margins fluctuate significantly across products	• Allow sellers to focus on more strategic products and opportunities • Consider a spiff to ensure cross-portfolio execution
Industries and Geographic Markets Are in Different Growth Stages	• Emphasis on growing in x and y regions • Significant growth opportunity in x verticals • Established right to win in x vertical/region	• Incentivize revenue conversion or new logo conversion • Incentivize revenue retention and penetration
Margin/Price Erosion Is an Issue in Some Geos	• Sellers lower prices to boost top-line revenue, but can come at the expense of profitability	• Price realization spiff

Benchmark Practice: Spiff metrics do not compete with the standard compensation plan. Use sales output metrics as opposed to activity metrics (e.g., number of calls made, registrations generated for events, leads).

Reward Types

"Cash is king" for spiffs, with more than 73% of reported companies utilizing this reward type. While cash does have some drawbacks—generic, no additional perceived value effect, intangible, cash is less memorable—the benefits are overwhelmingly positive. Cash is scalable to accommodate different geographic locations with varying levels of pay and has broad appeal.

Other Reward Types and Examples

Reward Type	Benefits	Drawbacks
Merchandise *Examples:* electronics, crystal awards, plaques, watches, pens and clothing	• Effective for close-ended spiffs • Potentially higher buzz factor • Usually, more cost-effective, as perceived value often higher than the actual value • Less conflict with a cash compensation program	• Can have limited appeal • May not be used by winners • More difficult to distribute • Tax implications
Points (Third Party) *Examples:* salesdriver.com, AMEX, airline mileage	• Can be used to accommodate multiple spiffs • Allows individuals to choose award type (and potentially cash) based on their interest	• Need multiple spiff owners to use the system for its benefit to be realized
Trips *Examples:* team trips, extended paid time after sales meeting, and individual paid weekend getaways	• High perceived value • Can provide personal access to executives • Able to invite personal guest • Group trips increase morale and foster idea sharing	• May dilute the prestige of the other recognition programs outside of the spiff • Might be a higher cost • Timing dictates the ability to participate • Tax implications
Services *Examples:* hotel/air upgrades, car lease, dinner certificates, gift certificates	• Effective for close-ended spiffs • Less conflict with a cash compensation program	• Can have limited appeal • May not be used by winners • More difficult to distribute • Tax implications
Company Perks *Examples:* upgraded office, upgraded furniture, extra paid time off	• Generally no tax implications • Effective for close-ended spiffs	• May dilute the effectiveness of business processes and procedures

Cost and Budget

While an underfunded spiff may lead to a lack of interest, and may not drive the intent of the spiff, an overfunded spiff may prove to be detrimental. Not only can an overfunded spiff program cost a lot without the proper guardrails, but too much money on spiffs may also cause reps to lose focus on the core plan. The core plan and its associated measures, if done correctly, are designed to align reps to the go-to-customer strategy, how the company wants them to execute their jobs and overall company strategy. Too much budget allocated towards spiffs may prove to be a more significant distraction, and dilute the intent of the core compensation plan, rather than drive the sales reps towards targeted, short-term objectives.

Benchmark Practice: Budget about 5% of the total compensation budget (base plus target incentive). As a design objective, spiff payouts should not exceed 25% of the recipient's target incentive.

Participation

If too many people are winning the spiff, the prize pool/allotment may be reduced, and not be enough of an award next time around. Too many people winning may indicate that the spiff target goal was too easy, and not driving the strategic intent.

Conversely, low participation rates reduce employee engagement. If the spiff focuses around a new product launch, reduced employee engagement will further fuel rep uncertainty about selling the product. Sometimes, the new product is such a groundbreaking technology that customers want to talk about it, but to do this, the team needs to know the product. Reduced employee engagement will limit the team's ability to learn about the new product.

Center Practice: Everyone should have the opportunity to win, but not everyone should win. Target at least 30% participation—no demotivating "winner-take-all" contests.

Author/Promoter

Some companies are adamant that during implementation, any message to the sales force should be from the VP of sales. Other companies lean more towards first-line sales managers or regional leaders. Center practice says that the responsibility lies in the sales leadership.

Department	Reasoning
Sales Leadership	• Typically owns spiff promotion • Levers to drive strategy and profitable revenue growth • Public ownership and communication demonstrate leadership
Sales Operations	• Typically provides enabling solution to the salesforce like CRM • Communicating a spiff implies that the spiff is just an administrative program
Marketing	• Product management encourages the sales force to "sell their product" • Many marketing campaigns have a companion spiff for the sales team
Human Resources	• HR is not in a position to defend or enforce the spiff • Assist with the preparation of the communication material • Answer questions related to HR practices or employment-related policies
Finance	• Important oversight role with the spiff • If finance communicates the spiff, sales personnel will harbor suspicions regarding crediting, goals and earning opportunities

Benchmark Practice: Many parties can offer/sponsor contests/spiffs. Coordination among HQ sales management, field sales management, and product management/marketing ensures programs do not overlap or operate as cross-purposes.

Global Practices

Optimal spiff oversight exists along a spectrum. On one end, companies allow local country management to oversee local contests and spiffs. On the other end, a more centralized global approach will take shape.

Question	Considerations
Does the Spiff Need Business Specific Knowledge?	• Business-specific knowledge is critical when the go-to-market strategy is unique or requires a deep understanding of local market conditions
What is the Appetite for Consistency and Governance Around the Spiff?	• Dependent on the strength of culture and organizational ability to drive accountability across regions/business from global HQ
Is the Spiff Unique to a Region?	• Unique capabilities with a broad application should be located centrally

Program Management

A spiff charter promotes governance around the process for launching, budgeting and executing against the spiff. Consider a charter like the following one.

High-Level Spiff Guidelines	
1. Define a Goal	Ensure spiffs align with the organization's sales and performance strategy.
2. Identify the Target Population	Whom will the spiff motivate? Who can affect its desired results? Are managers included? Is it global? (Define the narrowest population to drive results.)
3. Choose an Appropriate Award	Determine if the spiff is open-ended (open to all eligible participants) or close-ended (a limited number of winners or awards).
4. Set a Budget and Expected Return	Ensure that each spiff comes with a predetermined budget and a forecasted return.
5. Create a Buzz	Develop a formal communication plan, messaging and collateral to create a buzz.
6. Plan Ahead	Create a calendar outlining the number, timing and duration of any proposed spiffs. Only one spiff at a time.

Parker Hoffman is a manager at the Alexander Group.

SALES COMPENSATION: HOW TO REDUCE BASE PAY AND INCREASE PAY AT RISK

By Mark O'Donnell

Can a sales force become too complacent? Do high-base salaries as a portion of target total earnings reduce seller ambitions? Can reducing the base pay element and increasing the target incentive improve sales output? Consider one company's experience.

The Current Situation—Sales Stagnation

Sales growth has stalled. Everyone is scrambling to figure out why. Leadership believes the company is well positioned to grow.

- The industry is growing.
- The company is a market leader with superior products.
- The company continues to win quality awards outpacing its competitors.
- The company has a proven sales process with a well-paid, tenured sales team.

A growing consensus has formed over the past few years that sales incumbents are not motivated enough to sell the company's products. Many believe that the sales team sits back and waits for orders to come to them. Sales leadership has decided to invest in increasing the sales team's motivation. Research into the condition reveals:

- The sellers are not achieving reasonable quotas.
- Assigning quotas that are more aggressive did not improve performance, either.
- Target total compensation is above industry levels.
- The portion of base pay is much higher than industry levels.
- There is little pay distinction between low and high performers.

These observations suggest pay mix—the ratio of base pay and target incentive as a portion of target total compensation—needs to be more aggressive: lower base pay and higher incentive portion.

The Solution—Increasing Pay Mix By Lowering the Base Pay Element

Since the incumbents are already earning pay levels above the benchmark, the only way to achieve a more motivating pay mix is to reduce base pay and increase pay at risk. However, there are risks associated with adjusting the incumbent's base pay levels.

Inherent Risks

Although adjusting the pay mix may improve the sales team's motivation, it can have unintended consequences. Reducing base pay and increasing pay at risk introduces inherent risks to the sales organization. Pay mix adjustments will affect the overall sales plan design, the sales culture and the stability of the incumbent's pay.

Design Accuracy

With more pay at risk, the plan design must meet high standards: performance measure alignment and quota allocation accuracy. When redistributing base pay to more pay at risk, management should ensure the performance measures are tied to individual seller efforts. Furthermore, accurate quota allocation for the assigned measures becomes even more critical for both the company and the incumbent. Quotas should be achievable if incumbents are performing their jobs effectively. If quotas are too aggressive, management runs the risk of under-compensating effective incumbents. Alternatively, if management sets quotas too easily, the firm runs the risk of overpaying for performance. Increasing pay at risk magnifies the risk of sales compensation overpayment from quotas set too easily. Management should develop a strategy for a pay mix transition that considers the effectiveness of the current sales compensation program.

Culture

Pay mix directly influences behavior. The more money incumbents have at risk, the more reward they will receive for achieving their goals. A shift in pay mix can have a significant cultural impact, influencing how incumbents interact with one another. When firms increase pay at risk, team collaboration can decrease. For highly collaborative sales organizations, there is a risk that a shift in culture can destabilize a sales team. A more aggressive pay mix will motivate sellers to increase sales, but not all incumbents will initially have the skill sets required to grow their book of business.

Cash Flow Uncertainty

Management introduces more pay uncertainty by reallocating base pay to pay at risk. An incumbent who earned a fixed amount every two weeks will now have that amount decreased. To earn back the amount lost, the incumbent must meet performance expectations. This increases their pay and cash flow uncertainty. Additional pay uncertainty exists from the timing of incentive payments. Firms often pay base salary on a biweekly basis and incentive compensation either monthly, quarterly or even annually. Increasing pay uncertainty can lead to unexpected cash flow issues for incumbents.

Transition Strategies

Management has many strategies for pay mix transition. Selecting the right transition strategy depends on the current environment of the sales organization and the expected risks associated with adjusting the pay mix. The following are seven proven strategies describing when to use the strategy and the risks associated with each.

To help illustrate each strategy, we will assume that an incumbent's current target pay level is $100K with a pay mix of 90/10 ($90K in base pay and $10K in pay at risk). The pay level is competitively set and does not need adjustment. However, the desired pay mix is 70/30, and the current pay mix requires correction. Specifically, we must reduce base pay by $20K to $70K and increase pay at risk by $20K to $30K.

Cold Cut

The cold cut strategy is by far one of the simplest, most straightforward strategies to pick. Simply put, this strategy adjusts incumbents pay mix all at once. Management often chooses a meaningful date to implement the pay mix adjustment, such as the first day of a new fiscal year or quarter. The benefit of using a cold cut strategy is a quick transition and administration simplicity. Management aligns all eligible incumbents to the desired pay mix quickly and at the same time. This approach creates consistency, fairness and transparency.

However, this strategy can create a shock to the sales ecosystem, which can be both motivating and destabilizing depending on the current sales organization's skill sets and culture. A cold cut pay mix transition can significantly alter an incumbent's cash flow depending on current pay levels and the degree of pay mix shifting required. Current incumbents may object strenuously to the new pay mix. Ultimately, a cold cut strategy can lead to unexpected turnover due to a rapid increase in pay uncertainty. Finally, some countries may not allow adjustments to base pay or require a time-consuming approval process with works councils.

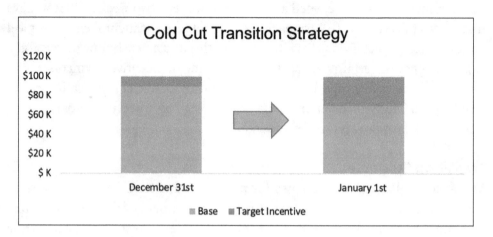

Buyout

The buyout strategy is similar to the cold cut strategy, except management provides a one-time buyout payment to incumbents affected by the pay mix adjustment. The buyout amount is typically equivalent to the amount of base pay that management has reduced. However, the payout could be any amount management has chosen. This strategy minimizes the immediate pay uncertainty associated with a cold cut strategy, but risks remain. Although this strategy mitigates the initial impacts of pay uncertainty, the quick nature of the pay mix transition still creates a shock to the sales ecosystem. This strategy can also be costly, increasing the cost of sales for the transition year.

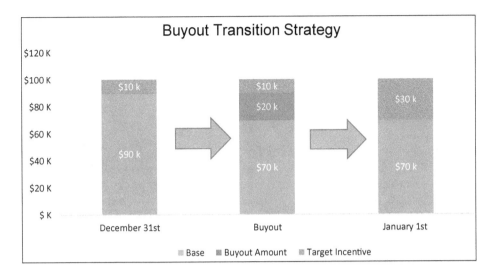

Non-Recoverable Draw

The non-recoverable draw strategy guarantees incumbents a set amount of variable pay for a fixed transition period. Management often sets the non-recoverable draw amount equal to the incumbent's base pay reduction. For example, if an incumbent currently has a base pay of $90K and after the pay mix adjustment has a base pay of $70K, a non-recoverable draw of $20K is common. This strategy allows for a quick pay mix adjustment without rapidly increasing pay uncertainty. Specifically, the non-recoverable draw allows incumbents to receive upside earnings for exceeding their sales goals but does not have a penalty for underperforming during the transition period. However, this strategy does come with risks. The approach is not motivating for incumbents to achieve their sales goals during the transition period. It also increases a company's cost of sales during the transition period.

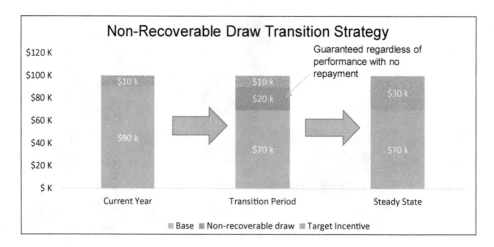

Recoverable Draw

The recoverable draw strategy is very similar to the non-recoverable draw strategy, except the company can recuperate draw payments made, reducing the program costs. Management often sets the recoverable draw amount equal to the incumbent's base pay reduction. Management guarantees the draw amount regardless of an incumbent's performance during a transition period. However, incumbents must repay draw payments provided for periods in which they did not achieve their sales goals. Incumbents will refund the draw repayments with their incentive payouts from periods where they exceeded their sales objectives.

This strategy transitions incumbents to a desirable pay mix quickly. The recoverable draw reduces incumbents pay uncertainty and still motivates incumbents to achieve their goals. This transition strategy is less costly compared to a non-recoverable transition strategy. Although there are clear advantages to a recoverable draw transition strategy, there are some disadvantages. The approach is much more complex to understand and has the highest administrative burden out of the seven transition options.

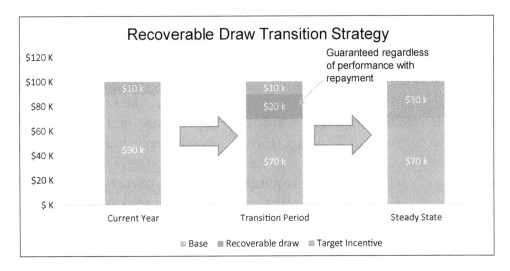

Migrate Over Time

The migrate over time strategy aims to reduce shock introduced to the sales ecosystem by gradually migrating incumbents to the desired pay mix over a more extended period. Management often selects a target date for pay mix to reach the desired ratio and then determines several intermediate dates for partial pay mix adjustments. This approach is relatively easy to administrate and reduces the level of pay uncertainty to the sales organization due to gradual pay mix adjustments. However, it does take more time to adjust an incumbent's pay mix to the desired ratio. The more extended the transition period is, the longer it will take to notice a change in an incumbent's behavior. Additionally, incumbents with the same job may have different pay mixes during the transition period, creating inequality.

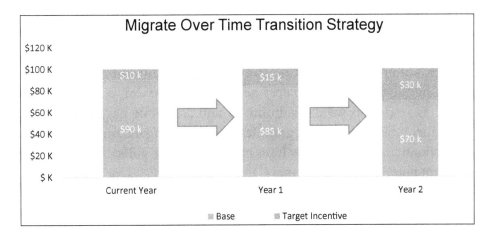

Migrate With Merit Increase

The migrate with merit increase strategy aims to eliminate shock to the sales ecosystem by not reducing base pay levels. Incumbents reach the desired pay mix by having all merit-based pay increases granted as a bonus. Each following year, management assigns this merit bonus amount to the variable portion of pay. Management will not provide base pay increases until incumbents have achieved the desired pay mix. This approach is simple to administer and eliminates all incumbents pay uncertainty. However, the method can take many years to accomplish if the required pay mix adjustments are significant. For example, it would take five years for an incumbent with an annual merit increase of 5% to go from a pay mix of 90/10 to 70/30. Due to the lengthy nature of the approach, behavior impacts will take longer to materialize. Also, if merit increases are not uniform, some reps will obtain the desired pay mix before others, creating inequality.

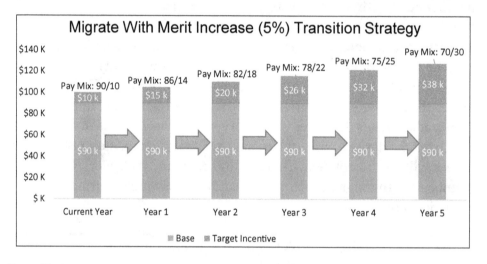

Grandfather

The grandfather approach focuses on keeping the current pay mix design for existing incumbents and places new hires on the desired pay mix. This approach is straightforward to administer and creates no pay uncertainty for existing incumbents. However, grandfathering existing incumbents will delay the behavioral impacts until new hires have replaced a significant portion of the incumbent population. Furthermore, this approach creates inequality between incumbents who hold the same job. New hires will have more pay uncertainty. Management will financially reward and penalize new incumbents more based on their performance compared to their grandfathered counterparts. Over time, this can create some undesirable cultural dynamics within a sales organization.

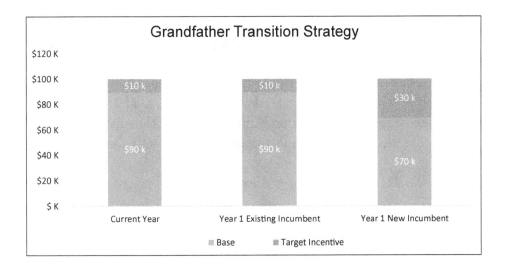

How to Choose

With sales stalling and sales motivation slipping, it is wise for sales management to address concerns around pay mix as quickly as possible. Management can now choose from several effective pay mix transition strategies. The right transition strategy depends on several key considerations. One, how quickly management wants to drive behavioral changes. Two, the expectation of sales team retention. Three, management's appetite to invest financially in the transition. The simplest and quickest transition option is a cold cut strategy. Management should select this strategy if they expect a minimal impact on sales team retention. If sales team retention is concerning, transitioning pay mix with draws is the next best option. Draws are very effective and relatively quick. However, draws can increase sales costs. If retention and sales costs are both concerns, management should migrate pay mix over time or via merit increases. However, with these transition options, the impact on sales behavior will take much longer to realize.

Effective Messaging

Although adjusting base salary increases pay uncertainty from the reduction of base pay, it allows for more upside. Incumbents will now have their pay more closely reflect their performance. Over performers will now earn more than they could have under the previous compensation structure. Firms that effectively transition pay mix via base reductions are those who can clearly communicate the benefits of such a transition to their incumbents.

Conclusion

Ensuring a sales organization has the right pay mix for its sales jobs can be critical for motivating the correct sales behavior. However, when organizations must achieve the right pay mix by reducing base salary, complications are inevitable. It is essential to understand the impacts such a pay mix transition will introduce into the organization. Choose the right transition strategy that will mitigate unnecessary risks and will drive the desired behavioral changes.

Mark O'Donnell is a manager at the Alexander Group.

SALES COMPENSATION: REWARDING TEAM SELLING

By Kelly Rue

What Is A Sales Team?

A sales team refers to multiple individuals working to achieve a common, sales close. Companies employ sales teams in many forms and for different reasons. For example, dedicated sales teams consist of permanent team members, who have assigned tasks. Pursuit teams are temporarily configured to pursue specific opportunities. Digital sales teams feature multiple touch points, some human, others digital; and functional teams include individuals from different functions who have different responsibilities, but do not necessarily interact with each other. These four examples are just the start. Now, the question remains: What is the best way to compensate sales teams?

What Drives A Company to Build and Employ Sales Teams?

Market shifts such as global competition, better-informed customers, technological developments, and increased connectivity are some of the factors driving team sales efforts. Employing team-based selling is an increasingly common sales strategy.

While sales teams serve different purposes and come in many forms, they all raise the same question: How does one compensate multiple individuals for closing a single sale? Sales compensation plans must adapt for this change in seller deployment. Embracing team selling can help drive growth more efficiently. Supporting and enabling sellers via the proper technology, tools, resources, and compensation will pay dividends.

Why Team-Based Selling?

Team-based selling refers to a collaborative sales approach where multiple team members work to close business rather than individual account owners who work independently. With team-based selling, the idea is that with increased coverage, a team is better equipped to serve a customer than a single resource. Teams are often made up of individuals with unique skill sets to better equip the team to address customer questions or close new opportunities that arise during the sales process. The value of a team approach is the unique perspective that each team member brings. In other instances, organizations create teams of multiple individuals within the same role. This increases coverage on an account to address multiple buyers, locations or other factors. The types of resources required differ based on the type of sale and customer. An effective team-based sales approach matches the customer's buying journey. If the organization is selling to different types of customers with unique buying journeys, it is important to configure the sales process to each. Organizations may deploy a sales team to target certain customers, while maintaining sole account ownership for others. Team selling is often useful when selling to sophisticated buyers with complex needs. A team-based sales approach provides the broadest knowledge and highest chance of effectively meeting the customer's needs.

Is Team Selling the Right Answer?
The organization may need to change its sales deployment if:

- Sales close rate is low
- Revenue (or margin) dollars associated with individual sales are declining
- Customer satisfaction rate is low

Team selling can increase the chances of closing additional deals by aligning increased resources to each deal. Specialized resources providing deeper knowledge can increase an organization's ability to up-sell and cross-sell to existing customers. With additional resources, sales teams are more likely to successfully answer tough questions that a singular seller might not have the knowledge base to answer.

Key Considerations for Employing Team-Based Selling
Team-based selling involves an important cultural shift for the traditional sales organization. Historically, account-based sales were owned by an individual responsible for the customer throughout the entire sales process. Additionally, they were the sole earner of incentive compensation associated with that customer. Team selling alleviates some of the workload from each team member, but also reduces the incentive compensation earned.

With a team structure, the key is to ensure each member has a specific role as a part of that team. Clearly documented and communicated rules of engagement and responsibilities will minimize the amount of overlap and gaps in duties.

For team-based selling to be successful, team members must work together. Sellers must have "bought in" to the concept that the team is more successful together than apart. This mindset encourages focus on the goal to expand business rather than compete with teammates for credit and earnings. The incentive plan must strike a balance between individual efforts and team success.

How To Compensate for Team-Based Selling?

As more resources are involved in each sale, the sales compensation program needs to accommodate the contributions by these individuals. Key questions that arise are:

- How to effectively align the objectives of all of these resources with customers?
- How to incent the right behaviors while ensuring the company does not overpay on a single sale?
- Who gets credit for closing each sale?

Team members must embrace a common goal. While this process begins with communication and training, sales compensation plans help reinforce the desired behavior. Sales compensation plans must first and foremost align to the job. To design the right compensation plans to support this redeployment, it is important to first step back to the basics of sales compensation.

Eligibility: Who should have the opportunity to earn incentive compensation?

Only those sales team members who have influence over a sale and contribute to the sales results should be eligible to earn incentive compensation upon close of the sale.

Pay Mix: What portion of an individual's target total compensation should be tied to sales performance?

Pay mix should align to the degree of influence an individual has on a sale. The team members with the most influence should have the most aggressive pay mixes.

Measures and Metrics: What activities/results should be used to assess and pay each role?

The measures of an individual's sales compensation plan should align directly to the individual's role in closing the sale. Compensation for each individual should be tied to their direct impact. Company sales strategy dictates the type of performance measures that should be employed in sales compensation plans. Examples of performance measure types include the following.

- Outcome measures pay employees based on results achieved (e.g., total revenue or gross profit dollars produced), and emphasize the results produced by sales representatives, no matter the means for achieving them.

- Input measures pay employees based on the activities put forth during the sales process (e.g., number of customer touch points or tool usage). Companies employ these measures when they stand to gain from specific sales activities that may not be employed by the sales force if not tracked.
- Sequential measures pay employees based on milestones met or progress made throughout the sales cycle (e.g., contractual agreement signed, or first order placed).

Mechanics: How does the sales compensation plan pay its recipients?

Sales commissions and quota-based bonuses are two of the most common mechanics employed. Both mechanics can be used to effectively compensate individuals on a team if designed and utilized properly.

A quota-based bonus makes it easy to account for team selling in the quota-setting process. Team members could each have a quota designed to include all of the sales they touch. This involves double crediting team members on a single sale; however, the double crediting equalizes since their initial quotas were inflated to account for this. Using a quota-based bonus provides flexibility to pay based on performance to quota no matter what the quota. A quota-based bonus plan with an increased quota should motivate the intended behavior from team members, and eliminate any competitive nature in the collaboration process.

If paying via a commission where each team member gets a portion of credit for each sale based on their role, it's important to drive collaboration and engrain teaming culture in the organization. The commission compensation plan won't inherently drive teaming as much as a quota-based bonus. With a commission structure, either the total commission is split among team members, or the commission rate or base is adjusted to pay out multiple individuals on a single sale.

To avoid overpaying, the total pool of incentive dollars available for a sale should not change based on the number of resources involved. The sales compensation split among the team members should instead add up to the total pool.

Crediting: Who is paid for a successful result?

With team-based selling, crediting is especially important. Establishing crediting rules up front to ensure sellers understand how they are paid and what they will earn is important. Clear crediting rules increase seller motivation and reduce confusion. Crediting options include, for example, equal credit among team members or proportional credit based on involvement. However, it is also important to develop a process for exceptions.

Conclusion

To adapt to the current (and still rapidly evolving) sales environment, team selling can be a useful tool to effectively reach customers and increase sales. When implementing team selling, there are a couple key components that should be considered to help drive success:

- Clearly outlined overall team objectives
- Individual role and responsibilities as part of the team
- Sales compensation alignment to role objectives
- How team success coincides with individual success

With clear communication, guidelines and tailored sales compensation, an organization can effectively train, implement and reinforce the team selling culture.

Kelly Rue is a manager at the Alexander Group.

SALES COMPENSATION COST MODELING: DETERMINING METHODOLOGY AND COMPONENTS

By Andrea Farinelli

Organizations often spend months designing strategic sales compensation programs for their sales team. These efforts need to be complemented by a thoughtful, accurate and well-articulated cost analysis.

To best answer the cost question behind a plan design, best-in-class organizations build a precise and adaptable compensation cost model. A model can also help explain a plan design to individuals by allowing them to see multiple examples of pay calculations.

For those new to cost modeling, the task may seem daunting. Where do I start? First, we will review the two main types of cost models and when to use which. Next, we will describe how to get started with data collection. Then, we will explain what to look for in the data and how to analyze it. Lastly, we will take a deep dive into the two different model types and how to set them up.

Determining Which Model to Use

There are two main cost-modeling methods. The first is an individual custom structure and the second is a pre-configured performance model. A custom cost model utilizes historical performance data for each incumbent and predicts future sales compensation costs. A pre-configured cost model utilizes a pre-established set of performance distributions, unrelated to any historical performance data, to predict sales compensation costs through regression analysis. The results of data analysis will be the guide in determining which model is right.

To utilize a custom cost model, it is necessary to be working with a stable sales force. For example, inconsistent performance, lack of data, significant organization change, or high turnover indicates instability. We will review how to test for stability in greater detail later. If faced with these issues, there is an alternative methodology to use: a pre-configured model. This model utilizes pre-configured performance scenarios, as opposed to historical performance scenarios, to predict sales compensation costs for the designed plans.

Getting Started: Data Collection

Data collection and organization is a meticulous step in the process of cost modeling. Cost modeling requires detailed plan design elements, incumbent HR data, and pay and performance data.

Plan Design Elements

Begin by understanding plan design elements including:

1. **Thresholds:** minimum performance to earn incentive pay.
2. **Accelerator Rates:** increase in payout rate above quota target.
3. **Caps:** maximum amount of earnings available.
4. **Decelerator Rates:** decrease in payout rate after pre-defined performance level.
5. **Performance Measures:** metrics against which incentive pay is awarded (e.g., revenue, profitability, key sales objectives).
6. **Modifiers/Links:** modify primary measures' payouts by a factor to increase or reduce payout based on secondary measures' performance.

Human Resources Data

In order to build out a cost model that includes total sales compensation costs to the organization, it is necessary to have certain elements of human resources data and additional information, too:

Required

1. Full Sales Team Roster
   - Names, role, compensation plan, hire date
2. Target Incentive Dollars by Incumbent

Additional

1. Salary by Incumbent
2. Annual Quota by Incumbent (required for pre-configured model)
3. Historical Compensation Payouts by Incumbent
4. Hiring Plan
5. Historical Turnover

Historical Performance Data

To gain an understanding of the historical payouts and performance of the sales organization, it is ideal to gather two-to-three years' worth of performance data, by measure. This data should be at the incumbent level and link to any previous years' payout data as available.

Analyzing Data: Understanding Its Accuracy and Efficacy

We now turn to the analysis of the data. Accuracy and relevancy of the data is the driver behind which of the two cost model types to use. Test the stability of the human resources' data and the sales performance data.

Human Resources Data Analysis

When reviewing the human resources data, a stable sales force will be quite evident. Here, look for low turnover and a tenured sales force. If there is consistency in the sales force, the data is aligned to a custom cost model build, assuming the performance data is available. If not, look to the pre-configured model.

Finally, review any quota information that is available. Are quota expectations for the year being modeled? Does the information provided take into account growth expectations or territories changes? Is the quota information available for all the sales roles in the organization?

Sales Performance Data Analysis

Understanding the historical sales performance data available is a key step in determining the viable options for modeling. Review if the overall performance is relatively consistent year over year. If there is consistent performance history, this means we can assume similar performance in the future, all else being equal. This is commonly the case and ideally used when an organization is looking to test changes to its detailed payout formula (thresholds, upside levels, etc.), but little else changing organizationally (job definitions, territories, etc.).

Stable historical performance can only apply to consistent measures across old and new plans. If the plan designs have changed from previous years, it is important to understand if the historical data is relevant at all. If the plan measures, their definitions, or crediting rules have changed substantially, this indicates that the data may no longer be relevant for consideration of future years' performance. When this is the case, it is best to align with key stakeholders on the use of any proxy performance data before moving forward. Without a stable situation, historical performance data should not be used to model future cost and the custom cost model becomes an inaccurate methodology. A pre-configured build will provide a more reliable cost forecast.

Building A Model

Custom Cost Model

Step one of building a custom cost model is to build out a detailed inputs tab. Build the inputs tab in a dynamic format instead of "hard coded." By doing this, it is easy to make updates to the model should the plan designs change. The primary components of the inputs tab are the mechanics of the sales compensation plan designs themselves.

Next, create a second tab to populate with the sales force incumbent data. This tab will include the full sales roster, including new hires if applicable. This is where target incentives are added, which compensation plan the individual is on, their role in the organization, and their historical performance data.

The model is now ready to run various performance scenarios. It is unlikely that historically your sales team's average performance against quota was equal to 100% attainment. Therefore, the first scenario to set up is to replicate this exact 100%. To do so, index every individual's performance so the average of everyone's performance is 100%.

In order to understand the full range of cost scenarios, it is important to next test for total cost above and below 100% average performance. Index the historical performances for two to three scenarios for both above and below. For example, choose 85%, 95%, 105%, and 110%. Testing for this broad range of performance helps to determine the implications of certain plan components, such as thresholds and accelerator rates.

Pre-Configured Cost Model

Setting up a pre-configured cost model is similar in many ways to the custom model in the early steps. The first step is still to set up an inputs tab. The initial steps of populating the second tab, the sales force incumbent data, is also very similar to the custom model. However, the pre-configured model also requires quota information for each individual. This is important because the pre-configured model utilizes the correlation between total sales performances against quota to the incentive dollars paid out for the achievement level (i.e., the plan structure itself). The model creates a regression line to estimate total costs at various levels of overall company performance.

In simplest terms, a regression analysis is an analytical method that examines the relationship of two variables. For our purposes, those two variables are quota performance and incentive payout. The pre-configured model uses the regression analysis against a wide variety of performance scenarios. First, define which performance scenarios to utilize. Utilizing one individual as an example, run that individual's quota and incentive payouts through all performance scenarios and calculate the average percent of quota and target incentive for each bell curve. Repeat this exercise for various performance points on each bell curve. Then, use these values to develop a regression line that compares quota performance to percent of target incentive paid out.

Conclusion

Designing, aligning and implementing new sales compensation plans can be time consuming but rewarding. However, understanding how a detailed cost model can support these efforts will alleviate some of these stresses. If working with a stable sales force as described above, prepare a custom cost model and test for various performance scenarios to answer any questions the organization has. This will position the model to provide an accurate forecast of sales compensation costs. If faced with an unstable sales force for any variety of reasons, execute on a pre-configured cost model structure to employ a regression line calculation of the annual sales compensation costs.

Andrea Farinelli is a manager at the Alexander Group.

ARTICLES LISTING

SALES COMPENSATION ALMANAC • 2022

RECENT ARTICLES OF INTEREST

This section provides a listing of the latest published sales compensation articles.

IN THIS SECTION
- 2020 Articles Listing
- 2021 Articles Listing

2020 ARTICLES

"2020 XaaS sales compensation symposium session recaps," Alexander Group

"2021 sales compensation planning—ready for major changes?" Alexander Group

"3 ex-Wells Fargo executives at center of fake accounts fined, one banned from banking," The Charlotte Observer

"5 facts about big new spending package for annuity sellers," Think Advisor

"68% of media execs consider sales comp adjustments," Alexander Group

"A deeper look at pay equity and sales compensation," Workspan

"A sales compensation plan that will inspire and reward reps," Learning Hub

"A sales compensation response to COVID-19," Joseph DiMisa, LinkedIn

"Aligning sales compensation with bottoms-up sales motions in a COVID-19 world," Forbes

"Are tech companies changing their sales comp program?" Alexander Group

"Avoiding the cost of imprecise language in incentive compensation plans," Lexology

"Avoiding the fallout, managing sales compensation changes for a dynamic economy," Workspan

"Bring them into the fold: what your CEO and board should know about your sales comp plan," Workspan

"California financial advisors lacking fixed and predetermined salary not subject to administrative salaried exemption," JD Supra

"Changing California commission and bonus plans in the time of COVID," JD Supra

"Changing sales jobs: Why and the impact on sales comp," Alexander Group

"COVID-19 shakeup: Organizations adjusting sales strategy," Workspan

"COVID-19: Adjustments to sales quotas," Alexander Group

"COVID-19: Sales departments seek to protect sellers' incentive pay," Workspan

"COVID-19: Should you protect sellers' pay?" Workspan

"Digitizing revenue growth: Align management systems," Alexander Group

"Do you have the right sales channels for a downturn?" Harvard Business Review

"DOJ, SEC settle with national bank for $3 billion over incentive compensation," Lexology

"DOL sales standard proposal could backfire: ACLI," Think Advisor

"Feds allege Wells Fargo-like practices by Fifth Third," Crain's Chicago Business

"Fifth Third Bank accused of opening fake accounts," News Dispatch

"Financial industry retools compensation plans for trust and growth," Forbes

"Finra clarifies sales contest restrictions for proposal to align suitability, Reg BI," Investment News

"Finra to probe effect of waning commissions on firm practices," Advisor Hub

"Formalize your sales compensation planning process," Alexander Group

"Four retail sales compensation imperatives for 2020," Alexander Group

"Gartner identifies three key objectives for sales leaders to best prepare for Coronavirus-related disruption," Yahoo Finance

"How far will asset management pay fall?" Institutional Investor

"How to guide your sales force through difficult times," Grand Rapids Business Journal

"How to reset your sales compensation plan in the New Year," MDM

"Is sales compensation just for sellers?" Alexander Group

"Key ingredient for 2021 sales compensation plan design," Gartner

"Let's talk about salespeople," Snow Magazine

"Life sciences roundtable recap: Aligning sales comp plans," Alexander Group

"Major sales compensation changes could be on the horizon," Workspan

"Managing sales through COVID-19: Immediate actions and long-term tactics," MDM

"Manufacturers: Motivate your sales teams to embrace ecommerce," Digital Commerce 360

"Manufacturing and sales comp: Adapt plan designs to current market dynamics," Alexander Group

"Manufacturing: Revise roles & sales comp plans to drive growth," Alexander Group

"Manufacturing: Sales comp strategies for COVID-19 disruption," Alexander Group

"Sales compensation: COVID-19—save the sales force," Alexander Group
"Sales compensation: rewarding sales profits," Alexander Group
"Sales compensation: What COVID-19 found in the shallows," Workspan
"Sales compensation's silent partner: Base pay," Workspan Daily
"Sales incentive design to drive growth in software sales," Workspan
"Sales leaders attempting to save the salesforce during COVID-19,"
  Workspan
"SEC charges bank execs over sales-compensation practices," Lexology
"Second-half actions for tech revenue leaders—Part 2," Alexander Group
"Seven actions for sales comp success," Alexander Group
**"Tech sales compensation predictions: More changes ahead," Alexander
  Group**
"Tesla sales employees launch petition to increase their salary following
  commission cuts," Electrek
"The art of quota setting," Forbes
"The evolution of radio: Where does sales comp fit in?" Alexander Group
"The future of sales comp: 5 predictions," Workspan
"The ultimate guide to profiting from cloud-based access control," Security
  Sales and Integration
**"Three sales compensation lessons COVID-19 has taught distributors,"
  Alexander Group**
"TV sales: A strong compensation profession?" RBR
"Wells Fargo raises monthly comp hurdle for 2021," Think Advisor
"Wells Fargo reaches $3 billion settlements related to fraudulent sales
  practices," The Associated Press
"Wells Fargo to pay $500 million for misleading investors about the success
  of its largest business unit," SEC
"What is sales performance management—And where is it going?" Forbes
"What tech leaders must do in the second-half of 2020," Alexander Group
"What's the best way to handle SaaS sales compensation?" Xaas Journal

2021 ARTICLES
"Aligning media sales compensation plans for growth," Alexander Group
"Are salespeople coin-operated?" Alexander Group
**"Changing your sales compensation plan for 2021? So is everyone else!"
  Alexander Group**

"Fired IBM manager's lawsuit over racial bias at the company heads to court," News Observer

"Gig workers may become eligible to receive equity compensation," National Law Review

"Global sales compensation—Is there such a thing?" Alexander Group

"Global vs. localized sales compensation," Workspan

"Homebuilder's agent challenges industry pay program," MRT

"Insurance regulators fall short on annuity sales rules, consumer advocate says," Financial Advisor

"Managing change: Sales compensation takes the lead," Workspan

"Media sales: Aligning sales comp with company goals," Alexander Group

"Multiple firsts for sales comp plans in 2021," Workspan

"Pandemic relief: Pharma sales rep salaries—and job satisfaction—actually increased in 2020," Fierce Pharma

"Quota busters!" Alexander Group

"Sales compensation victims," Alexander Group

"Sales goals in an uncertain economy: Mistakes can sabotage profits," Forbes

"Sales motivation goes beyond compensation," Workspan

"The digital revenue organization's impact on sales compensation," Alexander Group

"The future of sales compensation is insight-driven," Forbes

"The positive effect of using hurdles in sales comp," Workspan

"Variable compensation and salesperson health," American Marketing Association

"Why is omnichannel sales attribution still a problem?" RetailWire

About Alexander Group—Revenue Growth Consultants

The Alexander Group (www.alexandergroup.com) provides go-to-customer consulting services to the world's leading revenue acquisition organizations. Founded in 1985, Alexander Group combines deep experience, a proven methodology and data-driven insights to help revenue acquisition leaders anticipate change, align their go-to-customer resources—sales, marketing and service—with company goals and make better informed decisions with one goal in mind—to grow revenue. The Alexander Group has offices in Atlanta, Chicago, London, New York, San Francisco, Scottsdale, and Vero Beach.

Our Consulting Services

The Alexander Group provides the world's leading revenue acquisition organizations with management consulting services for the full spectrum of sales, marketing and service needs, as well as performance benchmarking based on the industry's richest repository of revenue program performance data. We apply years of experience and our Revenue Growth Model™, a proven methodology for evaluating go-to-customer organizations, to provide insights that are rooted in facts. We not only deliver insights—we understand sales, marketing and service business challenges. We roll-up our sleeves to work alongside our clients, whether they are realigning revenue acquisition programs or transforming their go-to-customer models. Our keen focus on high-impact and actionable recommendations ensures that we deliver value and results to our clients.

About Alexander Group Events

The Alexander Group produces and facilitates a specialized portfolio of events that help the world's leading revenue teams to drive growth. From our Women Revenue Leaders, Operations and Executive Forums to Symposiums and Executive Roundtables, Alexander Group's Leadership Series topics range from big-picture strategy to hands-on execution. Participants benefit from connecting with other top sales, marketing and service leaders, and gain exclusive access to the latest ideas and deeper insights needed to create high-performance revenue-growth organizations.

CPSIA information can be obtained
at www.ICGtesting.com
Printed in the USA
BVHW010341090322
630895BV00007B/89

9 781735 864648